SENSORCOMM 2016

The Tenth International Conference on Sensor Technologies and Applications

July 24 - 28, 2016

Nice, France

SENSORCOMM 2016 Editors

Carlos Becker Westphall, University of Santa Catarina, Brazil

Claus-Peter Rückemann, Westfälische Wilhelms-Universität Münster / Leibniz Universität Hannover / North-German Supercomputing Alliance, Germany

Muhammad Shakeel Virk, Narvik University College, Norway

Umair Najeeb Mughal, Institute of Industrial Technology, Norway

Printed from e-media with permission by:

Curran Associates, Inc.
57 Morehouse Lane
Red Hook, NY 12571

Some format issues inherent in the e-media version may also appear in this print version.

Printed by Curran Associates, Inc. (2016)

International Academy, Research, and Industry Association (IARIA)
412 Derby Way
Wilmington, DE 19810

Phone: (408) 893-6407
Fax: (408) 527-6351

petre@iaria.org

Additional copies of this publication are available from:

Curran Associates, Inc.
57 Morehouse Lane
Red Hook, NY 12571 USA
Phone: 845-758-0400
Fax: 845-758-2633
Email: curran@proceedings.com
Web: www.proceedings.com

Table of Contents

GREEN 2016

Forward

The First International Conference on Green Communications, Computing and Technologies (GREEN 2016), held between July 24-28, 2016 in Nice, France, was an inaugural event focusing on current green solutions, stringent requirements for further development, and evaluations of potential directions. The event targeted and brought together academia, research institutes, and industries working towards green solutions.

Expected economic, environmental and society wellbeing impact of green computing and communications technologies led to important research and solutions achievements in recent years. Environmental sustainability, high-energy efficiency, diversity of energy sources, renewable energy resources contributed to new paradigms and technologies for green computing and communication.

Economic metrics and social acceptability are still under scrutiny, despite the fact that many solutions, technologies and products are available. Deployment at large scale and a long term evaluation of benefits are under way in different areas where dedicated solutions are applied.

The conference had the following tracks:

- Green computing and communication technologies
- Smart grid
- Energy awareness

We take here the opportunity to warmly thank all the members of the GREEN 2016 technical program committee, as well as all the reviewers. The creation of such a high quality conference program would not have been possible without their involvement. We also kindly thank all the authors that dedicated much of their time and effort to contribute to GREEN 2016. We truly believe that, thanks to all these efforts, the final conference program consisted of top quality contributions.

Also, this event could not have been a reality without the support of many individuals, organizations and sponsors. We also gratefully thank the members of the GREEN 2016 organizing committee for their help in handling the logistics and for their work that made this professional meeting a success.

We hope GREEN 2016 was a successful international forum for the exchange of ideas and results between academia and industry and to promote further progress in the field of green communication, computing and technology. We also hope that Nice, France provided a pleasant environment during the conference and everyone saved some time enjoy the beautiful French Riviera.

GREEN 2016 Advisory Committee

Steffen Fries, Siemens AG, Germany
Carlos Becker Westphall, Federal University of Santa Catarina - Florianópolis, Brazil
Daisuke Mashima, Advanced Digital Sciences Center, Singapore
Bo Nørregaard Jørgensen, University of Southern Denmark, Denmark
Enrique Romero-Cadaval, University of Extremadura, Spain
Camille Salinesi, Université Paris 1 Panthéon - Sorbonne, France
Sotirios Ziavras, New Jersey Institute of Technology, USA

GREEN 2016 Special Area Chairs

Green Computing and Internet of Things
Sandra Sendra Compte, University of Granada, Spain

SENSORCOMM 2016

Committee

SENSORCOMM Advisory Committee

Jean Philippe Vasseur, Cisco Systems, Inc., France
Jaime Lloret Mauri, Polytechnic University of Valencia, Spain
Jens Martin Hovem, Norwegian University of Science and Technology, Norway
Pascal Lorenz, University of Haute Alsace, France
Sergey Yurish, IFSA, Spain

SENSORCOMM 2016 Industry Liaison Chairs

Sarfraz Khokhar, Cisco Systems, Inc., USA
Michael Niedermayer, Siemens AG, Germany
Harkirat Singh, Samsung Electronics Co., Korea

SENSORCOMM 2016 Research/Industry Chairs

Hristo Djidjev, Los Alamos National Laboratory, USA Teng Rui, National Institute of Information and Communication Technology, Japan
S. Biju Kumar, Philips Research - Eindhoven, The Netherlands
Ivan Ndip, Fraunhofer-Institut fuer Zuverlaessigkeit und Mikrointegration / Technische Universitaet (TU) Berlin, Germany

SENSORCOMM 2016 Special Area Chairs

Embedded systems
Joshua Ellul, University of Malta, Malta

Security
Yenumula Reddy, Grambling State University, USA

Body networks
Alessandro Pozzebo, Università degli Studi di Siena, Italy

Underwater systems
Mylène Toulgoat, Communications Research Centre - Ottawa, Canada

Applications
Elena Gaura, Coventry University, UK

Social sensing
Abdulrahman Alarifi, King Abdulaziz City for Science and Technology (KACST), Kingdom of Saudi Arabia

Atmospheric Icing and Sensing
Muhammad Shakeel Virk, Narvik University College, Norway

SENSORCOMM 2016 Technical Program Committee

Qusai Al-Hamdan, University of the Highlands & Islands, Perth College, UK
Aziz Al-Mahadin, Mu'tah University, Jordan
Abdulrahman Alarifi, Computer Research Institute - King Abdulaziz City for Science and Technology, Saudi Arabia
Carlo Alberto Boano, Graz University of Technology, Austria
Mothanna Alkubeily, Université de Technologie de Compiègne, France
Boushra Alkubily, Université de Technologie de Compiègne, France
Maykel Alonso Arce, CEIT and Tecnun (University of Navarra), Spain
Mansour Alsaleh, King Abdulaziz City for Science and Technology (KACST), Saudi Arabia
Adil Al-Yasiri, University of Salford, UK
Isabelle Augé-Blum, INSA Lyon - Laboratoire CITI -Villeurbanne, France
Sebastian Bader, Mid Sweden University, Sweden
Dominique Barthel, Orange Labs Division R&D - Meylan, France
Majid Bayanil Abbasy, Universidad Nacional de Costa Rica, Costa Rica
Rezaul K Begg, Victoria University, Australia
Paolo Bellavista, University of Bologna, Italy
Stephan Benecke, Technische Universitaet Berlin | Fraunhofer Institut Zuverlässigkeit und Mikrointegration, Germany
Mingsong Bi, Samsung Research America, USA
Karabi Biswas, Indian Institute of Technology - Kharagpur, India
Alessandro Bogliolo, University of Urbino, Italy
David Boyle, Imperial College London, UK
Lina Brito, Madeira Interactive Technologies Institute (M-ITI) - University of Madeira, Portugal
Ioannis Broustis, AT&T Labs Research, U.S.A
Tiziana Calamoneri, "La Sapienza" Università di Roma, Italy
Maria-Dolores Cano Baños, Technical University of Cartagena, Spain
Juan Vicente Capella Hernández, Universidad Politécnica de Valencia, Spain
Alexandru Caracas, IBM Research - Zurich, Switzerland
Matteo Ceriotti, University of Duisburg-Essen, Germany
Amitava Chatterjee, Jadavpur University, India
Sang H. Choi, NASA Langley Research Center, USA
Hugo Coll Ferri, Polytechnic University of Valencia, Spain
Daniel Curiac, "Politehnica" University of Timisoara, Romania
David Cuartielles, Malmö University, Sweden
Juarez Bento da Silva, Universidade Federal de Santa Catarina, Brazil
Debabrata Das, International Institute of Information Technology - Bangalore, India
Danco Davcev, University for Information Science & Technology "St. Paul the Apostle" - Ohrid, Republic of Macedonia
Eli De Poorter, Ghent University - iMinds, Belgium
Jerker Delsing, Lulea University of Technology, Sweden

Behnam Dezfouli, University of Iowa, USA
Akshaye Dhawan, Ursinus College, USA
Vincenzo Di Lecce, Politecnico di Bari, Italy
Mari Carmen Domingo, Barcelona Tech University, Spain
Wan Du, Nanyang Technological University (NTU), Singapore
Sylvain Durand, LIRMM/Université Montpellier II, France
Imad H. Elhajj, American University of Beirut, Lebanon
Joshua Ellul, University of Malta, Malta
Vincent Emeakaroha, University College Cork, Ireland
Xiang Fei, Coventry University, UK
Paulo Felisberto, Institut for Systems and Robotics-Lisbon / Universidade do Algarve, Portugal
Gianluigi Ferrari, University of Parma, Italy
Armando Ferro Vázquez, Universidad del País Vasco - Bilbao, Spain
Paul Fortier, University of Massachusetts Dartmouth, USA
Leonardo Franco, Universidad de Malaga, Spain
Pedro Furtado, University of Coimbra, Portugal
Elena Gaura, Coventry University, UK
Hamid Gharavi, National Institute of Standards and. Technology (NIST) - Gaithersburg, USA
Chris Gniady, University of Arizona, USA
Stephane Grumbach, INRIA, France
Jayavardhana Gubbi, TCS Innovation Labs, India
Per Gunningberg, Uppsala University, Sweden
Jianlin Guo, Mitsubishi Electric Research Laboratories - Cambridge, USA
Malka N. Halgamuge, The University of Melbourne, Australia
Mohammad Hammoudeh, Manchester Metropolitan University, UK
Vincent Huang, Ericsson Research - Stockholm, Sweden
Muhammad Ali Imran, University of Surrey, U.K.
Abhaya Induruwa, Canterbury Christ Church University, UK
Vasanth Iyer, International Institute of Information Technology, India
Shaghayegh Jaberi, Islamic Azad University - Tehran, Iran
Imad Jawhar, United Arab Emirates University - Al Ain, UAE
Zhen Jiang, West Chester University, USA
Miao Jin, University of Louisiana at Lafayette, U.S.A.
Adrian Kacso, University of Siegen, Germany
Kyoung-Don Kang, Binghamton University, USA
Reinhardt Karnapke, Brandenburg University of Technology Cottbus – Senftenberg, Germany
Dimitrios A. Karras, Chalkis Institute of Technology, Hellas
Fotis Kerasiotis, University of Patras / Rio-Patras, Greece
Yaser Khamayseh, Jordan University of Science and Technology, Jordan
Abdelmajid Khelil, Huawei European Research Center, Germany
Sarfraz Khokhar, Cisco Systems Inc., USA
Kwangsoo Kim, Electronics and Telecommunications Research Institute (ETRI), Korea
Boris Kovalerchuk, Central Washington University, USA
Thorsten Kramp, IBM Research Zurich, Switzerland
Dilip Krishnaswamy, Qualcomm Research - San Diego, U.S.A.
Danny Krizanc, Wesleyan University - Middletown, USA
Sisil Kumarawadu, University of Moratuwa, Sri Lanka
Erlend Larsen, The Norwegian Defence Research Establishment (FFI) - Kjeller, Norway

Animesh Pathak, Inria Paris-Rocquencourt, France
Leonidas Perlepes, University of Thessaly, Greece
Dirk Pesch, Cork institute of Technology, Ireland
Patrick Pons, CNRS-LAAS, France
Miodrag Potkonjak, University of California - Los Angeles, USA
Shrisha Rao, International Institute of Information Technology - Bangalore, India
Shahid Raza, Swedish Institute of Computer Science (SICS) – Stockholm, Sweden
Yenumula Reddy, Grambling State University, USA
Mark Reed, Yale School of Engineering & Applied Science, USA
Juan Reig Pascual, Polytechnic University of Valencia, Spain
Càndid Reig, University of Valencia, Spain
Tor Arne Reinen, SINTEF ICT, Norway
Biljana Risteska Stojkoska, University "Ss. Cyril and Methodius", Macedonia
Joel Rodrigues, University of Beira Interior, Portugal
Laura Margarita Rodríguez Peralta, Universidad Popular Autónoma del Estado de Puebla - UPAEP, Puebla, México
Lorenzo Rubio-Arjona, Universidad Politécnica de Valencia, Spain
Ulrich Rückert, Bielefeld University, Germany
Teng Rui, National Institute of Information and Communication Technology, Japan
Jorge Sá Silva, University of Coimbra, Portugal
Tapio Saarelainen, Army Academy, Finland
Sicari Sabrina, University of Insubria, Italy
Husnain Saeed, National University of Sciences & Technology (NUST), Pakistan
Addisson Salazar, Polytechnic University of Valencia, Spain
Francisco Javier Sánchez Bolumar, ADIF, Spain
Olga Saukh, ETH Zurich, Switzerland
Kamran Sayrafian, National Institute of Standards & Technology, USA
Elad Michael Schiller, Chalmers University of Technology, Sweden
Leo Selavo, University of Latvia, Latvia
Sandra Sendra Compte, Polytechnic University of Valencia, Spain
Kuei-Ping Shih, Tamkang University - Taipei, Taiwan
Simone Silvestri, Sapienza University of Rome, Italy
Francesco Simeone, University "Sapienza" of Roma / INFN-Roma, Italy
Andrzej Skowron, University of Warsaw, Poland
K M Sunjiv Soyjaudah, University of Mauritius, Mauritius
Grigore Stamatescu, University Politehnica of Bucharest, Romania
Yannis Stamatiou, University of Patras, Greece
Razvan Stanica, National Polytechnic Institute of Toulouse, France
Kris Steenhaut, Vrije Universiteit Brussel, Belgium
David Stork, Rambus Labs, USA
David Sundaram, University of Auckland, New Zealand
Ewa Szynkiewicz, Warsaw University of Technology, Poland
Muhammad Tariq, Waseda University - Tokyo, Japan
Rolf Thomasius, Technische Universität Berlin, Germany
Vassilis Triantafillou, Technological Educational Institution of Messolonghi, Greece
Neeta Trivedi, Aeronautical Development Establishment- Bangalore, India
Wilfried Uhring, University of Strasbourg, France
Fabrice Valois, INRIA SWING / CITI, INSA-Lyon, France

Copyright Information

VANETs Networking Protocols: An Analytical Study

Samira Harrabi
ENSI University
Mannouba, Tunisia
Email: samira.harrabi@gmail.com

Ines Ben Jaffar
ESCT University
Mannouba,Tunisia
Email: ines.benjaafar@gmail.com

Khaled Ghedira
ISG University
Tunis, Tunisia
Email: khaled.ghedira@anpr.tn

***Abstract*—Vehicular Ad hoc NETworks (VANETs) are considered as a class of Mobile Ad hoc NETworks (MANETs). The VANETs are a set of vehicles that are capable of exchanging data dynamically and without needing any pre-existing and fixed network infrastructure. Each node sends and receives messages in its communication area. Thus, message routing is done through a routing protocol. Despite the fact that the VANETs are a subgroup of the MANETs, they possess exceptional network behaviors like high mobility and dynamic topology, which make the MANETs routing protocols unsuitable for the VANETs. This paper summarizes the different protocols used for routing in the VANETs that focuses on a vehicle-to-vehicle communication. Utilizing an OMNET++ simulator, the experimental results are discussed to compare the presented routing protocol categories.**

Keywords–VANET; Routing protocols; OMNET++.

I. INTRODUCTION

A Vehicular Ad hoc NETwork (VANET) is a communication network between vehicles equipped with computers, network devices and various types of sensors [1]. In the VANET, vehicles communicate with each other via a Vehicle-to-Vehicle (V2V) communication and with the roadside through a Vehicle-to-Infrastructure (V2I) communication. Fig. 1 shows an example of the VANET.

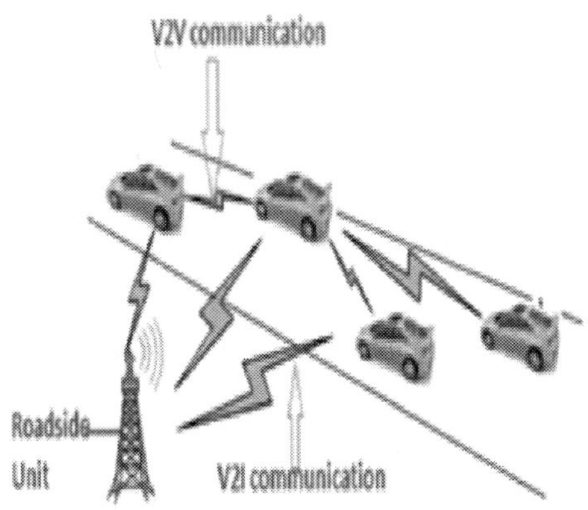

Figure 1. Example of VANET scenario.

Even though the VANET is a subclass of a Mobile Ad-hoc NETwork (MANET), it has specific network characteristics, as follows [2]:

- **High mobility**
  The VANETs are characterized by a high mobility of vehicles. Therefore, a node may join or leave the network in a very short time, which makes a very frequent change of the topology. In addition, routing problems can occur when communication links are broken suddenly due to an important velocity value, i.e., an intermittent connectivity problem.
- **Communication environment**
  The environments considered by the VANET are often unfavorable particularly in urban areas. Vehicle movements are related to road structures (intersections, traffic signs, etc.) and road base stations (infrastructure) in highways or within a metropolitan area. The constraints imposed by this type of environment, such as radio obstacles and impacts of multipath propagation, affect the quality of services as well as radio transmissions.
- **Constraint of energy**
  Unlike the MANET, where the energy constraint is an addressed challenge issue, the VANETs energy is not a critical behavior because the components of the VANET have no limit in terms of energy and may have multiple communication interfaces.
- **Density Variation**
  The density of nodes in the VANET is not uniform. For example, in an urban environment the density is much higher than in rural areas. The number of vehicles in an intersection or in a traffic jam is more important than in another area where traffic is often fluid. In addition, the density is different depending on the night or the day, and / or peak or break hours. This density diversity makes it difficult to design routing protocols.
- **Network partitioning**
  This problem mainly occurs when the node density is low. Then, the vehicles move in isolated and non-connected groups. Therefore, it becomes difficult in this case to ensure end-to-end communications.

From the above characteristics, it is evident that designing a suitable routing protocol for the VANET is a big challenge. In addition, the presented behaviors make the MANET routing algorithms unsuitable for the VANET [3]. Hence, routing in the VANET has been the subject of many research works and several protocols have been proposed [4][5][7][8][9][10]. Based on the path creation manner, as well as the maintenance of routes, we can classify the VANET routing protocols into two major categories: hierarchical and non-hierarchical protocols. The aim of this paper is to study the impact of the

VANETs properties on all routing protocols.

The remainder of this paper is structured as follows. Section 2 deals with the classification of the routing protocols. Section 3 presents the simulation results and gives a comparison of the various algorithms. In Section 4, we conclude the paper.

II. Routing Protocols in VANETs

Routing is an important mechanism for the VANET, through which vehicles can communicate together, even if they are not in a direct communication range. To route a message, each protocol possesses a specific strategy to find and maintain a path. Based on this specificity, we can classify the VANET routing protocols into two major categories: hierarchical and non-hierarchical protocols.

A. Non - Hierarchical Protocols

This family of protocols is known as uniform or flat routing protocols which consider that all the nodes are equal, in the same hierarchical level, having the same roles and functions. Therefore, no hierarchy is defined between the network nodes. Each node sends and receives routing control messages [11]. Based only on its position, the node takes a decision to route packets. They are further divided into two classes: topology-based routing protocols and geographical position-based protocols.

1) Topology Based Routing Protocols

There are three routing categories that define this family, which are proactive, reactive and hybrid routing protocols.

(a) Proactive Routing Protocols

In proactive protocols, each node keeps knowledge of the entire network topology. This image is updated periodically or every topological modification by an exchange of control messages. Routing tables are maintained through these packages and routes are determined on the basis of this knowledge [12]. The proactive routing protocols are investigated as follows [13]:

- Global State Routing protocol (GSR)
  The GSR [14] is a link-state protocol where each node knows the global network topology saved in the routing table, which enables it to calculate routes and reach each destination. Unlike other protocols, the GSR nodes do not broadcast their links-state to all the network nodes, but only send its neighbors. This link-state includes the delay to reach every neighbors node. Consequently, the rate of control packets flooding in the network can be reduced. However, due to the high mobility of nodes that provide instability of links, the control overhead can increase.
- Destination-Sequenced Distance-Vector (DSDV)
  The DSDV [15] is a distance vector protocol, where each node maintains a routing table containing information about all reachable destinations. This information includes the intermediate nodes used to join the destination, the number of hops between the source and the destination node as well as the Sequence Number (SN) stamped by the recipient node, which can be an intermediate node or the destination node itself. The SN is used to differ the novel established route from the old one. Each node sends, periodically, its routing table to its neighbors. Other update packets are also sent after changing in the network topology. These packages include only the routing information affected by this variation.
  Once a node receives an update packet, it compares it with the existing information stored in its routing table. An updating in the entire routing table starts if the received information is newer with a larger sequence number or if they have the same sequence number but with a shorter distance (lower hops number). Nevertheless, the routing problem, in terms of performance, is that the DSDV engenders a large volume of control packets and consumes a large part of the available bandwidth.
- Optimized Link State Routing (OLSR)
  The main goal of the OLSR [16] is to provide the shortest possible path to reach a destination in terms of hops number based on the Dijkstra algorithm [17]. Its contribution is in using the Multi-Point Relaying (MPR) method. The idea behind this method is as follows. To reach all of its 2-hop-link neighbors, each node builds a set of nodes called the MPR. Every MPR node is used to route and forward the received messages. The other neighbors which are not MPRs can only read and execute packets.

(b) Reactive Routing Protocols

These protocols are known as on-demand routing protocols because the routes are established only when a node wants to join a destination and only the used routes are maintained [12]. In this case, unlike proactive protocols, an additional delay is required at the beginning of each search; i.e., when a node intends to transmit packets, a route discovery phase is initiated by broadcasting a route search message. Any node that receives this message and does not have information about the destination broadcasts the message. Consequently, a route search packet is transmitted from point to point in all or part of the network. This mechanism is called the flooding technique [18]. The reactive routing protocols are reviewed as follows:

- Dynamic Source Routing (DSR)
  This protocol uses the source routing technique in which the source node includes the complete route in the packet header to reach the destination node [19]. Therefore, the intermediate nodes do not need to update the information on the crossing path. The DSR is based on two phases that are the route discovery and the road maintenance.
- Ad hoc On-demand Distance Vector (AODV)
  The AODV [20] uses the number of hops as a metric to select an available route. Like the DSDV, this reactive protocol utilizes the principle of the sequence number in order to use the most new or fresh roads. There are three types of packets utilized by the AODV which are: the Route REQuest (RREQ) packet, the Route REPly (RREP) packet and the Route ERRor (RERR) packet. In addition, the AODV invokes a HELLO control packet that verifies the route connectivity. Like the DSR, the AODV uses two mechanisms which are the route discovery and the road maintenance. While the first step is used to find a route to reach a destination, the second mechanism is necessary to detect

and announce broken links caused by the mobility of nodes.

(c) Hybrid Routing Protocols
Hybrid protocols combine the two previous categories. A proactive technique is used in a limited network area around the source node where the number of hops is not more than four hops. Otherwise, the reactive method is used for the distant nodes [21]. The advantage of the hybrid protocols is that they adapt better to large networks. However, this type of protocol combines the cons of proactive and reactive routing protocols such as the regular exchange of control packets and the flooding of the whole network in order to find a route and join a distant node.

- Zone Routing Protocol (ZRP)
It divides the network into different zones. For each node, it defines a routing zone expressed in a maximal number of hops. Inside this area, the ZRP uses a proactive protocol; and outside of this routing zone, it uses a reactive protocol [22]. Based on various comparative and behavioral studies of topology-based routing protocols in the VANET [23][24][25], the previous protocols are compared and tabulated in Table 1.

2) Geographical Position Based Protocols
Geographical protocols are based on two phases: the location of the destination node and the routing of packets to this node [26]. However, these protocols require a node location service for the routing packets in the network. Yet, most of these protocols generate a lot of control packets which can increase the network congestion. Various protocols belong to this type.

(a) Greedy Perimeter Stateless Routing (GPSR)
The routing technique of the GPSR [27] is based on two phases. The first step is to select of the next transmitter node which will have the role to retransmit packets. This procedure is based on the position information of the neighboring and destination packet. This step is necessary to choose the nearest node to the destination. The second part of the GPSR is to get around the obstacles as well as the empty geographical areas where no transmitter node exists.

(b) Movement-based Routing Algorithm (MORA)
To take an adaptable retransmission decision, MORA [28] used the position and movement direction of vehicles. This method takes into consideration the dynamic changes in the network.

(c) Vehicle-Assisted Data Delivery (VADD)
The VADD [29] uses the predictable movement of vehicles to take a retransmission decision. It particularly uses the information on the traffic road to estimate the transmission delay. Therefore, the packets will be routed along a path with the lowest time.

(d) Greedy Traffic-Aware Routing protocol (GyTAR)
The main goal of this protocol is to route data to the nearest node considering the specific factors to this kind of network environments. The GyTAR [30] protocol assumes that each vehicle knows its current position using the GPS service. In order to make routing decisions, a source node has to know the destination position.

(e) Urban Multi hop Broadcast Protocol (UMB)
In order to reduce collisions problems and effectively utilize the bandwidth, the UMB [31] is based on the multi-hop diffusion algorithm for inter vehicular networks. Unlike the flooding protocols, the UMB assigns a sending packet process to the most distant nodes without knowing any information about the network topology.
The UMB is based on two phases: the first is called directional broadcast where the vehicle selects a source node for relaying a data without any information about the network topology. The second is called intersection broadcast where the packet disseminates in all directions. The main advantage of the UMB protocol is that it performs well in terms of multi-hop broadcast reliability in urban channels.

TABLE I. A COMPARISON STUDY OF TOPOLOGY BASED ROUTING PROTOCOLS IN VANET.

	Pros	*Cons*
DSR	-Beacon less. -It has small overload on the network. -It reduces load on the network. -No periodical update is required in DSR.	- The control overhead is high. -Unnecessary flooding burden the network. -In high mobility pattern, it performs worse. -Unable to repair broken links locally.
AODV	-It uses destination sequence number. -It reduces excessive memory requirements and the route redundancy. -AODV responses to the link failure in the network. -It can be applied to large scale ad hoc network.	-More time is needed to establish a route compared to other approaches. - It provide a heavy control overhead. -It consumes extra bandwidth.
GSR	-Packet delivery ratio of GSR is better than AODV and DSR. -GSR is scalable than AODV and DSR.	- It neglects the situation like sparse network where there are not enough nodes for forwarding packets. -GSR shows higher routing overhead than GyTAR because of using hello messages as control messages.
DSDV	-It solves routing loop problem. -It reduces the count to infinity problem. -It maintains only the best route.	-It takes up a large volume of available bandwidth. -It is unsuitable for high density and dynamic networks.
OLSR	-It is suitable for high density and dynamic networks. -The number of transmission is less.	-The control packet overhead is high.
ZRP	-It reduces the control overhead.	-It combines the drawbacks of reactive and reactive protocols.

(f) Anchor-based Street and Traffic Aware Routing (A-STAR)
This protocol uses particularly the information about city bus routes in order to identify a route anchor with a high connectivity for routing packets. The A-STAR [32] adopts a routing approach based on the anchor, which reflects the characteristics of the streets. A point is associated with each street according to its capacity (large or small Street serviced by a number of different buses). Information about the roads provided by buses give an idea on the

charge of the vehicular network in each street. This gives an image of the city in different times.

(g) Distributed Vehicular Broadcasting (DV-CAST)
The DV-CAST [33] is designed to be used for a multi-hop routing technique. This protocol shows three scenarios of movement for broadcasting vehicles: dense traffic scenario, sparse traffic scenario, and regular traffic scenario. Lots of studies have demonstrated that the DV-CAST provides an elevated control overhead and delay in end-to-end packet transmissions.
Their used essential characters, illustrated in different survey papers, deal with position-based routing protocols in the VANET [34][35]. The previous protocols are compared and presented in Table 2.

TABLE II. A COMPARISON STUDY OF POSITION BASED ROUTING PROTOCOLS IN VANET.

	Pros	*Cons*
GPSR	-To forward the packet a node needs to remember only one hop neighbor location. - Forwarding packet decisions are made dynamically.	- For high mobility characteristics of node, stale information of neighbors position is often contained in the sending nodes neighbor table. - Though the destination node is moving its information in the packet header of intermediate node is never updated.
MORA	-It performs well in high dynamic topology.	- Complex metrics used to forwarding packets.
VADD	- It is suitable for multi-hop packet transmitting. - Packet delivery rate is high.	- Traffic road is high.
GyTAR	- Number of transmission is less. - Efficient for high dynamic network.	- Control packet overhead is high. - It is on the basis of a roadside units to define vehicle number.
UMB	-It performs well at high packet loads and vehicle traffic densities. - It solves packet collision problem.	- It broadcasts message without any topology information that can increase rate of dropped packet.
A-STAR	- In low traffic density, A-STAR ensures for finding an end-to-end connection. - A-STAR uses a new local recovery strategy which is more suitable for city environment. - Path selection of A-STAR ensures high connectivity though its packet delivery ratio is lower than GSR and GPSR.	- The packet delivery ratio of A-STAR is lower than GSR and GPSR. -To find a path from source to destination it uses static information based on city bus routes which causes connectivity problem on some portion of streets.
DV-CAST	-By using flag variable check whether the packet is redundant or not.	- Control overhead is high. - End to end data transfer delay is high.

B. Hierarchical Routing Protocols

In this type of routing protocols, the neighboring vehicles form a group of nodes or a cluster. Each cluster is managed by a leader node, called the cluster-head [36]. Each cluster head is responsible for managing the nodes, not only in the same group but also between the neighboring clusters. The clustering operation and the manager node selection are of two necessary steps. Several protocols are classified under this routing type, namely:

1) Hierarchical Cluster Based (HCB)
This protocol is designed especially for high mobility networks and it is based on a two-layer communication architecture. While in the first layer the nodes can communicate with each other via a multi hop path based on their unique interface radio, there exist [37] nodes in the second layer that also have another radio communication interface.

2) Cluster Based Location Routing (CBLR)
For this protocol, each cluster head maintains a routing table containing the addresses and geographical locations of the nodes in its own group and for the neighboring clusters [38]. When a source node wants sending a data to a destination, the leader node checks if the destination is in the same group or not. If it is, it sends the packet to the nearest neighbor of the destination.

3) Cluster-Based Directional Routing Protocol (CBDRP).
To form a cluster, this protocol uses the vehicle movement direction as a metric. Consequently, the nodes get the same direction form a group [39]. The source node sends the packet to its cluster head, which forwards the message to the leader node of the destination group, which in turn transmits it to the destination.

4) Cluster Based Routing Protocol (CBRP)
The CBRP [40] uses geographical information to form a cluster. To locate a node, the geographical areas are divided into a grid form. The node existing in a grid will be selected as a cluster head., The selected node must broadcast a LEAD message to inform its neighbor vehicles or a LEAVE message if it leaves the grid. Both the LEAVE and LEAD messages contain the position of their grid.
On the basis of diverse behavioral studies of hierarchical protocols in the VANET [41][42], the above cited methods are compared and presented in Table 3.

TABLE III. A COMPARISON STUDY OF HIERARCHICAL ROUTING PROTOCOLS IN VANET.

	Pros	*Cons*
HCB	- Intra-cluster routing is performed independently in each cluster. -Cluster heads exchange membership information periodically to enable inter-cluster routing.	- Number of retransmission is high. - packet loss rate is high.
CBLR	-It is suitable for high mobility network. - Digital map is used. -Control packet overhead is low.	- Number of retransmission is high.
CBDRP	-Link stability problem solve in VANET. -Reliable and rapid data transfer.	-Control packet overhead is average. -Number of retransmission is high.
CBR	-Routing overhead is less.	- It doesnt consider velocity and direction of a vehicle.

Fig. 2 summarizes the taxonomy of different routing protocols in the VANET.

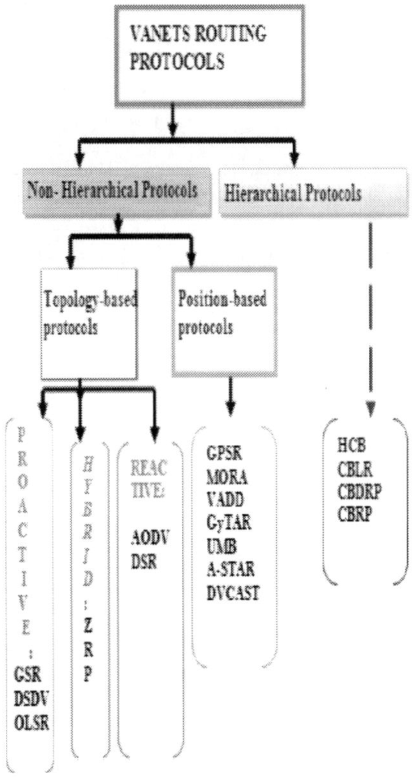

Figure 2. Toxonomy of different routing protocols.

As one can see in Fig. 2, a VANET routing protocol may be classified according to various criteria reflecting a fundamental design.

III. Simulation Results and Analysis

Unlike the previous part, where we compared the various routing protocols of the same category based on their important parameters, in this section we compare the different routing categories on the basis of simulation results. To achieve this goal, we chose from each routing family a single protocol. Consequently, we evaluated the performance of the AODV [20], the DSDV [15], the GPSR [27] and the CBRP [40] routing protocols using OMNET++ [43] and MATLAB [44] tools.
We selected three performance metrics, which are the average of the end-to-end delay, the throughput, and the Packet Deliver Ratio (PDR).

- The end-to-end delay (E2E delay): It defines all the delays caused during the routing process, such as transmission/re-transmission delays at the MAC layer, the transfer delay, and the route discovery delay.
- Throughput: The throughput is the most important metric because we are concerned with the number of transmitted messages. It is described as the total number of received packets at a destination out of the total simulation time.
- Packet deliver ratio (PDR): The rate of the number of delivered packets to the best destination defines the PDR.

The simulation parameters are listed in Table 4.

TABLE IV. Simulation parameters.

Parameter	*value*
Transmission rate	54Mbps.
Simulation time	200-1400s.
Playground Dimensions	1300m x 1300m.
Routing protocols	AODV,DSDV,GPRS, and CBRP.
Transmission range	150m.
Number of nodes	30.
Mac type	IEEE 802.11p

A. E2E Delay

Fig. 3 depicts the E2E delay average measured for the previously discussed methods with a variation in the simulation time from 200 to 1400s. In this routing case, the number of vehicles is fixed to 30. We can notice that at [200,800], and despite the increase in the E2E delay average value of the GPSR from 5% at 500 to reach 13% at 800 s, it outperforms the AODV, DSDV and CBRP protocols. Nevertheless, at [800, 1400], the CBRP demonstrates a good behavior. On the other hand, the topology-based routing protocols represented by both the AODV and DSDV methods show a bad performance in terms of E2E delay in the entire simulation time.

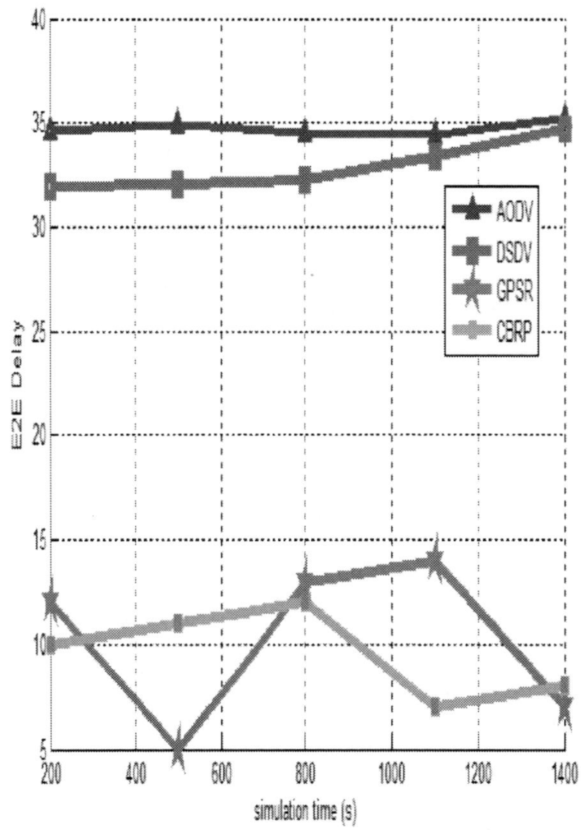

Figure 3. E2E Delay vs. simulation time.

B. Throughput

In Fig. 4, the results of the measured throughput for the four methods depend on the simulation time. The results indicate a more efficient behavior of topology-based routing protocols in comparison with the GPSR and the CBRP when the simulation time grows. As illustrated in the figure below, the AODV exhibits the highest throughput value in spite of the fluctuations from different simulation times.
We observe also that although its throughput value is mostly half of the AODV value, the DSDV shows good results compared to the GPSR and CBRP protocols which demonstrates a bad behavior in terms of throughput rate.

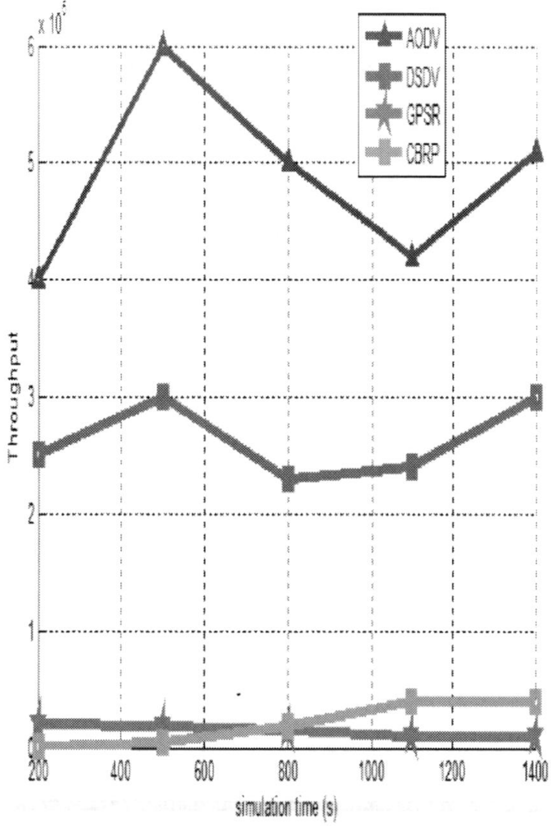

FIGURE 4. THROUGHPUT VS. SIMULATION TIME.

C. Packet Delivery Ratio (PDR)

In Fig. 5, the PDR of the AODV, the DSDV, the CBRP and the GPRS are presented when the simulation time is varied from 200 to 1400s. It can be seen that the CBRP, the DSDV and the AODV demonstrate a better performance than the GPSR, with a slight difference counted for the CBRP.
As compared to the cluster-based routing protocol and the topology-based methods, the GPSR exhibits the lowest performance level. The reason behind the bad behavior in terms of packet delivery ratio is due to the feature of the GPSR in which it takes into consideration the geographical position of nodes that cannot be an ideal metric. However, the clustering technique provides a more stability for the CBRP. As a result, Fig. 5 shows a PDR over 1 for the CBRP.

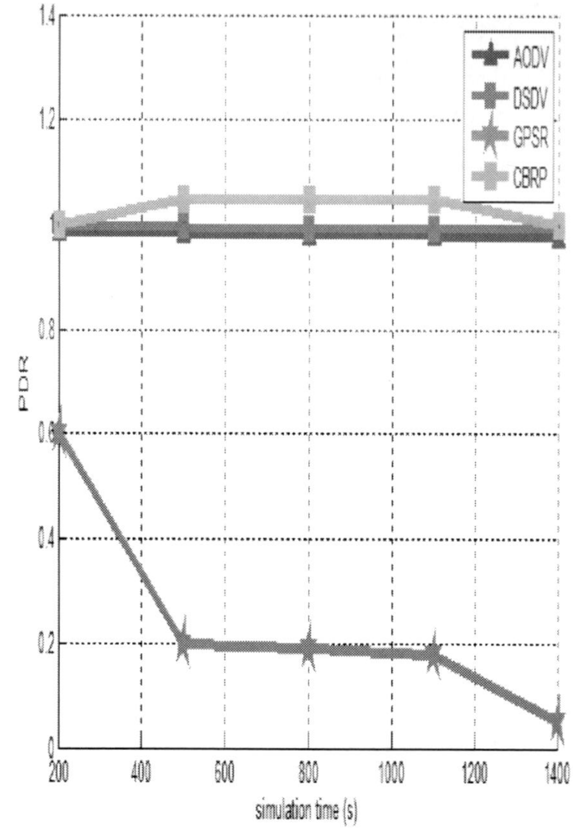

FIGURE 5. PDR VS. SIMULATION TIME.

Table 5 presents a numerical comparison of the AODV, DSDV, CBRP and GPSR routing protocols in terms of throughput, E2E delay and packet delivery ratio in the cases where the simulation time has minimum and maximum values.

TABLE V. NUMERICAL COMPARISON BETWEEN AODV, DSDV, CBRP, AND GPSR PROTOCOLS.

	Simulation time is 200s			Simulation time is 100s		
	Throughput (byte/s)	E2E Delay)	PDR	Throughput (byte/s)	E2E Delay)	PDR
AODV	400000	34.9%	1	500000	35%	1
DSDV	250000	31%	1	300000	34.8%	1
GPSR	20000	11%	0.6	10000	7%	0.1
CBRP	520	10%	1	40000	7.5%	1

IV. CONCLUSION AND FUTURE WORK

The key difference of Vehicular Ad hoc Network (VANET) and Mobile Ad hoc Network (MANET) is the exceptional mobility pattern and quick variability variable of network topology. Thus, the most important aim of this paper is to categorize different mobile ad hoc routing protocols and to evaluate these methods in the VANET. In this paper, we have

reviewed and compared the different routing categories. From the results of our comparative study, we have examined the topology-based routing protocols, the AODV and the DSDV, against the position-based routing protocol, the GPSR, as well as the cluster-based routing protocol, the CBRP. We have demonstrated that the GPSR outperforms the AODV, the DSDV and the CBRP in terms of E2E delay with a low simulation speed. Nevertheless, the CBRP demonstrates a good behavior when the simulation time grows. We have also found that the topology-based routing protocols show a bad performance in the entire simulation time.
On the one hand, the results of the measured throughput have depicted a more efficient behavior of topology-based routing protocols in comparison with the GPSR and the CBRP despite the fluctuations from different simulation times. On the other hand, the GPSR have exhibited the lowest performance level in terms of packet delivery ratio compared to the CBRP, the DSDV and the AODV. From this study, it is evident that each routing protocol category has its network specificity, which makes it efficient in one case and inefficient in another.
The novelty of this paper is to compare and evaluate all the categories routing protocols and show the impact of the VANET properties on each class.
As a future work, we intend to improve the AODV protocol to make it more efficient and effective in vehicular networks.

ACKNOWLEDGMENT

The authors are thankful to the anonymous reviewers for their useful comments and suggestions that helped us to improve the quality of this paper.

REFERENCES

[1] H. H. Hartenstein and K.P. Laberteaux, "A tutorial survey on vehicular ad hoc networks," IEEE Communications Magazine, vol. 46, no. 6, June 2008, pp. 164-171.

[2] Venkatesh, A. Indra, and R.Murali, "Vehicular Ad Hoc Networks (Vanets): Issues and applications," Journal of Analysis and Computation, vol. 8, no. 1, (January-June 2012), pp. 31-45.

[3] P. Ranjan and K.- K. Ahirwar, "Comparative Study of VANET and MANET Routing Protocols," Proc. of the International Conference on Advanced Computing and Communication Technologies (ACCT 11), India, 2011, pp. 517-523.

[4] P. Salvoa, F. Cuomoa, A. Baiocchia, and I. Rubinb, " Investigating VANET dissemination protocols performance under high throughput conditions," Vehicular Communications, vol. 2, Issue 4, October 2015, pp. 185-194.

[5] A. Gorrieri and G. Ferrari, " Irresponsible AODV routing," Vehicular Communications, vol. 2, Issue 1, January 2015, pp. 47-57.

[6] C. Li, C. Zhao, L. Zhu, H. Lin, and J. Li, "Geographic routing protocol for vehicular ad hoc networks in city scenarios: a proposal and analysis "International Journal of Communication Systems, vol.27, Issue 12, December 2014, pp. 4126-4143.

[7] Y.-S. Chen, Ch.-S. Hsu, and Ch.-H. Cheng, "Network mobility protocol for vehicular ad hoc networks, " International Journal of Communication Systems ", vol. 27, Issue 11, November 2014, pp. 3042-3063, doi: 10.1002/dac.2525.

[8] W. Xiaonan and Q. Huanyan, "Constructing a VANET based on cluster chains," International Journal of Communication Systems, vol. 27, Issue 11, November 2014, pp. 2497-2517, doi: 10.1002/dac.2484.

[9] S. Harrabi, W. Chainbi, and K. Ghedira, " A Multi-Agent Proactive Routing Protocol for Vehicular Ad Hoc Networks," The 2014 International Symposium on Networks, Computers and Communications (ISNCC 14) , Hammamet- Tunisia, June 2014, pp. 1-6, doi:10.1109/SNCC.2014.6866523.

[10] K.-Z. Ghafoor, K. Abu Bakar, and H.-N. AL-Hashimi, "A Novel Delay- and Reliability-Aware Inter-Vehicle Routing Protocol," International Journal of Network Protocols and Algorithms, vol. 2, no. 2, 2010, pp. 66-88, doi: 10.5296/npa.v2i2.427.

[11] K. Petteri, " Classification of ad hoc routing protocols, " Finnish Defence Forces, Naval Academy, Finland, 2002.

[12] B. D. Shivahare, C. Wahi, and Shalini Shivhare, "Comparison Of Proactive And Reactive Routing Protocols In Mobile Adhoc Network Using Routing Protocol Property", International Journal of Emerging Technology and Advanced Engineering, vol.2, Issue 3, March 2012, pp. 356-359.

[13] S. Dhankhar and S. Agrawal "VANETs: A Survey on Routing Protocols and Issues, "International Journal of Innovative Research in Science, Engineering and Technology, vol. 3, Issue 6, June 2014, pp. 13427-13435.

[14] T. -W. Chen, and M. Gerla, "Global state routing: A new routing scheme for ad-hoc wireless networks," In IEEE International Conference on Communications (ICC 98), Atlanta, GA, June 1998, pp. 171-175, doi: 10.1109/ICC.1998.682615.

[15] R. R. More and S.V. Sankpal, "Performance evaluation of an efficient dsdv routing protocols for ad hoc networks", ITSI Transactions on Electrical and Electronics Engineering, vol.1, Issue 4, 2013, pp. 15-18.

[16] T. Clausen and P. Jacquet "Optimized Link State Routing Protocol (OLSR)," RFC 3626, Network Working Group, Oct. 2003.

[17] J. Yi, E. Cizeron, S. Hamma, B. Parrein, and P. Lesage, " Implementation of multipath and multiple descriptions coding in olsr," In Proceeding of 4th OLSR Introp/Workshop, Ottawa- Canada, 2008.

[18] G.-C, Gilbert, J.-W. Branch, and B.-K. Szymanski," A Self-selection Technique for Flooding and Routing in Wireless Ad-hoc Networks," International Journal of Network and Systems Management, vol. 14, no. 3, September 2006, pp. 359-380.

[19] D. -B. Johnson and D.-A. Maltz," Dynamic Source Routing in Ad Hoc Wireless Networks, " In Mobile Computing, chapter 5, Vol. 353 of the series. The Kluwer International Series in Engineering and Computer Science, 1996, pp. 153-181.

[20] C. Perkins, E. Belding-Royer, and S. Das, " Ad hoc on-demand distance vector (AODV) routing" IETF RFC, 3561, July 2003, doi: 10.17487/RFC3561.

[21] B. Maria, B. Nabil, S.- K. Deep, EL. Driss, "Recent study of routing protocols in VANET: survey and taxonomy," In The 1st International Workshop on Vehicular Networks and Telematics (WVNT 13), Marrakech-Morocco, 2013.

[22] Z. J. Haas, "The Zone Routing Protocol (ZRP) for ad hocnetworks," Internet Draft, Nov. 1997.

[23] A.-B. Kathole and Y. Pande," Survey Of Topology Based Reactive Routing Protocols In Vanet," International Journal of Scientific and Engineering Research, Vol. 4, Issue 6, June 2013, pp. 39-44.

[24] S. Negi and S. Rani," Comparative Study of Topology based Routing Protocols in VANET," International Journal of Computer Science and Information Technology and Security (IJCSITS), vol. 5, no. 3, June 2015, pp. 290-294.

[25] S. Makhija and S. Malik," Performance Evaluation Of Topology Based Routing Protocols In VANET," International Journal of Computer Science (IIJCS), vol. 1, Issue 2, July 2013, pp. 21-28.

[26] S. Allal and S. Boudjit, "Geocast Routing Protocol for Vanet: Survey and Geometry Driven Scheme Proposal," Journal of Internet Services and Information Security, vol. 3, 2013, pp. 20-36.

[27] B. Karp and H.-T. Kung, "GPSR: Greedy perimeter stateless routing for wireless networks," in Proceedings of the ACM/IEEE International Conference on Mobile Computing and Networking (MobiCom 00), Massachusetts, August 2000.

[28] F. Granelli, G. Boato, and D. Kliazovich, " MORA: A movement-based routing algorithm for vehicle ad hoc networks," In IEEE Workshop on Automotive Networking and Applications (AutoNet 06), San Francisco, 2006.

[29] J. Zhao and G. Cao, "VADD: vehicle-assisted data delivery in vehicular Ad hoc networks," IEEE Transactions on Vehicular Technology, vol. 57, no. 3, 2008, pp. 1910-1922.

[30] M. Jerbi, R. Meraihi, S.-M. Senouci, and Y. Ghamri-Doudane, "GyTAR: improved greedy traffic aware routing protocol for vehicular ad

hoc networks in city environments," in Proceedings of the 3rd ACM International Workshop on Vehicular Ad Hoc Networks (VANET 06), pp. 88-89, ACM, Los Angeles, September 2006.

[31] G. Korkmaz, E. Ekici, F. Ozgner, and U. Ozguner, "Urban multi-hop broadcast protocol for inter-vehicle communication systems," In Proceedings of the 1st ACM international workshop on Vehicular ad hoc networks(VANET 04), USA, 2004, pp. 76-85.

[32] B.-C. Seet, G. Liu, B.-S. Lee, C.-H. Foh, K.-J.Wong, and K.-K. Lee, " A-STAR: A mobile ad hoc routing strategy for metropolis vehicular communications," In Networking, Springer Berlin Heidelberg, 2004 , pp. 989-999.

[33] O. K. Tonguz, N. Wisitpongphan, and F. Bai, " DV-CAST: A distributed vehicular broadcast protocol for vehicular ad hoc networks" IEEE Wireless Communications, vol. 17, no. 2, 2010, pp. 47-57, doi: 10.1109/MWC.2010.5450660.

[34] A. Kurien and A. Diana," Survey on Various Position Based Routing Protocols in Vehicular Ad Hoc Network," International Journal of Engineering Research and Technology (IJERT), vol. 2, Issue 12, December 2013, pp. 3119-3123.

[35] A. Soni and D. K. Xaxa," Position Based Routing protocols in VANET for Better Link Quality: A Survey," International Journal of Science and Research (IJSR), vol. 4, Issue 4, August 2015, pp. 2493-2496.

[36] F. Li and Y. Wang, "Routing in vehicular ad hoc networks: A survey," IEEE Vehicular Technology Magazine, vol. 2, no. 2, June 2007, pp. 1222.

[37] Y. Xia, C. K. Yeo, and B. S. Lee, "Hierarchical cluster based routing for highly mobile heterogeneous MANET," in Proceedings of the International Conference on Network and Service Security (N2S 09), France, June 2009, pp. 1-6.

[38] R. A. Santns, R. M. Edwards, A. Edwards, and D. Belis, "A novel cluster-based location routing algorithm for inter-vehicular communication," Personal, Indoor and Mobile Radio Communications, IEEE proceedings of the 15th Annual Symposium, Barcelona- Spain, 2004.

[39] T. Song, W. Xia, T. Song, and L. Shen," A Cluster-Based Directional Routing Protocol in VANET," 12th IEEE International Conference on Communication and Mobile Computing (ICCT), Nanjing, 2010, pp. 1172-1175, doi: 10.1109/ICCT.2010.5689132.

[40] M. Jiang, J. Li, and Y. C. Tay, "Cluster Based Routing Protocol (CBRP) (Internet-Draft draft-ietf-manetcbrp- spec-01.txt)," in National University of Singapore, I. E. T. F. (IETF), Ed., 1999, pp. 1-27.

[41] U. Nagaraj, M. U. Kharat, and P. Dhamal," Study of Various Routing Protocols in VANET," International Journal of Computer Science and Technology (IJCST), vol. 2, Issue 4, (October- December 2011), pp. 45-52.

[42] V. A. Gajbhiye and R. W. Jasutkar,"A Review and Comparative Study of Routing Protocols for VANET," IJACKD Journal of research, vol. 2, Issue 1, February 2013 , pp. 11-16.

[43] OMNET++, URL : https://omnetpp.org/omnetpp/ [accessed: 2016-07-14].

[44] MATLAB, URL :http://www.mathworks.com/products/matlab/ [accessed: 2016-07-14].

A Low-Power, Tricky and Very Easy to Use Sensor Network Gateway Architecture with Application Example

Susanne Kenner
and Klaus Volbert

Technical University of Applied Sciences
Regensburg, Germany
Email: {susanne1.kenner, klaus.volbert}@oth-regensburg.de

Abstract—**Wireless Sensor Network gateways are key components to connect smart environments with Internet of Things and to support Wireless Sensor Network applications. With regard to the increasing amount of smart devices, communicating with each other in Home area networks or over the Internet, low cost and low power devices are desirable. In this paper, we present such a low cost and low power gateway and system architecture with an example application in the Smart Home environment to control smart devices with a mobile application. We show an easy way to use low cost and low power hardware to expand the existing home network just with an USB-Stick without any extra power supply. The gateway we developed needs only 0.3 % of the average power consumption of the used network router.**

Keywords–Sensor Networks; Sensor Network Architecture; Sensor Network Gateway; Low-Power Devices; Internet of Things.

I. Introduction

The Internet of Things (IoT) is the next Internet generation, which expands the present Internet and machine-to-machine communication of smart and active devices to a larger global network of connected devices and sensors. 24 billion devices are expected in 2020 [1], communicating with each other and making smart decisions based on huge amounts of data. For this reason, many research works are in process in the IoT field. The IoT consists of different sectors like home automation systems, health applications, logistic applications, warehousing, industrial production, smart grid and many other sectors. The Radio Frequency Identification (RFID) technology and Wireless Sensor Networks (WSN) are key technologies and wide-spread in the IoT sectors to collect sensor data and control and connect devices to the Internet [1]. WSNs are used for many applications. In health care sector, they can be used to analyze the sleep of people which have an infrequent breathing during sleep, for fall detection systems or a better and faster diagnostic through doctors. In the agriculture industry, WSNs can help to increase the harvest by tracking moisture, nutrients, lightning and temperature values. Energy monitoring, weather monitoring and use cases in the industry are only a few application areas. In [2], the authors give a detailed review of the named application areas. An example work for an agriculture industry use case is presented in [3] and in [4], an application in the Smart Home area is presented, which combines the RFID and WSN technologies. WSNs consist of many nodes, which track data from sensors and transmit them to a gateway. The gateway collects data from all sensors and often visualizes and analyzes them. In the IoT the gateway is a key component, which connects the WSNs to the Internet and therefore, the use cases named above were taken to the next level. The amount of nodes in WSNs and the expected amount of devices in the IoT are one of the reasons for developing low cost and low power devices in this environment. Another reason is the transition in energy policies, especially in Europe. The increasing power demand and the transition from conventional to renewable energy sources have an impact on the stability of the power grid [5]. Low power IoT gateways can support Smart Grid applications to stabilize the power grid or to analyze smart environments. For example, they can be used as gateways for collecting energy values in a low voltage grid as described in [6] or for monitoring data from energy analyzers in a small smart grid scenario as presented in [7]. Additionally, low power devices contribute to the reduction of the CO_2 emission, which was decided by the European Parliament [8]. In this paper we present a Wireless Sensor Network gateway architecture with focus on low cost hardware and low power functions.

This paper is structured as follows. Section II introduces the gateway design idea and names some similar works on this topic. Section III describes the eZ430 Development kit we used for developing the gateway and in Section IV the gateway architecture is explained in detail, followed by an application example in Section V. Section VI shows the power consumption of the gateway and finally, Section VII concludes this paper.

II. Motivation and Related Work

Smart devices like smart fridges, smart washing machines, automatic controllable heating systems, window shutters and switchable outlets, controlled by a radio control unit, are integrated in modern households. Several solutions for home automation systems like RWE Smart Home [9], Telekom Smart Home system [10] or HomeMatic [11] are offered in the market but each manufacturer develops their own closed system with a special communication protocol and gateway device. Additionally, the systems often are not power optimized and need an additional power supply. Besides the named Smart Home systems, the Startup Codeatelier first followed the same approach as we, but they do not describe how they couple the USB-Stick with the router [12]. In this paper, we show how simple a router could be expand by an USB gateway to get WSN functionality at the home network and connect them to the IoT. There are existing several gateway architectures in literature as named in the following. In [13] the authors describe the design and implementation of an embedded Linux gateway for monitoring smart home health system data. A flexible gateway with different communication interfaces is presented in [14]. The gateway architecture modules are replaceable depending on the application running at the system. Further gateway architectures and systems are presented in [15] and [16]. Another interesting approach show the authors in [17] by using a Smartphone as a (mobile) gateway. Combined with an Arduino hardware board the Smartphone receives data from sensors and transmits data to the Internet. However, this approach needs an extra hardware like the Arduino board, with extra power supply, for connecting sensors and transmitting data to the Smartphone.

In contrast to the referred works above, we present a gateway architecture without extra power supply by integrating the gateway in the existing home network infrastructure. Almost every household uses a router with an USB-Port, which provides USB devices like printers and external hard disks in the network. We exploit this feature to connect a USB-Stick as gateway for a home automation system via the USB-Port of the router with the home network. Through the usage of low cost hardware and free available software we present a low cost and very easy to use sensor network gateway. The most similar approach to our one is presented in [18]. The authors also develop a gateway, which communicates over the USB-Interface with an USB-Host like a PC or RaspberryPi to monitoring data from a WSN. Different USB communication classes are possible and they tested the system with the Virtual Serial Port and Ethernet Emulation classes. These USB communication classes need a system driver on the host which means that the usage is restricted on devices with driver support. In our system the USB Mass Storage class, which needs only a standard driver provided by all USB host devices, is used. Therefore, it is possible to connect our gateway to any host device without needing a driver. On this basis it is possible to expand existing network devices like routers in the home network so that they operate as the interface to the IoT as described in this paper. We combine different known technologies to design a gateway, which emulates a file system and communicates over the USB port of a router with the network.

III. eZ430-Chronos Development Kit

The eZ430-Chronos kit is a development kit from Texas Instruments including a programmable watch, an access point with radio module and a programming interface as shown in Figure 1. The kit is available for the following different ISM/SRD-Band frequencies: 915 MHz (America), 433 MHz (worldwide usable) and 868 MHz (Europe and India). The microcontroller in the watch case is a CC430F6137 with integrated sub-1GHz wireless radio module based on the CC1101. The eZ430 consists of a 96-segment LCD Display, a pressure sensor, three-axis accelerometer, temperature and battery voltage sensor. Additionally, a heart rate monitor can be connected, communicating over the BlueRobin protocol [19]. The Access point (middle usb device in Figure 1) is an USB-based microcontroller and consists of a MSP430F5509 microcontroller and a CC1101 radio module for communication with the watch [20]. There are two different access points available. We use the newer release of the eZ430 Chronos kit with the white access point. The older eZ430 Chronos kit with black access point contains an CC1111 radio module. The MSP430F5509 is an ultra-low-power 16-bit RISC CPU with USB interface, 24 KB flash memory and 6 KB RAM. The supply voltage is between 1.8 to 3.6 VCC. It supports one active (AM) and 6 low power (LPM0 - LPM4.5) operating modes. Table I shows power consumption according to interesting operating modes [21]. Due to the characteristics like low power (our application mainly runs in LPM 3), low costs and the free availability of hard- and software, we use this kit in our system. For developing a gateway for home automation systems we only need the access point of the kit.

Figure 1. Texas Instruments eZ430 Chronos - Development Kit

TABLE I. MSP430F5509 OPERATING MODES AND POWER CONSUMPTION [21]

Operating mode	Description	power consumption
AM	All clocks active	115 - 195 μA/MHz
LPM 3	Standby mode - CPU, MCLK, FLL loop control, DCOCLK, DCO's generator disabled	1.4 - 2.1 μA
LPM 4	CPU, MCLK, ACLK, FLL loop control, DCOCLK, DCO dc generator disabled, Crystal oscillator is stopped, Complete data retention	1.1 μA
LPM 4.5	Internal regulator disabled, No data retention	0.18 μA

IV. Gateway Architecture

In our work we create a low power gateway for home automation. This gateway should be integrated in existing network infrastructure to save energy and costs. To realize this, we designed the architecture shown in Figure 2. The access point described above was programmed as a gateway and coupled with a FRITZ!Box router. The gateway communicates over the USB interface with the router by emulating a file system and is mounted as USB flash device in the integrated NAS-System. At the other side the gateway is able to communicate over the radio module with different devices at home to monitor sensor data or control them. The FRITZ!Box router supports data access over FTP, HTTP and the Server Message Block (SMB) protocol, so it is possible to request data by different clients. The router is also able to make the data available through the Internet by registering the FRITZ!Box router at

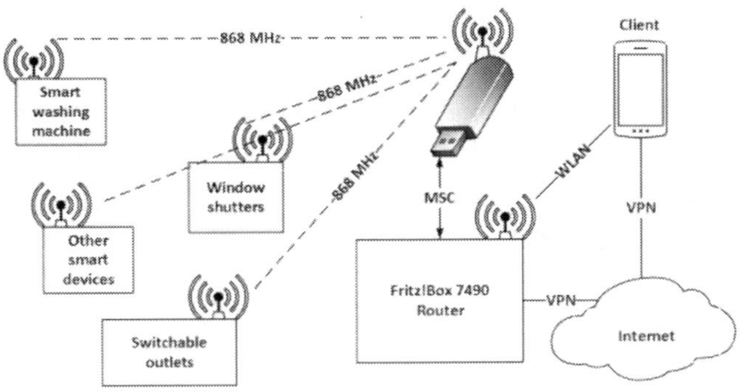

Figure 2. System architecture

the AVM domain service. In our scenario we implemented an Android application which uses the SMB protocol to request data. Additionally it is possible to set up a VPN (Virtual private network) connection between the FRITZ!Box router and the Android client, so we communicate over a secure channel from outside the home network.

A. USB Mass Storage Class (MSC)

The MSC is one of the USB device classes, which are defined for the communication between an USB-Device and an USB-Host. The device classes summarize devices with similar functions to standardize the communication interface. Each host provides a standard driver for each defined USB device class and so also for MSC devices. The MSC profile provides an interface for reading and writing file systems [22] [23].

Texas Instruments provides an example code package for training and testing with the different USB communication classes for free. This package is available for Windows, Linux and MAC systems and can be downloaded at [24]. The package demonstrates the USB-Development with MSP430 devices and provides the USB communication device class (CDC), human interface device (HID) and mass storage class (MSC). We used the included example for file system emulation `M1_FileSystemEmulation` and make some changes for our scenario. Some hardware settings were adjusted to the MSP430F5509 of the access point. The emulated file system in the example with a size of 83456 byte is too big for the available hardware. As described in Section III the access point only has a flash memory of 24 KB. Approx. 18 KB is needed for the program code, so we changed the emulated file system size to 4 KB by creating an FAT12 file system with 7 sectors, whereas each sector has a size of 512 byte. A FAT12 file system normally consists of 2 file allocation tables (FATs), but due to the limited flash memory size we set the value for provided FATs in the BIOS Parameter Block (BPB) to 1. The first three sectors are used by the FAT12 file system, sector 4 includes the "data_log.txt" file and the remaining sectors are free at the beginning. By connecting the gateway to a host, the free available space will be used by the operating system. At the FRITZ!Box router this makes some trouble for the reason that the FRITZ!Box router indexing the files and overrides the flash memory at the gateway. In addition, the FRITZ!Box sets the mounted flash drive as write-protected, so it is impossible to exchange data with the gateway. To avoid this situation we create one file for each sector so the free available space at the gateway is zero and the operating system cannot write index or temp data on sectors. Therefore, the FRITZ!Box do not set the mounted flash drive as write-protected and it is possible to exchange data between gateway and router via the file system.

B. Communication

There are two communication ways implemented as shown in Figure 3. At the first one the client writes data via the SMB protocol over the network into the file "data_log.txt" mounted at the router NAS for controlling smart devices at home network. The gateway reads the flash memory area for this file every 2 seconds, controlled by a timer, and read out the command codes. Independent on these codes it controls the smart devices by transmitting a radio sequence. The communication in the opposite direction is based on the smart devices. The smart devices like power outlets send data

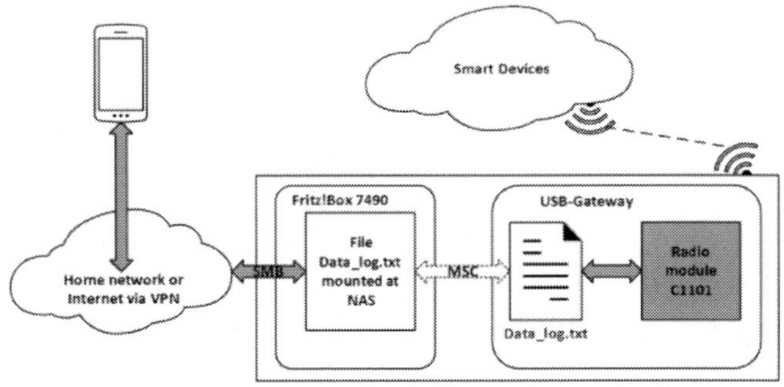

Figure 3. Gateway details

via radio sequence to the gateway. Subsequently the gateway software transforms the measurement in a human-readable value and writes this value into the flash memory area of a file. On the reason that the USB protocol is host driven the router as host takes no note of the changed file. The host caches the data read at USB plug in for the reason the host does not expect changes. A reset triggered through the Watchdog timer of the gateway forces the host to re-read the file system. In the case of using the FRITZ!Box router the remount of the USB flash drive has a duration time of $\sim$ 10 seconds. After this time the files are available again. To realize the radio communication between the gateway and the smart devices we integrate parts of the radio code from the original access point code example into the emulated file system example.

V. APPLICATION EXAMPLE

We test the low power gateway and the architecture described above in a small test environment. At this a little smart home environment with a switchable power outlet and 7 window shutters is used as proof of concept scenario. The switchable power outlet is a FS20 ST-4 with a Breaking capacity of 16 A at 230 V and a built-in timer to switch devices on or off depending on time [25]. The FS20 RSU-2 window shutters are flush-mounted sockets also with a built-in timer for time-depending operations [26]. The devices are controllable through the FS20 protocol via radio at the 868 MHz SRD band. This protocol is only used as example to demonstrate the low power gateway. In the following the FS20 system is described and the example application is presented.

A. FS20 System

The FS20 system is a smart home radio control system with many different devices in the home automation sector [27]. The system is distributed by the companies Conrad Electronics and ELV, which is the copyright holder of the FS20 protocol and devices. There are controllable devices like switchable power outlets, electric window shutters, rain sensors, temperature sensors, etc. These devices are controllable via transmitters like radio remote control or gateway devices. The receivers can be integrated in the home automation system through the following described addressing scheme. It consists of 4 different address types and a home code. Each remote control or gateway has its own home code address with a length of 8 digits, so it is possible to run more radio systems side by side in the same environment. The receivers are addressable with up to 4 addresses with a length of 4 digits, one for each address type. There are 225 single, 15 function group, 15 local master addresses and 1 global master address. With function group addresses it is possible to control several receivers of the same kind with one command. The local master address forms spatial groups, e.g., to switch all devices in one room on or off by sending one command. The global master address also forms one group with several receivers, e.g., all devices in a house [26]. The FS20 communication protocol operates at a

TABLE II. FS20 COMMAND CODES [26]

FS20 command	Description
0x00	device off
0x01	device on, 6.25% brightness level 1
0x02	device on, 12.5% brightness level 2
...	...
0x0f	device on, 93,75% brightness level 16 (max)
0x10	device on
0x11	device on, set to last brightness level
0x12	toggle between off and on with last brightness level
0x13	dim up to the next brightness level
0x14	dim down the brightness level
0x15	changing between dim up and down
0x18	device off, depending on timer
0x19	device on, depending on timer
0x1a	device on, last brightness level, depending on timer

frequency of 868.35 MHz and uses the amplitude modulation [25]. Table II shows some different commands for controlling smart FS20 devices as described in [26]. According to the device type some commands have different effects. At window shutters all commands for dimming up and for switching on are used to switch the device on and run them up. All commands for dimming down and for switching off are used to run the windows shutters down and switch them off. The commands can be expand by an extension byte. With this one it is possible to control the devices depending on time settings as described in [26]. A more detailed protocol description can be found at web.

B. Proof of concept application

For the proof of concept application, the access point of the eZ430 Chronos additionally was configured for FS20 data transmission. The main settings for the CC1101 radio module is listed in table III. For each device we create a control frame, for example to switch the power outlet on or off. The control of the devices and the access to the file system at the gateway is encapsulated through an Android application. The Android client is connected to the FRITZ!Box router via home network or over the Internet as described above. Each smart device is controllable through one button, which switches the power outlet on or off or pulls up and down the window shutters. The client application saves the commands of the buttons in the "data_log.txt" file, which are not visible for the user. We

TABLE III. CC1101 MAIN SETTINGS

Register	Value	Description
MCSM0	0x18	XOSC-Timeout 149-155μs, calibration at IDLE to TX
PKTLEN	0x23	Packet length: 35 Bytes
PKTCTRL0	0x04	Fixed packet length modus, CRC calculation disabled, data-whitening disabled
FREQ2 FREQ1 FREQ0	0x21 0x65 0xE8	Frequency: 868,35 MHz
MDMCFG4 MDMCFG3	0x87 0x93	Data rate: 5.00107 kBaud ~ 5 kBaud
MDMCFG2	0x30	Preamble disabled, Synchronization word disabled, Amplitude modulation
AGCCTRL2	0x43	Highest DVGA-asset can not be used
FREND0	0x11	Amplitude modulation: Setting for transmitting a 1 in PATABLE(1)

use 1 Byte for each command as described in table IV. After these 18 bytes there are 6 more bytes available. For example these could be used for pulling up and down the window shutters at set times, for time synchronization between gateway and USB-Host or for additional devices. The values saved at "data_log.txt" are checked periodically by a timer. Every two seconds the gateway checks if the values at the flash memory of the "data_log.txt" are changed. According to the changes the gateway triggers the equivalent action and transmits the control frame for the command via the radio module to the device. The command structure could be optimized by using

TABLE IV. APPLICATION CONTROL COMMANDS

Position in "data_log.txt"	Operation when Byte changed
Byte 1 / Byte 2	Pulls up/down all window shutters
Byte 3 / Byte 4	Pull up/down window shutter 1
...	...
Byte 15 / Byte 16	Pull up/down window shutter 7
Byte 17 / Byte 18	Turn power outlet on/off

just one bit for one command or by using XML-files. Further protocol extensions are possible to support different devices, communicating via other protocols, e.g., z-Wave [28]. Through the separation of control and data flow efficient low power energy monitoring is possible. As described above the gateway is able to write received data from radio devices into the flash memory. Received energy values from energy analyzers can be saved in a second file on the emulated file system and read out via the MSC Profile from the host respectively the Smartphone application.

VI. Power consumption

The MSP430F5509 microcontroller and the CC1101 radio module are low power devices as described above. In the following, we show typical current consumption values for the used hardware. Based on these values we show the power consumption of our developed gateway. The total amount of power consumption consists of the consumption of the MSP430F5509, depending on clock frequency and power mode, and the consumption of the radio module, depending on radio power output and operation mode. As shown in table I the current consumption of the MSP430F5509 in active mode is between 115 and 195 μA/MHz, and in LPM3 mode between 1.4 and 2.1 μA. Depending on these values, table V shows the power consumption at different supply voltage levels and clock frequencies for the active operation mode and LPM3. The maximum power consumption with frequency of 25 MHz and a supply voltage of 3.6 is 17.55 mW and in LPM3 mode the maximum value is 0.0076 mW. For the CC1101 radio module we consider the current consumption in IDLE State, receiving (RX) and transmitting (TX) mode. In IDLE state the radio module needs 1.7 mA, in RX mode 15 mA, in TX mode 30 mA (SLEEP state with 0.2 μA is negligible) [29]. Table VI shows the power consumption for these modes, depending on the different supply voltage levels. The maximum values are 6.12 mW for IDLE state, 108 mW for TX and 54 mW for RX mode. Due to the fact, that the application is in IDLE state most of the time, the total amount of power consumption of our system is approx. $17.55mW + 6.12mW = 23.67mW$. Depending on the frequency of sending commands, the power consumption for TX mode must be added. In our example application we mainly use window shutters. In a household the persons typically run up the window shutters at morning and run them down at evening. Under this assumption the TX mode is entered twice at a day for some microseconds. With regard to the statutory duty cycle, which limits time the gateway can transmit at 868 MHz band (1% transmitting time in 1 hour), the power consumption results as follows. A transmitter can only transmit data at 868 MHz band for 0.01 h in 1 h, so the maximum power consumption for RX in this time is $108 \cdot 10^{-3}W \cdot 0.01h = 0.00108Wh$. Additionally with the $23.67 \cdot 10^{-3}Wh$ from above we get a power consumption of 0.02475 Wh for our gateway. These values could be reduced by using a lower supply voltage as described in the tables or by using a lower radio output power level. However, in comparison with the power consumption of the FRITZ!Box router the values of the gateway are negligible. The FRITZ!Box router has an average power consumption of 9.3 Wh and a maximum of 27 Wh [30]. As described in the router manual, the average power consumption was determined with an active DSL connection, active WLAN, active DECT with one connected phone and one connected LAN device without data transfer.

TABLE V. POWER CONSUMPTION MSP430F5509

Clock Frequency	1.8 V Min / Max mW	3.0 V Min / Max mW	3.6 V Min / Max mW
8 MHz	1.66 / 2.81	2.76 / 4.68	3.31 / 5.62
16 MHz	3.31 / 5.62	5.52 / 9.36	6.62 / 11.23
25 MHz	5.18 / 8.78	8.63 / 14.63	10.35 / 17.55
LPM3	0.0025 / 0.0038	0.0042 / 0.0063	0.005 / 0.0076

TABLE VI. POWER CONSUMPTION CC1101

Supply Voltage	IDLE	TX	RX
1.8 V	3.06 mW	54 mW	27 mW
3.0 V	5.1 mW	90 mW	45 mW
3.6 V	6.12 mW	108 mW	54 mW

VII. Conclusion

In this paper, we presented a low power and low cost sensor network gateway, which could be integrated in existing network infrastructures at home. Due to the fact that the gateway is just a little USB-Stick and it communicates over the USB-MSC Profile with a router, we present a gateway, which needs no extra power supply. The power consumption of the gateway is just approx. 0.3 % of the power consumption of the router. Therefore, the consumption of the gateway is negligible. The application example shows the easy use of the system and further applications like monitoring of sensor data or controlling washing machines or alarm systems are possible. The gateway is also useable in the industry by energy service providers to read out power and water consumption over the internet or by utility companies to monitoring the power grid. The next steps are the optimization of the command structure, implementing a flexible application for different smart devices with different protocol stacks and analyzing performance parameters and the possible amount of concurrently supported sensors in the system.

Acknowledgment

This work was supported by the Regensburg Center of Energy and Resources (RCER) and the Technology- and Science Network Oberpfalz (TWO). Further information under www.rcer.de.

References

[1] J. Gubbi, R. Buyya, S. Marusic, and M. Palaniswami, "Internet of things (iot): A vision, architectural elements, and future directions," Future Generation Computer Systems, vol. 29, no. 7, 2013, pp. 1645–1660, DOI: 10.1016/j.future.2013.01.010.

[2] H. M. Ammari et al., "A survey of sensor network applications and architectural components," Ad Hoc & Sensor Wireless Networks, vol. 25, 2015, pp. 1–44, ISSN: 1551-9899.

[3] T. Gomes, J. Brito, H. Abreu, H. Gomes, and J. Cabral, "Greenmon: An efficient wireless sensor network monitoring solution for greenhouses," in Industrial Technology (ICIT), 2015 IEEE International Conference on. IEEE, 2015, pp. 2192–2197, DOI: 10.1109/ICIT.2015.7125420.

[4] S. Hussain, S. Schaffner, and D. Moseychuck, "Applications of wireless sensor networks and rfid in a smart home environment," in Communication Networks and Services Research Conference, 2009. CNSR'09. Seventh Annual. IEEE, 2009, pp. 153–157, ISBN: 978-1-4244-4155-6.

[5] X. Fang, S. Misra, G. Xue, and D. Yang, "Smart gridthe new and improved power grid: A survey," Communications Surveys & Tutorials, IEEE, vol. 14, no. 4, 2012, pp. 944–980, DOI: 10.1109/SURV.2011.101911.00087.

[6] G. Zenger, S. Kenner, K. Volbert, T. Waas, and M. Kucera, "Acquiring energy data from a medium-voltage grid for future smart grid solutions: A practical smart grid application example realized by use of cellular communication networks of the 2 nd and 3 rd generation," in Intelligent Solutions in Embedded Systems (WISES), 2013 Proceedings of the 11th Workshop on. IEEE, 2013, pp. 1–8, ISBN: 978-3-00-042899-9.

[7] S. Kenner, R. Thaler, M. Kucera, K. Volbert, and T. Waas, "Smart grid architecture for monitoring and analyzing, including modbus and rest performance comparison," in Intelligent Solutions in Embedded Systems (WISES), 2015 12th International Workshop on. IEEE, 2015, pp. 91–96, ISBN: 978-88-87548-06-8.

[8] "Europe 2020 - a strategy for smart, sustainable and inclusive growth," 2010, URL: http://eurlex.europa.eu/LexUriServ/LexUriServ.do?uri=COM:2010:2020:FIN:EN:PDF [accessed 2016-04-06].

[9] "Rwe smart home," URL: https://www.rwe-smarthome.de/web/cms/de/2768534/home/ [accessed 2016-04-06].

[10] "Telekom smart home," URL: https://www.smarthome.de/was-ist-smarthome [accessed 2016-04-06].

[11] "Homematic smart home," URL: http://www.homematic.com/ [accessed 2016-04-06].

[12] "Homee - Smart Home so easy as Lego," URL: http://www.siio.de/homee-smart-home-so-einfach-wie-lego/ [accessed: 2016-03-16].

[13] M. Mittek, J. D. Carlson, and L. C. Pérez, "Design and implementation of a low-cost embedded linux gateway for smart home health monitoring," in Electro/Information Technology (EIT), 2014 IEEE International Conference on. IEEE, 2014, pp. 485–490, DOI: 10.1109/EIT.2014.6871812.

[14] S. Guoqiang, C. Yanming, Z. Chao, and Z. Yanxu, "Design and implementation of a smart iot gateway," in Green Computing and Communications (GreenCom), 2013 IEEE and Internet of Things (iThings/CPSCom), IEEE International Conference on and IEEE Cyber, Physical and Social Computing. IEEE, 2013, pp. 720–723, DOI: 10.1109/GreenCom-iThings-CPSCom.2013.130.

[15] C. Kruger, A. Abu-Mahfouz, and G. Hancke, "Rapid prototyping of a wireless sensor network gateway for the internet of things using off-the-shelf components," in Industrial Technology (ICIT), 2015 IEEE International Conference on. IEEE, 2015, pp. 1926–1931, DOI: 10.1109/ICIT.2015.7125378.

[16] B. D. S. Campos et al., "Design and construction of a wireless sensor and actuator network gateway based on 6lowpan," in EUROCON-International Conference on Computer as a Tool (EUROCON), 2011 IEEE. IEEE, 2011, pp. 1–4, ISBN: 978-1-4244-7486-8.

[17] S. K. Dhar, S. S. Bhunia, S. Roy, and N. Mukherjee, "Enabling smartphone as gateway to wireless sensor network," in Recent Advances in Information Technology, RAIT-2014 Proceedings. Springer, 2014, pp. 19–26, ISBN: 978-81-322-1855-5.

[18] A. Voinescu, D. Tudose, and D. Dragomir, "A lightweight, versatile gateway platform for wireless sensor networks," in Networking in Education and Research, 2013 RoEduNet International Conference 12th Edition. IEEE, 2013, pp. 1–4, ISSN: 2068-1038, ISBN: 978-1-4799-2599-5.

[19] "Bm wireless ltd.&co.kg - bluerobin^{TM} technology," URL: http://www.bmwireless.com/index.php/references_bmwireless.html [accessed 2016-04-06].

[20] "ez430-chronos^{TM} development tool - user guide," URL: http://www.ti.com/lit/ug/slau292g/slau292g.pdf [accessed: 2016-03-21].

[21] "The msp430f5509 mixed signal microcontroller - datasheet," URL: http://www.ti.com/product/MSP430F5509/description [accessed: 2016-03-21].

[22] J. Axelson, USB complete: the developer's guide. Lakeview research LLC, 2015, ISBN: 978-1-931448-28-4.

[23] ——, USB mass storage: designing and programming devices and embedded hosts. lakeview research llc, 2006, ISBN: 978-1-931448-05-5.

[24] "Usb developer package 5.0.01," URL: http://software-dl.ti.com/msp430/msp430_public_sw/mcu/msp430/MSP430_USB_Developers_Package/latest/index_FDS.html [accessed: 2016-03-22].

[25] "Wireless switch socket "fs20 st"," URL: http://www.produktinfo.conrad.com/datenblaetter/600000-624999/623004-an-01-en-FUNK_SCHALTSTECKDOSE_FS_20_ST.pdf [accessed 2016-04-06].

[26] "Radio controlable window shutter," URL: http://www.produktinfo.conrad.com/datenblaetter/1000000-1099999/001093002-an-01-de-FS20_RSU_2_UP_FUNK_ROLLLADENSCHALTER.pdf [accessed 2016-04-06].

[27] "Fs20 - radio control system," URL: http://www.elv.de/fs20-funkschaltsystem.html [accessed 2016-06-13].

[28] "zwave alliance," URL: http://z-wavealliance.org/ [accessed 2016-04-06].

[29] "Cc1101 - low-power sub-1ghz rf transceiver," URL: http://www.ti.com/lit/ds/swrs061i/swrs061i.pdf [accessed: 2016-06-13].

[30] "Fritz!box manual," URL: https://avm.de/fileadmin/user_upload/DE/Handbuecher/FRITZ_Box/Handbuch_FRITZ_Box_7490.pdf [accessed 2016-06-13].

IoT-based Wireless Access Point for Underground Safety Services

Taewook Heo, Sanggi Hong*, Jaehum Lee and Inhwan Lee
UGS Convergence Research Division, IoT Convergence Research Division*
ETRI (Electronics and Telecommunications Research Institute)
Daejeon, Korea
e-mail: {htw398, sghong*, ljh, ihlee}@etri.re.kr

***Abstract*— Recently, many researchers have focused on solving problems related to sinkholes, exploring both natural and artificial options. To address this problem, researchers need to work with land subsidence related to groundwater. In this paper, we consider outdoor environmental factors such as groundwater, water supply, and sewer and propose an Underground SAfety Hybrid (USAH) architecture. Specifically, the WAPUS (Wireless Access Point for Underground Safety services for Sinkhole detection) exploits a periodic monitoring and an aperiodic sensing. To increase the accuracy and reliability, we propose a hybrid architecture which merges these techniques. Furthermore, in our proposed architecture, the sensor nodes collect sensing data as part of periodic monitoring and our platform carefully examines it using aperiodic sensing. Our simulation results show that WAPUS enhances the reliability in the hybrid special condition.**

Keywords—sink hole; underwater detection; wireless sensing

I. Introduction

Recently, there has been an increasing interest in the processes going on under the ground in Korea. Humans can not see the natural sinkholes that form underground. Because of artificial water supply and sewer leaks, a subsidence of the ground occurs. This phenomenon has given rise to social issues [8] [9].

In particular, if water leaks occur underground, they are likely to cause sinkholes. For this reason, several sinkhole technologies have been proposed. Many proposals [4] dealt with how to connect the information gathered from the sensors of the central server. In general, smart meters using ZigBee method have wireless networks (900MHz, 2.4GHz ISM band). LoRaWAN is a Low Power Wide Area Network (LPWAN) specification intended for wireless battery operated Things in regional, national or global network [2]. LoRa technology has over 1Km RF (Radio Frequency) range and the LoRa alliance wants to achieve reliable networks.

This paper explains that WAPUS has several networks simultaneously connected to the central server using several connecting methods, such as WiFi network, Ethernet, and Long Term Evolution (LTE) [6].

Secondly, WAPUS supports IEC/ISO 30128 specification to connect to the server and IEEE 802.15.4 standardization to link reliable RF connectivity.

Due to its support for standard interfaces, WAPUS has a merit of dynamic extensibility.

Periodic sensing has to use an existing technique via the various wireless sensor networks, which will be expanded into the Internet of Things applications. Further, these applications include a lot of aperiodic and non-destructive techniques.

The rest of this paper is structured as follows. In Section II, we present USAH architecture, which can be used for wireless sensing. Section III describes the application and the architectural benefits of WAPUS. In Section IV, we introduce a system design that takes into consideration the hybrid wireless sensing data. In Section V, we evaluate the WAPUS based on the simulation environment. Finally, in Section VI, we provide some concluding remarks along with directions for future research.

II. USAH and WAPUS Architecture

The architecture presented in this paper is a sensor network infrastructure that is used by the general wireless sensor network architecture [1]-[3]. Current legacy infrastructure provides a common standard interface and a core infrastructure of the sensor network [7].

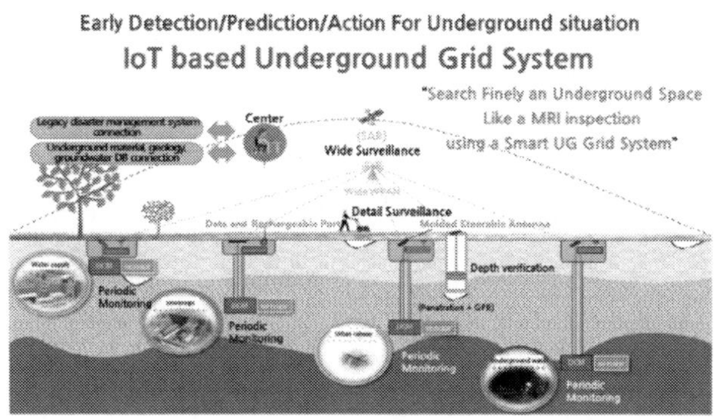

Figure 1. USAH system scenario [5].

The main idea provided in this paper is a method of collecting periodic and aperiodic sensing information at the same time. Periodic sensing has long break periods to achieve low power consumption. It performs aperiodic sensing if slightly suspicious information is reported from periodic sensing. By using this method, it is possible to perform hybrid sensing by utilizing low power consumption.

We propose a hybrid structure with the aperiodic sensing information and periodic sensing information serving at the same time (see Figure 1 [5]).

Our WAPUS has several features;

1. Multi network connections (LTE, WiFi, Ethernet, etc.)
2. Two RF modules with dynamic ranges
3. NXP Cortex-A7 dual processor with 1GHz DDR 3 memory
4. 4+ UART ports

A. WAPUS Hardware Architecture

First, WAPUS supports several interfaces to be able to have multi networks (LTE, WiFi, Ethernet, etc.). In Figure 2, our platform has 2 RF ports, WiFi port, and LTE port. Also, WAPUS supports dual RF modes to know dynamic situations simultaneously.

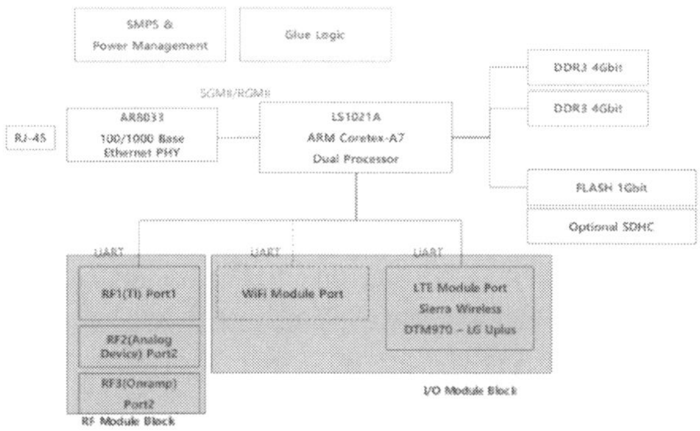

Figure 2. WAPUS Hardware Block Diagram.

B. WAPUS Software Architecture

The software architecture of WAPUS is as follows: WAPUS has multi-thread blocks and fundamental functions of logging, configuration, UART connection and network connections.

WAPUS has N2S (Node to Server) thread block that processes the messages transferred from PANC (PAN coordinator) through UART (Universal Asynchronous Receiver/Transmitter), and S2N (Server to Node) thread block that processes the messages transferred from the server through TCP (Transmission Control Protocol).

Also, WAPUS has a system initialization function and an AP (Access Point) main function (see Figure 3).

III. APPLICATION AND ARCHITECTURAL BENEFITS OF WAPUS

Our WAPUS proposal has several advantages, as follows. The WAPUS, unlike existing AP, has a structure that supports two or more RF devices. The AP with two or more RF components has an advantage in scalability. Another WAPUS advantage is the stability of the network. Furthermore, by supporting the ISO standard, WAPUS provides compatibility with other devices.

- ✓ WAPUS provides an aperiodic sensing function, periodic monitoring and a merged hybrid platform using these methods.
- ✓ WAPUS proposes a dual RX/TX queue architecture to remove a bottleneck of gateway.
- ✓ WAPUS provides extensibility with the ISO standard interface adaptation.
- ✓ WAPUS has several interfaces to allow aperiodic data sensing such as moving images.

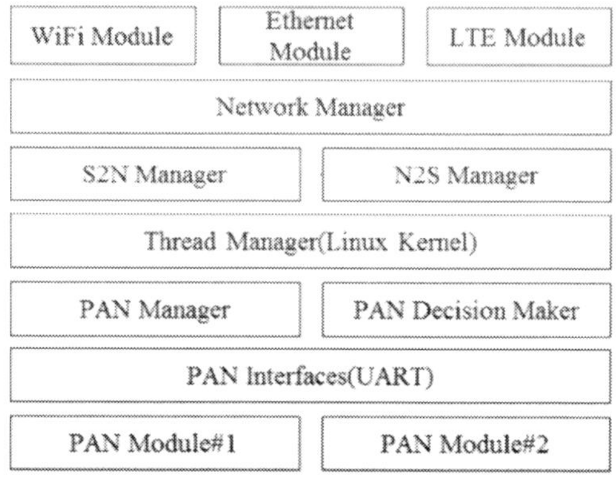

Figure 3. WAPUS Software Block Diagram.

A. PAN Decision Maker Algorithm

The proposed algorithm used in the PAN Decision Maker is as follows: The PAN Manager selects the better PAN module from the available networks, as shown in Figure 4.

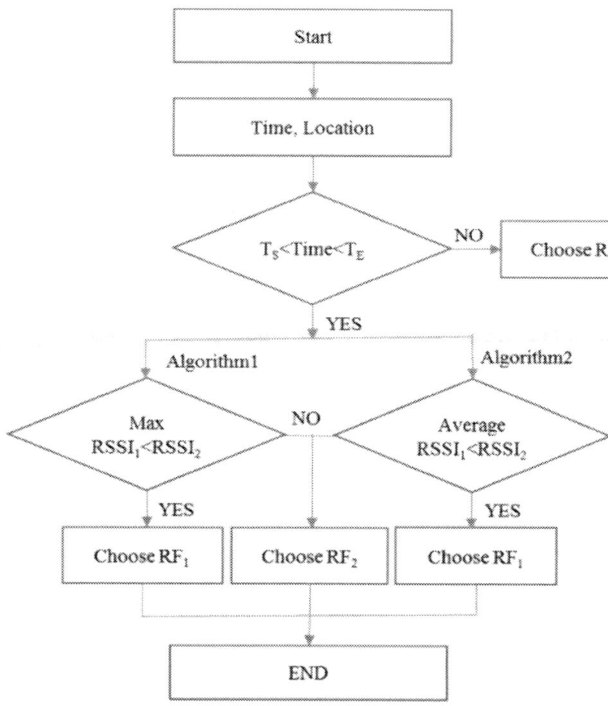

Figure 4. PAN Decision Maker Algorithm.

Referring to Figure 5, while managing two or more RF modules AP gateway corresponding to the spatial domain,

WAPUS communicates with the sensor nodes using the RF1 module at point A and RF2 module for communication of the C point.

Basically, it will be responsible for different communication modules in Zone1 and Zone2.

Since the sensor node's RF characteristics vary at point B existing between the Zone1 and Zone2, the WAPUS selects the RF module according to the RSSI (Received Signal Strength Indicator) and RF characteristics.

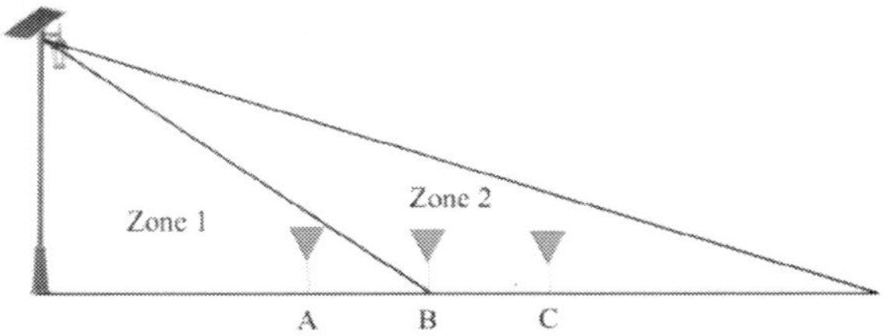

Figure 5. Sensor nodes spatial layout.

The method of RF selection is as follows. Firstly, we propose that average RSSI values are accumulated N times in selecting an RF module. We consider a method of selecting by using maximum and minimum values. If the difference between maximum value and minimum value is large, we will change to the better RF module. If the difference value is minimal, we keep the original RF module.

Also, we select the RF module depending on the determined angle, the obstacles and other settings between the sensor node and the WAPUS.

Normally, we have a choice of RF modules that gives a better RSSI value. We measure the average RF signal strength of at least N times, analyze the optimization characteristics of the communication, and choose to use the optimal RF module. We choose to collect N times or more RF signal strength, in consideration of the location and time change. This will select the RF module. Also, it will be determined in consideration of 2.4GHz method and 900MHz modulation scheme.

IV. EVALUATION

To evaluate our proposal, we used the Matlab toolkit. Simply, we propose a sensor accuracy model, as seen in Figure 6. We can calculate several parameters from equations (1)-(3).

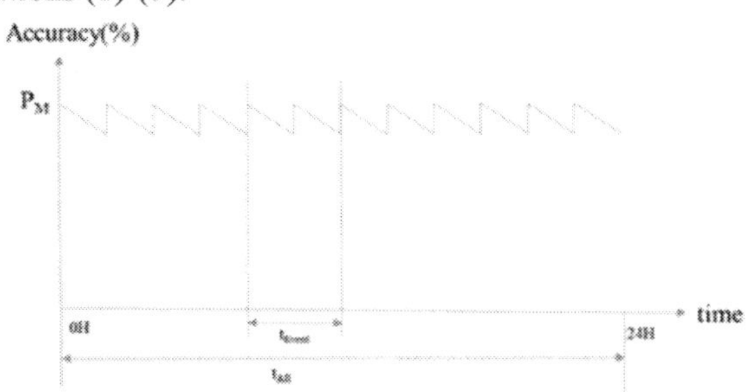

Figure 6. The sensor accuracy model with time interval.

$$R_{Event} = \frac{t_{Event}}{t_{All}} \quad (1)$$

$$P_{Accuracy} = P_M(1 - \delta(t - t_M)) \quad (2)$$

$$\delta = -5\%/hour \quad (3)$$

We show the average accuracy as a function of sensing rate (sensing counts/hour) in Figure 7 and the sensing cost versus aperiodic sensing over total sensing ratio in the simulation in Figure 8.

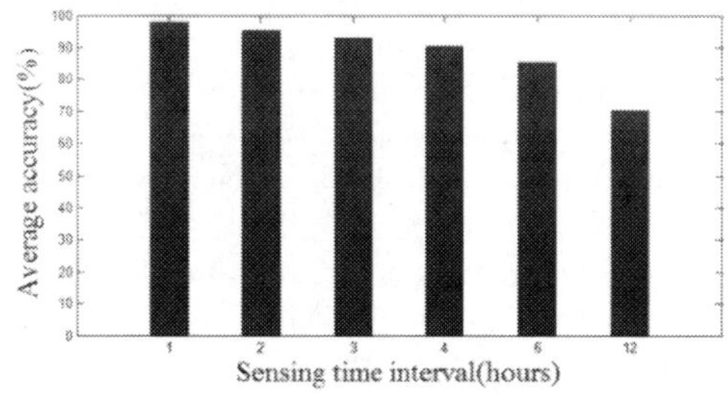

Figure 7. Average accuracy via sensing rate (sensing counts/hour).

As shown in Figure 7, the accuracy decreases in time after it is measured. When the measured value is corrected again, the system has high accuracy. Therefore, the average accuracy decreased when the sensing time interval increases, as shown in Figure 7 and Figure 8.

The sensing cost, as shown in Figure 8, also increases as aperiodic sensing over total sensing ratio also increases.

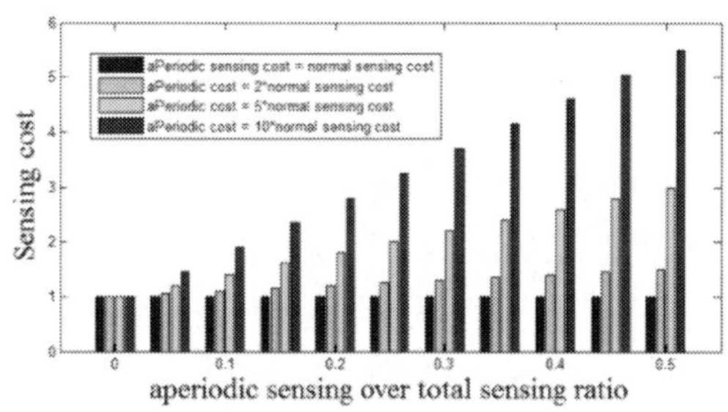

Figure 8. Sensing cost via R_{Event}.

For this reason, we do not select a large aperiodic sensing period. It is necessary to use the aperiodic sensing with the proper aperiodic sensing period.

V. CONCLUSION AND FUTURE WORK

This paper showed that WAPUS includes the sensing information to be acquired from various sensing devices in the underground facility management subsystem to transfer from the gateway to the upper platform. The sensing period of the gateway device dynamically varies according to the value of the sensing information.

Also, through a variety of RF modules in a long distance and a short distance, we dynamically select the better RF module.

In this paper, we introduced the WAPUS designed for sink

hole detection applications. The WAPUS exploits its hybrid sensing characteristic to form a networked system that effectively increases the accuracy of the sensing measurement. We believe that this study is an effort to diversify our thoughts on IoT (Internet of Things) architectures and quantitatively notice that with new capabilities added on to the wireless sensor networks, a new perspective of network architecture design is required.

ACKNOWLEDGMENT

This work was supported by the National Research Council of Science & Technology (NST) grant by the Korea government (MSIP) (No. CRC-14-02-ETRI, Development of Internet of Things (IoT)-based Urban Underground Utility Monitoring and Management System)

REFERENCES

[1] Sang Gi Hong, Nae Soo Kim, and Whan Woo Kim, "Reduction of False Alarm Signals for PIR Sensor in Realistic Outdoor Surveillance," ETRI Journal, vol. 35, no. 1, Feb. 2013, pp. 80-88.

[2] Lora Alliacne, http://lora-alliance.org, Jun. 2016.

[3] T. Heo, et al., "Adaptive dual prediction scheme based on sensing context similarity for wireless sensor networks," IET Electronics Letters, vol. 50, 2014, pp. 467-469.

[4] J. A. Stankovic. "When sensor and actuators cover the world," ETRI Journal, vol. 30, no. 5, 2008, pp. 627–633.

[5] ISO/IEC 30128:2014, "Information technology – Sensor networks – Generic Sensor Network Application Interface"

[6] ETSI TS 136211, "LTE; Evolved Universal Terrestrial Radio Access (E-UTRA); Physical Channels and Modulation," Nov. 2008.

[7] T. Heo, et al., "Escaping From Ancient Rome, Finally! Applications and Communication Infrastructures for Designing Smart Cities". Wiley Transactions on Emerging Telecommunications Technologies (ETT), vol. 25, Issue 1, January 2014, pp. 109-119.

[8] P. Kwak, et al., "IoT(Internet of Things)-based Underground Risk Assessment System Surrounding Water Pipes in Korea," International Journal of Control and Automation, vol. 8, no. 11 (2015), pp. 183-190.

[9] K. Kim, D. H. Park, J. Lee, and S. I. Jin, "UGS Middleware for Monitoring State of Underground Utilities," in Proceedings of the International Conference on Information and Communications Technology Convergence (ICTC) Oct. 28–30, 2015, Jeju, Rep. of Korea. The Korean Institute of Communcations and Information Sciences, Oct. 2015, pp. 1186–1188.

Improved Lossless Compression Algorithm in HEVC

Kibaek Kim and Jechang Jeong
Department of Electronic and Computer Engineering
Hanyang University
Seoul, South Korea
e-mail: k2b0002@hanyang.ac.kr; jjeong@hanyang.ac.kr

Abstract—**The state-of-the-art video-coding standard is High Efficiency Video Coding (HEVC), which achieves significant compression performance relative to H.264/AVC. HEVC is designed for lossy compression, however, and it is not ideal for lossless compression. To overcome the limitations of conventional coding in HEVC, we focus on the improvement of entropy coding for lossless compression. In this method, entropy coding is modified based on the characteristics of residuals in a lossless environment. The experimental results show that the bit savings of the proposed entropy coding is 1.46% on average when compared to HEVC lossless coding. Modified entropy coding with block-based intra prediction shows a bit savings of 7.99% on average. We observe that the combination of intra prediction and entropy coding is effective in screen-contents sequences.**

Keywords-HEVC; RDPCM; intra prediction; entropy coding; lossless compression.

I. INTRODUCTION

High Efficiency Video Coding (HEVC) is a state-of-the-art video-coding standard that outperforms other standards in several ways. HEVC aims to achieve significant compression improvements in the range of 50% output bit-rate reduction while still offering the same subjective quality as the previous video-coding standard, H.264/AVC (Advanced Video Coding). HEVC has been widely exploited for many uses, including in tablets, mobile phones, and high-definition televisions [1-3].

Lossy and lossless compression are two major classes of compression [4]. When compared with an original image, some data loss in the reconstructed image is allowed for in lossy compression. In lossless compression, in contrast, the reconstructed image is identical to the original image. Although HEVC supports both lossy and lossless compression, most of the coding techniques that are used in HEVC were designed for the improvement of coding performance in lossy compression. It is thus difficult to improve on the performance of lossless compression in the current HEVC structure.

Since lossless compression bypasses the transform, quantization, and in-loop filtering processes such as de-blocking filter and sample adaptive offset (SAO), the remaining processes are prediction and entropy coding, as shown in Fig. 1. The roles of prediction and entropy coding are therefore key for achieving higher compression. Intra prediction can be divided into block-based prediction and pixel-based prediction. Since the reconstructed image is identical to the original image, pixel-based prediction is generally more effective than block-based prediction, although pixel-based prediction may cause harmony-related problems with block-based structures in HEVC.

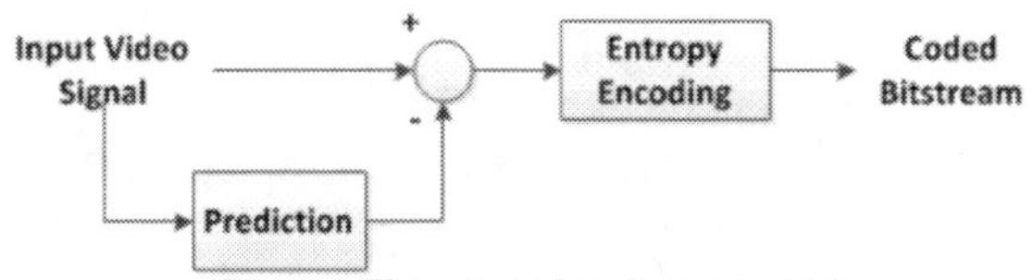

Figure 1. Flow chart of lossless compression

Entropy coding in HEVC focuses on the efficient coding of the coefficients that occur in lossy compression environments. The coefficients in lossless compression environments have different statistical characteristics than those in lossy compression environments. Considering the statistical characteristics of lossless compression, several researchers have proposed modifications related to entropy coding [5-7].

This paper focuses on the improvement of compression performance. For the prediction setup, a block-based scheme was considered as the intra prediction in this work. In the case of entropy coding, the level coding setup was modified based on the characteristic of the coefficient in a lossless compression environment. When intra prediction and entropy coding are combined to maximize compression performance, some compression improvement can be expected. In this paper, a block-based intra prediction method based on differential pulse-code modulation (DPCM) and several modifications of entropy coding have been combined and tested experimentally.

The remainder of this paper is organized as follows. Section 2 explains related work related to the proposed algorithm; Section 3 provides the proposed method for the entropy-coding process in a lossless coding environment. Section 4 includes an experimental evaluation, and Section 5 offers conclusions on the work.

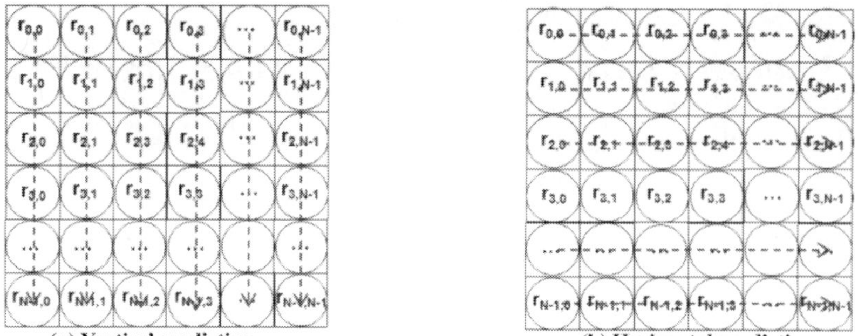

(a) Vertical prediction (b) Horizontal prediction

Figure 2. Example of NxN RDPCM

II. RELATED WORK

A. *Block-based Intra Prediction*

In the case of block-based prediction, reference pixels that are located farther away than neighboring pixels may be used for prediction. In terms of prediction accuracy, block-based prediction may be reduced because of the block-based structure. In order to solve this problem, several studies on applying DPCM to the residual signals have been conducted; the output of these studies is based on "residual DPCM," or RDPCM [8-12]. While RDPCM is used to apply DPCM on the residuals to ensure pixel-based performance, it is also possible to maintain a block-based structure.

When intra prediction in HEVC is applied, the prediction pixels can be obtained from the reference pixels. We may then acquire differences between the original pixels and the prediction pixels, which are denoted as the residuals $r_{i,j}$ ($i,j \in \{0,1,\ldots N-1\}$).

As shown in Fig 2, RDPCM can be applied to the residuals $r_{i,j}$ that are obtained after intra prediction when the intra-prediction mode is vertical or horizontal. Suppose an NxN array R with elements $r_{i,j}$ in an array that includes the residual pixels obtained after intra prediction. When DPCM is applied to the NxN array R, we may attain the modified NxN array R' with elements $r'_{i,j}$ as a result of RDPCM.

The elements $r'_{i,j}$ obtained from the modified NxN array R' can be represented as follows when the intra-prediction mode is vertical:

$$r'_{i,j} = \begin{Bmatrix} r_{i,j}, & i=0, 0 \le j \le (N-1) \\ r_{i,j} - r_{i-1,j}, & 0 < i \le (N-1), 0 \le j \le (N-1) \end{Bmatrix} \quad (1)$$

or as follows when the intra-prediction mode is horizontal:

$$r'_{i,j} = \begin{Bmatrix} r_{i,j}, & 0 \le i \le (N-1), j=0 \\ r_{i,j} - r_{i,j-1}, & 0 \le i \le (N-1), 0 < j \le (N-1) \end{Bmatrix} \quad (2)$$

The elements $r'_{i,j}$ of R' are sent to the decoder instead of the elements $r_{i,j}$ of R. Through inverse RDPCM, the elements of $r_{i,j}$ of R can be reconstructed as follows, with the elements $r'_{i,j}$ of R' sent from the encoder when the intra-prediction mode is vertical:

$$r_{i,j} = \sum_{k=0}^{i} r'_{k,j}, 0 \le i, j \le (N-1) \quad (3)$$

or as follows when the intra-prediction mode is horizontal:

$$r_{i,j} = \sum_{k=0}^{j} r'_{i,k}, 0 \le i, j \le (N-1) \quad (4)$$

Algorithms related to RDPCM were proposed in [13-17]. To further improve prediction accuracy, the authors applied an additional prediction after the RDPCM process; they applied an additional prediction based on the spatial characteristic that the difference between neighboring pixels would be linearly increased or decreased according to the prediction direction in a block.

B. *Entropy Coding of HEVC*

After residuals are obtained from the prediction process, the residuals are then grouped into multiple square transform units (TUs). Though the basic unit of coefficient coding is TU, the coefficients are encoded per 4x4 sub-blocks. The syntax elements for the coefficient coding include *sig_coeff_flag/coeff_abs_level_g1_flag/coeff_abs_level_g2_flag/coeff_sign_flag/coeff_abs_level_remaining*. Each syntax element shows (respectively) whether or not (a) the coefficient is non-zero, (b) the absolute value of the coefficient is larger than one, and (c) the absolute value of the coefficient is larger than two; they also show (d) the sign information and (e) the remaining absolute-level value [18].

For the remaining absolute level of coefficient (except for 1 or 2), *coeff_abs_level_remaining* is binarized by a *k*-th order truncated Rice and a (*k*+1)th order Exp-Golomb (EG*k*). HEVC supports a range from 0 to 4 for the Rice parameter *k*, as shown in Table 1. When an absolute level of coefficient is greater than the threshold, EG*k* is added. The initial value of the Rice parameter *k* is zero. During the coding process, the Rice parameter depends on the current parameter and the previously coded value of *coeff_abs_level_remaining*.

TABLE I. BINARIZATION TABLES ACCORDING TO K-TH ORDER TRUNCATED RICE CODE

v	Codeword				
	$k=0$	$k=1$	$k=2$	$k=3$	$k=4$
0	0	0.0	0.00	0.000	0.0000
1	10	0.1	0.01	0.001	0.0001
2	110	10.0	0.10	0.010	0.0010
3	1110	10.1	0.11	0.011	0.0011
4	11110	110.0	10.00	0.100	0.0100
5	111110	110.1	10.01	0.101	0.0101
6	1111110	1110.0	10.10	0.110	0.0110
7	11111110	1110.1	10.11	0.111	0.0111
8	111111110	11110.0	110.00	10.000	0.1000
9	1111111110	11110.1	110.01	10.001	0.1001
10	11111111110	111110.0	110.10	10.010	0.1010
11	111111111110	111110.1	110.11	10.011	0.1011
12	1111111111110	1111110.0	1110.00	10.100	0.1100
13	11111111111110	1111110.1	1110.01	10.101	0.1101

The updated Rice parameter k is always greater than the previous k. The increment of the parameter is determined as per the following condition:

$$If\,|x|>3\cdot 2^k,\ then\ k'=\min(k+1,4) \tag{5}$$

where k' denotes the updated Rice parameter and $|x|$ is an absolute value of the current coefficient [18].

III. PROPOSED METHOD FOR LOSSLESS CODING

In lossy compression, the magnitudes of the scanning position with a low index are relatively high compared to the magnitude of the scanning position with a high index [18][19]. The magnitude of each scanning position is similar, however, since lossless compression bypasses the transform and quantization processes. This means that the magnitudes of each coefficient in lossless compression are independent of the scanning position; it has also been observed that the range of non-zero coefficients in lossless compression is generally wide in comparison to lossy compression [6]. This insight allows us to know that the current design of the entropy coding in HEVC does not work efficiently in lossless compression environments.

Several algorithms have been proposed to achieve efficient coding in lossless compression [5-7]; these studies include (respectively) changing the scan order according to prediction mode, extending the binarization tables for level coding, and changing the rule of binarization-table selection. A binarization table related to these algorithms is shown in Table 1.

We propose a modified binarization-table-selection method based on the characteristics of residuals in a lossless compression environment; this method is based on decision the updated Rice parameter [6].

In HEVC, an absolute value of current coefficient is used for renewal of Rice parameter. In [6], the previous coefficients in addition to current coefficient are used for the renewal. The renewal is based on the weighting sum of the previous encoded coefficients. In calculation of weighting sum, the previous zero coefficients may influence according to distribution of non-zero coefficients. In the proposed method, only the previous non-zero coefficients of current coefficient position influence the prediction of the next non-zero coefficient and the binarization-table selection. This point is different from that proposed in [6]. We explain the details of the proposed method in the following sub-section. We also briefly describe other modifications.

A. *Proposed Entropy Coding*

Absolute levels of previous non-zero coefficients in addition to the current coefficient are used to calculate $T(s_i)$ in the proposed method. Since $T(s_i)$ is considered for the prediction of the next non-zero coefficient, zero coefficients may have a negative influence on the prediction. In the proposed method, the absolute levels of the previous non-zero coefficients are considered in the calculation of $T(s_i)$.

The decision procedure of $T(s_i)$ for determining the level-binarization table is described as follows:

$$T(s_i) = \frac{1}{w_i}\sum_{k=p}^{i} s_k \quad (6)$$

$$w_i = \begin{cases} b, & if\ nz_i = 1 \\ b+1, & if\ nz_i = 2 \\ b+2, & if\ nz_i = 3 \\ b+3, & otherwise \end{cases} \quad (7)$$

In Equation (6), i and p denote the current scanning position and the past non-zero scanning position, respectively. In Equation (7), nz_i is the number of non-zero coefficients that contain the current coefficient in a 4x4 sub-block. According to nz_i, the sharing value w_i is then determined; in addition, p is influenced by w_i. The (w_i-1)-th previous non-zero coefficient is the starting position p for the summation. The parameter b for influencing w_i reflects the sharing value and is determined empirically (b = 1).

For the renewal of Rice parameter, the calculated T is used as the input value instead of $|x|$ in (5). According to the result, Rice parameter is determined for encoding of the absolute level of the next non-zero coefficient. In contrast with HEVC, the Rice parameter k for the binarization-table selection can increase or decrease according to the decision procedure.

B. Other Modifications of Entropy Coding

TABLE II. MODIFIED SCANNING PATTERN ACCORDING TO MODE

Mode	Block size			
	4x4	8x8	16x16	32x32
Mode (H)	Diag	V->H	H->V	Diag
Mode (V)	Diag	H->V	V->H	Diag
Remainder	Diag	Diag	Diag	Diag

Three scanning patterns are supported in HEVC: (1) diagonal upright, (2) horizontal, and (3) vertical [18]. The scanning pattern is adaptively determined according to intra mode. In lossless compression, a correlation in the prediction direction remains. As shown in Table 2, the adaptive-scanning patterns are thus changed in our method [5]. Considering the characteristic that some coefficients with a very high magnitude will appear, the range of the Rice parameter k is extended from 0 to 6 [7].

IV. EXPERIMENTAL RESULTS

In order to evaluate the performance of the proposed method, we implemented the method using HM 10.0 reference software; the experimental condition was "Intra, Main," which is one of the most common test conditions, discussed in [20][21].

In order to apply a lossless coding mode, the quantization parameter (QP) was set to 0, while the TransquantBypassFlag, CUTransquantBypassFlagValue, and LosslessCUEnabled parameters were set to 1. The transform and quantization processes were skipped. Other details of the experimental conditions are shown in Table 3. Various HEVC test sequences were used for the simulations. In Table 3, CU and LCU mean coding unit and largest coding unit, respectively.

TABLE III. EXPERIMENTAL CONDITION

Parameter	Value	Description
CUWidth	64	LCU size (64x64)
CUHeight	64	
IntraPeriod	1	All intra coding
QP	0	Lossless coding
Reference Sample Smoothing	off	
Block Boundary Filtering	off	
LoopFilterDisable	1	No in-loop filtering
SAO	0	

The compression performance was evaluated for bit savings as follows. In bit savings, positive values denote an improvement in coding efficiency.

$$\Delta Bit\ saving(\%) = \frac{Bitrate_{HEVC} - Bitrate_{proposed}}{Bitrate_{HEVC}} \times 100 \quad (8)$$

Several techniques for lossless compression were either evaluated independently, or a combination of tools was evaluated. In terms of intra prediction, the block-based method [17] in addition to RDPCM was exploited in our technique. Three components of entropy coding from section 3 were combined as the proposed entropy coding. In order to evaluate the compression performance, five categories were partitioned: proposed entropy coding (M1), RDPCM (M2), block-based prediction [17] (M3), a combination of A and B (M4), and a combination of A and C (M5). Table 4 summarizes the experimental results of the bit-savings tests. The table shows the results of M1, M2, M3, M4, and M5, which are compared with HM 10.0 lossless intra coding.

As shown in Table 4, the bit savings of M1 were 1.46% on average in total test sequences. Especially, the test did show meaningful results in class F. Class F shows that the bit savings were 3.48% on average. The sequences in that class consisted of screen contents. Compared to natural images, screen-content images tend to experience many changes between adjacent pixels. Some coefficients therefore may have a very high magnitude. Since the proposed entropy-coding method considers the characteristics in a lossless compression environment, the method can prevent wasteful bits from representing non-zero coefficients that have a very high magnitude.

In the case of block-based prediction, the bit savings of M2 and M3 were 5.83% and 7.29%, respectively. Since intra prediction is comprised of pixel-by-pixel DPCM, intra prediction can provide better coding efficiency compared to HM10.0 lossless coding. M3 achieved a small improvement over M2, since M3 applies additional prediction after the RDPCM process.

In order to optimize lossless compression, we experimented with a combination of intra prediction and entropy coding. As shown in Table 4, the bit savings of combinations M4 and M5 were 6.43% and 7.99% on average, respectively. When compared with M2 and M3, test results showed additional coding gains of 0.6% and 0.7% (respectively) on average in total sequences. In addition, M4 and M5 showed significant improvement in class F of screen content. The difference of bit savings compared to M2 and M3 were 2.13% and 2.11%, respectively.

TABLE IV. EXPERIMENTAL RESULTS OF BIT SAVINGS

Bit savings (%)						
Class	Sequence	M1	M2	M3	M4	M5
A	Traffic	1.58	8.20	11.34	8.88	12.22
	PeopleOnStreet	1.74	7.57	11.85	8.41	12.98
	Nebuta	-0.19	5.65	10.12	4.79	9.64
	SteamLocomotive	1.21	6.04	11.39	6.78	12.53
Average of class A		1.09	6.87	11.18	7.22	11.84
B	Kimono	1.67	4.28	6.30	5.17	7.36
	ParkScene	0.87	5.01	7.55	5.26	7.94
	Cactus	0.38	2.17	2.73	1.99	2.56
	BQTerrace	-0.02	2.67	3.32	2.04	2.66
	BasketballDrive	0.67	2.49	2.80	2.64	2.99
Average of class B		0.71	3.33	4.54	3.42	4.70
C	RaceHorses	1.15	5.17	7.51	5.53	8.09
	BQMall	1.33	4.47	4.86	4.93	5.27
	PartyScene	0.54	3.60	3.89	3.31	3.59
	BasketballDrill	1.50	1.79	2.07	2.71	2.98
Average of class C		1.13	3.76	4.58	4.12	4.98
D	RaceHorses	0.97	6.06	8.88	6.02	9.09
	BQSquare	1.15	2.68	2.62	3.19	3.15
	BlowingBubbles	0.45	3.82	4.01	3.28	3.45
	BasketballPass	1.86	8.98	10.71	9.69	11.54
Average of class D		1.11	5.38	6.55	5.55	6.81
E	FourPeople	1.67	8.75	10.87	9.49	11.77
	Johnny	1.29	7.59	8.53	8.22	9.26
	KristenAndSara	1.35	8.48	9.69	9.15	10.44
Average of class E		1.43	8.28	9.70	8.95	10.49
F	BasketballDrillText	1.91	2.56	2.69	3.70	3.77
	ChinaSpeed	2.83	11.54	10.23	13.41	11.91
	SlideEditing	6.00	7.97	6.05	12.14	10.43
	SlideShow	3.18	12.35	14.96	13.69	16.24
Average of class F		3.48	8.61	8.48	10.74	10.59
Total average		1.46	5.83	7.29	6.43	7.99

TABLE V. COMPARISON OF CODING TIMES

Overall	M2	M3	M4	M5
Encoder	99%	99%	103%	104%
Decoder	92%	89%	95%	93%

Table 5 describes the encoding time and decoding time of each method when each was compared with HM 10.0 lossless intra coding. In the case of block-based prediction, there was no increase in coding time, since high prediction accuracy leads to the reduction of residual data to be encoded or decoded in our method. The proposed entropy coding, when combined with block-based prediction method, led to increases in coding time because of the additional processes we use related to entropy coding.

V. CONCLUSION

In order to overcome the limitations of the conventional coding structure based on lossy coding, we have proposed a method for improving performance in lossless compression environments. In this method, entropy coding was modified based on the characteristic of residuals in a lossless environment. In comparison with HEVC, the experimental results showed that the proposed method achieved a bit reduction of 1.46% on average. Modified entropy coding with block-based intra prediction achieved bit reductions of 7.99% on average. In particular, the combination of intra prediction and entropy coding showed good compression performance in screen-contents sequences.

There is still a need to improve on the coding gains in some of the sequences, however. Further study is thus required to improve coding performance in lossless coding environments.

ACKNOWLEDGMENT

This work was supported by Institute for Information & communications Technology Promotion(ITP) grant funded by the Korea government(MSIP) (No.2016-B0101-15-1377, Development of 16-channel Multi-viewer, H/W Encoder, and Transcoder Systems for 4K UHD Broadcasting)

REFERENCES

[1] G. J. Sullivan, J. Ohm, W. Han, and T. Wiegand, "Overview of the high efficiency video coding (HEVC) standard," IEEE Trans. Circuits Syst. Video Technol., vol. 22, no. 12, Dec. 2012, pp. 1649-1668.

[2] B. Bross et al, "High Efficiency Video Coding (HEVC) text specification draft 10," JCTVC-L1003, Geneva, Switzerland, Jan. 2013.

[3] J. Ohm, G. J. Sullivan, H. Schwarz, T. K. Tan and T. Wiegand, "Comparison of the coding efficiency of video coding standards including High Efficiency Video Coding (HEVC)," IEEE Trans. Curcuits Syst. Video Technol., vol. 22, no. 12, Dec. 2012, pp.1649-1668.

[4] K. Sayood, Lossless Compression Handbook, San Diego, Academic Press, 2003.

[5] W. Gao, M. Jiang, and H. Yu, "On lossless coding for HEVC," in: Proc. SPIE, Feb. 2013, pp. 8666–8674.

[6] J. Choi and Y. Ho, "Improved residual data coding for high efficiency video coding lossless extension," in Proc. RIVF, 2013, pp. 18-21.

[7] J. Choi and Y. Ho, "Differential pixel value coding for HEVC lossless compression," Advanced video coding for next-generation multimedia services, INTECH; 2013.

[8] Y. Lee and K. Han, "Lossless coding for professional extensions," JVT-L017, Redmond, USA, Jul. 2004.

[9] Y. Lee, K. Han, and S. Lim, "Lossless intra coding for improved 4: 4: 4 coding in H. 264/MPEG-4 AVC," Geneva, Switzerland, JVT-P016, Geneva, Switzerland, Jul. 2005.

[10] Y. Lee and K. Han, "Complexity of the proposed lossless intra," JVT-Q035r1, Nice, France, Oct. 2005.

[11] Y. Lee, K. Han, and G. J. Sullivan, "Improved lossless intra coding for H. 264/MPEG-4 AVC," IEEE Trans. Image Process., vol. 15, no. 9, Sep. 2006, pp. 2610-2615.

[12] S. Lee, I. Kim, and C. Kim, "AHG7: Residual DPCM for HEVC lossless coding," JCTVC-L0117, Geneva, Switzerland, Jan. 2013.

[13] J. Kwak and Y. Lee, "Secondary residual transform for lossless intra coding in HEVC," J. of Broadcast Eng., vol. 17, no. 5, Sep. 2012, pp. 734-741.

[14] S. Hong and Y. Lee, "CR-DPCM for lossless intra prediction method in HEVC," J. of Broadcast Eng., vol. 19, no. 3, Sep. 2014, pp. 307-315.

[15] S. Hong, J. Kwak, and Y. Lee, "Cross residual transform for lossless intra-coding for HEVC," Signal Process. Image Commun., vol. 28, no. 10, Nov. 2013, pp. 1335-1341.

[16] Y. Lee and S. Hong, "Cross residual DPCM for HEVC lossless coding," JCTVC-N0113, Vienna, Austria, Aug. 2013.

[17] K. Kim, G. Jeon, and J. Jeong, "Improvement of implicit residual DPCM for HEVC," in Proc. SITIS, 2014, pp. 652-658.

[18] J. Sole et al, "Transform coefficient coding in HEVC," IEEE Trans. Circuits syst. video technol., vol. 22, no. 12, Dec. 2012, pp. 1765-1777.

[19] D. Marpe, H. Schwarz, and T. Wiegand, "Context-based adaptive binary arithmetic coding in the H.264/AVC video compression standard," IEEE Trans. Circuits Syst. Video Technol., vol. 13. no. 7, Jul. 2003, pp. 620-636.

[20] HEVC Test Model. Available: https://hevc.hhi.fraunhofer.de/svn/svn_HEVC Software/tags/HM-10.0/.

[21] F. Bossen, "Common HM test conditions and software reference con figurations," JCTVC-K1100, Shanghai, China, Oct. 2012.

Field Study of Ice Detection on Structures Using Passive Thermal Infrared Imaging

Muhammad S. Virk

Arctic Technology Research Team
Institute of Industrial Technology, University of Tromsø, Norway
Email: muhammad.s.virk@uit.no

Abstract--**Different techniques have been used by researchers to detect ice accretion on structures, but most of these techniques detect ice on a particular (point) location and detecting the ice on large surface areas is still a problem. This paper describes a passive thermal infrared-based ice detection technique for large surface areas. A field study has been carried out to detect ice accretion on various large structures such as roads, bridges, communication towers and fishing vessels. Results from this preliminary field study show that passive thermal infrared-based non-intrusive ice detection method can be a promising way to detect ice on large surface areas, where typical point based icing sensors do not work effectively.**

Keywords- Atmospheric ice detection; Structure; Passive thermal infrared; Temperature distribution.

I. INTRODUCTION

One of the difficulties of atmospheric ice detection on structures is how to accurately detect and analyze the intensity of accreted ice on a surface. Most ice detectors are point devices and measure required icing parameters only at one particular location, while the interest of operators is often to detect ice accretion over a large surface area. At the same time, ice detector technology must not interfere with the ice accretion process, so that the measurements are accurate, nor should it be affected by the icing event itself, which is one of the problems with the present point based ice detection methods. Generally four ice detection technologies; imaging, remote, conformal and probe are used for annunciating the presence of ice, automatically triggering ice protection technologies and indicating whether ice has been removed or not [1]. A system based on the processing of thermal images acquired in the infrared spectra can be a possible way to monitor the ice accretion in a non-intrusive manner, while covering all these areas of interest.

The infrared spectrum lies below the visible band. Infrared (IR) imaging can be divided into two main categories: *active imaging and passive imaging*. Active imaging techniques use artificial IR lighting source to illuminate the target image where icing might be present, then an infrared sensor collects the reflecting signal. A plethora of successive images over a number of sub-bands are collected, which are then processed to determine whether or not ice is present. One example on the active method is the "*Ice Camera*" which has been developed by MacDonald, Dettwiler and Associates Ltd. (MDA). The "Ice Camera" system utilizes a multi-spectral infrared camera that detects both ice and water. It employs a reflectance spectroscopy technique to detect ice of 0.5 mm thickness or above [2].

Passive thermal infrared image captures the naturally radiated infrared from the target to construct an image. In this technique, a thermal image is constructed using a *Focal Plan Array* (FPA) sensor that captures the radiated IR energy from the object. The FPA is designed to sense a certain band of IR radiation depending on the application for which the thermal image camera will be used. Every object in the world emits thermal radiations, which are mainly the function of object temperature and surface emissivity. When the object's temperature increases, the radiation also increases. Thermal imaging devices capture these thermal radiations and allow one to study variations in surface temperature. During ice accretion process, the region where ice accretion occurs becomes warmer than the surrounding surface due to release of latent heat of fusion while water freezes. In case of an area already covered with ice, the iced surface will have low temperature as compared to the un-iced surface area. By measuring the intensity of thermal radiation from the surface material and emissivity, it then become possible to infer the surface temperature in icing conditions. For thermography analysis *emissivity of the object, reflected apparent temperature, distance between radiated object and thermal camera, relative humidity and atmospheric temperature* are the important parameters that need to be taken into consideration for reliable results [3]. Very little work has been reported to detect the ice on surface using thermal infrared techniques, as most work in this regard has been done using the active infrared approach. Adam et al.[4] used the passive thermal infrared technique to investigate the atmospheric ice accretion on helicopter rotor blade, where a prototype detector system was built consisting of a single point infrared pyrometer. The characteristic chord wise temperature distribution was observed during the icing event. Virk & Ghani [5] conducted a lab based experimental study to detect ice on wind turbine blades using a passive thermal infrared approach.

The paper describes the preliminary field study to analyze the non-intrusive passive thermal IR based approach for detection of ice on large structures in cold regions. The remainder of the paper is structured as follows. Section II covers the field measurement setup used for this study. Section III describes the results & discussion of the field measurement study. The acknowledgement and conclusions close the article.

II. FIELD EXPERIMENTAL SETUP

The field study was carried out in the northern part of Norway during winter 2013/2014, using simple experimental setup consisting of a very long wave (17 µm) thermal infrared camera (*FLIR A615*), data logger, image processing software (IRControl) and a laptop computer. Analyses were carried out for different structures (*bridge, communication towers, roads and fishing vessels*). The thermal infrared images were processed to measure the surface thermal signature and these surface temperature distributions helped in identifying the ice distribution along surfaces of these large structures. Figure 1 shows a schematic overview of the experimental setup used for this field study.

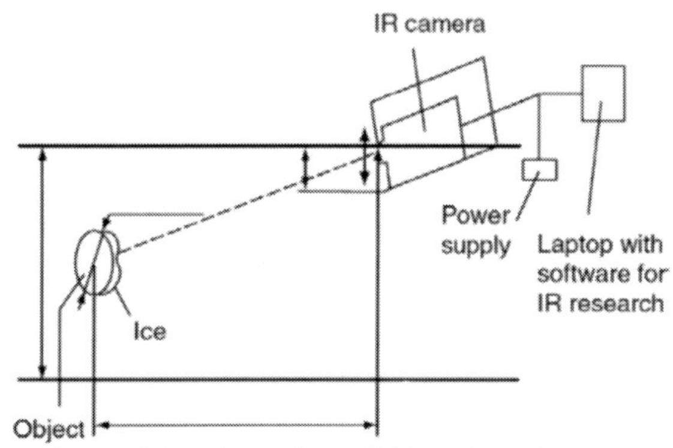

Figure 1. Schematic overview of field experimentation setup

In this setup, the IR camera measures infrared radiation in a specific spectral range. The radiation originating from structural surface is directly related to its temperature and makes it possible to calculate the temperature distribution on structural surfaces based on the radiation measured. This information was reproduced as an image. The radiation measured from IR camera is not only a function of temperature, but also the emissivity of the measured object. Emissivity is often not uniform across the entire surface of the object. IRControl software used in this study has the capability to measure emissivity. A locally generated emissivity map is calculated and recorded. Other factors effecting the IR radiation like reflected ambient radiation, object distance, relative humidity and the atmospheric damping has also been compensated within IRControl software used in this study for IR image processing.

III. RESULTS & DISCUSSION

A. *Road Bridge*

In recent years, the relevance of ice accretion for wind-induced vibration of structural bridges has been recognize as a safety hazard. Two main topics of concern in this regards are, 1) icing on road surface of bridge, 2) icing on bridge structural components mainly on cables. As an overall, ice accretion on bridge effects both static and dynamic stabilities due to added mass effects of accreted ice and changes in wind induced aerodynamic effects. In addition, ice chunks falling from bridge members/cables can also cause traffic accidents, direct damages to passing vehicles and generally place human safety at risk [6].

A field study has been carried out to detect the ice accretion on a hanging bridge structure by using passive thermal IR approach. Figure 2 shows the results of surface temperature distribution along each selected location of the bridge.

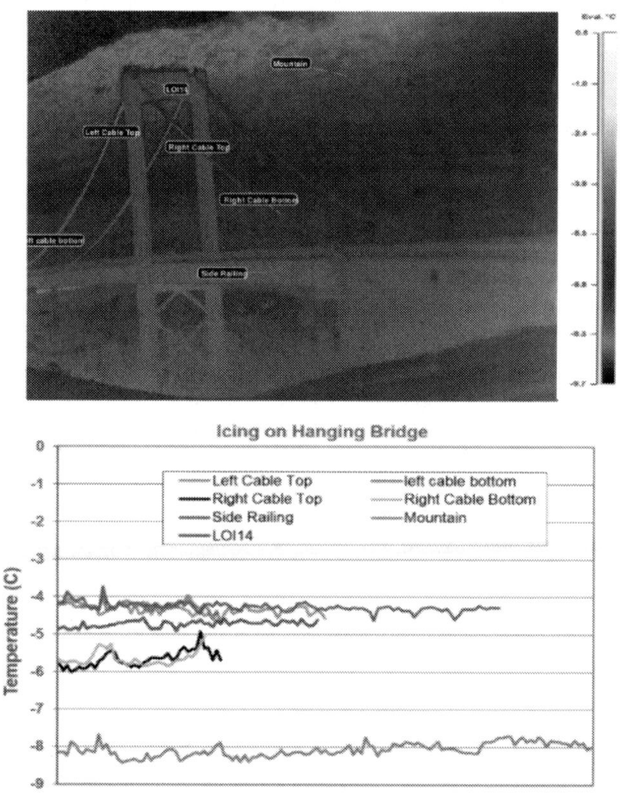

Figure 2. Surface temperature distribution along different sections of iced bridge

Surface temperature distribution at seven different locations was analyzed and compared with the visual observations of iced areas. Results showed a significant variation in surface temperature distribution along these selected locations. The lowest surface temperature was found along the top end of the bridge, where ice was accreted. More ice was found on windward (right) side of the bride. Ice detection by IR thermal images was also found in agreement with the visual observations. A systematic application of this approach can help to routinely monitor the ice accretion along bridge and avoid any possible incidents effecting the safety of the bridge structure and pedestrians.

B. *Road Surface*

In regions with subzero temperatures, severe road conditions are common, therefore a good knowledge of the road conditions is important for performing effective and environmental friendly safe road maintenance. Water freezes to ice causing a drastic decrease of road surface friction, which can lead to an increase in the possibility of traffic accidents [7]. The importance of finding the point at which a wet road surface will freeze implies that a correct monitoring of road surface is necessary. The limitations of existing technology is not the ability to get qualitative data at single point, but to get data that represents the actual road conditions over a large surface area. It is difficult to accurately estimate the road condition from a single point freezing point sensor, therefore additional efforts are required to better detect the presence of ice and differentiate between different types of accumulated ice on the road. There is a good potential in non-intrusive infrared (IR) based technology for monitoring the road weather conditions in cold and icing conditions. This technique can give detailed information about the top surface temperature of the road, which is crucial for finding possible icing locations.

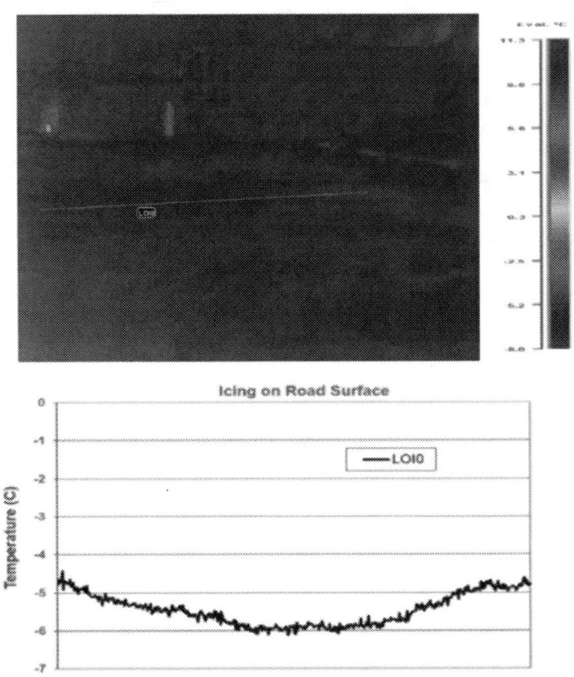

Figure 3. Surface temperature distribution along iced road surface.

Figure 3 shows the results of surface temperature distribution along an iced road surface in northern Norway, where it can be seen that the iced surface areas are marked in blue color and have lowest temperature as compared to un-iced surfaces. Such information about distribution of surface temperature also helps to identify among different types of ice, which eventually can help to improve the road safety. The results shown in Figure 3 represent the case, where ice has already accumulated on the road surface, therefore the iced surface area has the lowest temperature. However, while ice accumulation is in process and super cooled water droplets are hitting the road surface, in that case, latent heat will releases while the droplets freeze and the iced surface area will show the highest temperature. With the help of point based ice detection method, it is not easy to get such detailed information about road surface condition in icing condition.

C. *Shipping Vessels*

Icing can be a safety hazard for offshore shipping vessels as weight of accreted ice can possibly effect both its safety and stability, therefore actions necessary to improve safety must be considered [1]. Thermal imaging technique of ice detection may be useful for application in marine environment also, especially where incipient icing could cause slipping hazards on deck, stairs and other work areas. Figure 4 shows some results of temperature distribution along different sections of a fishing vessel.

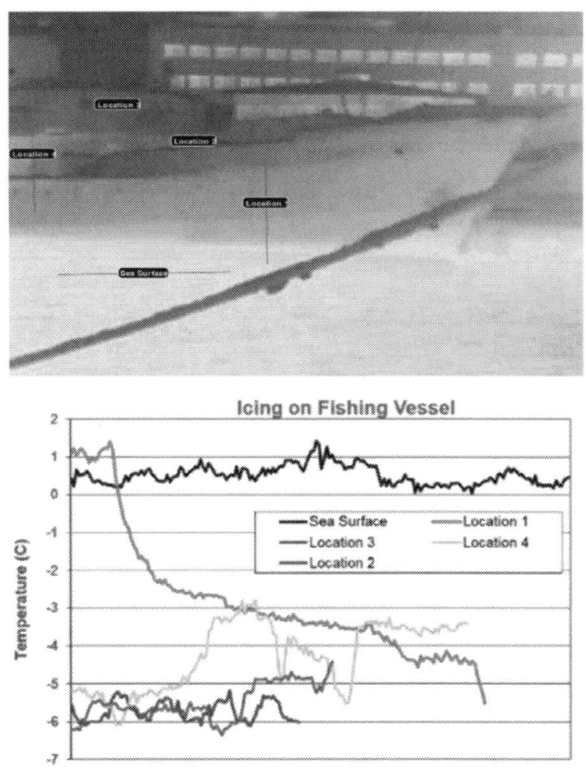

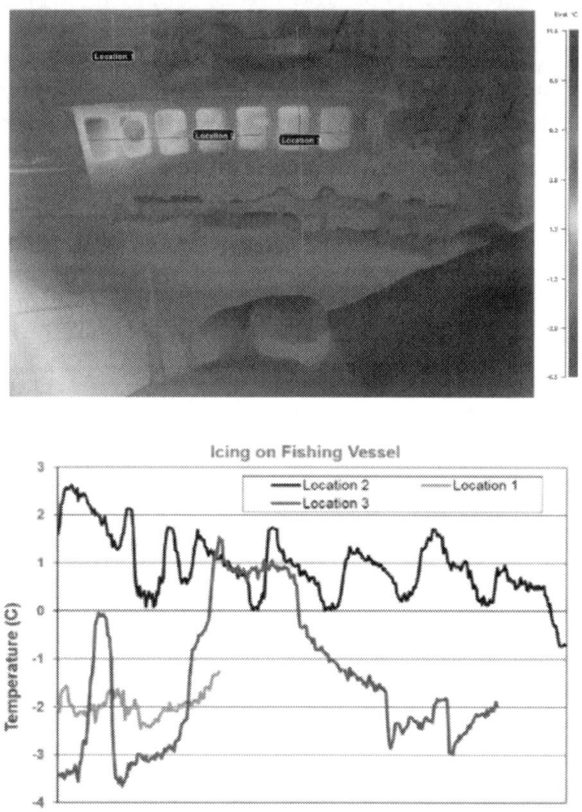

Figure 4. Thermal image of fishing vessels and temperature distribution along selected locations.

It can be seen in Figure 4 that the distribution of temperature is not constant along the selected locations and iced locations have significantly low temperature compared to un-iced surfaces. Such information of temperature distribution is vital to identify the iced surfaces and initiate the de-icing operation accordingly. With the help of passive thermal IR approach, it is possible to monitor the ice accretion along various sections of ships, where ordinary point based icing sensor does not work. A coupled continuous monitoring of significant locations along ships can help to optimize the operation of the anti/deicing systems, which can also help to save the required energy for anti/deicing systems.

D. Communication Towers

Atmospheric icing is a design constraint for the communication towers in cold regions, as these are typically elevated and exposed. Ice buildup on communication towers can cause signal interference, structural fatigue from dynamic loading, guy wire stretch, ice chuck fall and complete tower failure [8]. Due to complex structural integration and installation at remote locations, ice detection and mitigation on communication towers is difficult, but non-intrusive passive thermal IR approach can be a good way to detect the ice on communication tower and initiate the ice mitigation accordingly. Figure 5 shows the thermal IR image of communication tower and respective distribution of ice along the specified locations.

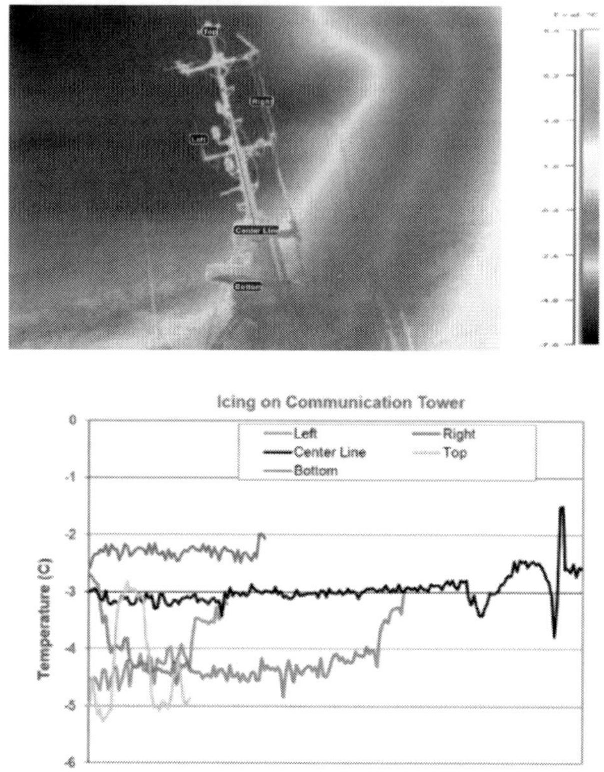

Figure 5. Thermal image of communication antenna and temperature distribution along selected locations.

In this field study, five different locations were selected along a radio communication tower, where based upon thermal radiation and surface emissivity temperature distribution was analyzed to get a perspective about accumulated ice. Results showed different temperature distribution profiles along each location, which indicated that ice is not symmetrically distributed along these locations and maximum ice was observed near the top and right locations of the communication antenna. Such information about distribution of ice along antenna surface can help to optimize the design of communication antenna and design the ice mitigation approach accordingly.

IV. CONCLUSION

This preliminary research work was focused on to use of non-intrusive passive thermal infrared based intelligent sensor technology to analyze the ice distribution along surfaces of different structures in cold regions. Preliminary analysis showed a potential in this technique to better predict the ice distribution along different structures. This technique has an advantage over the available techniques for detection of ice at single point, as with this technique we can successfully predicted the dynamic icing conditions over large surface areas, but it is necessary to further evaluate this methodology by a comprehensive study to build a large dataset from different scenarios before its final implementation.

ACKNOWLEDGEMENT

The work reported in this research paper is funded by the WindCoE (Nordic Wind Energy Centre) project funded within Interreg IVA Botnia-Atlantica, as part of European Territorial Cooperation (ETC).

REFERENCES

[1]. C. Ryerson, "Ice protection of offshore platforms", Cold Regions Science and Technology, 2011, p. 97-110.

[2]. D. Gregoris, S. Yu and F. Teti, "Multispectral imaging of ice", IEEE CCECE Conference, 2004, Niagara, Ontario, Canada, p. 2051-2056.

[3]. M. S. Virk, "Application of Passive Thermal Infrared Imaging to Study Ice and Snow Accretion on Automobiles in Cold Regions", Advanced Materials Research, 2013, vol. 739: p. 481-485.

[4]. A. Dershowitz and R. J. Hansman, "Experimental investigation of passive infrared ice detection for helicoptr applications", AIAA-91-0667,1991, Massachusetts Institute of Technology, USA: Reno, NV.

[5]. R. Ghani and M. S. Virk, "Experimental Study of Atmospheric Ice Detection on Wind Turbine Blade Using Thermal Infrared Technique", Wind Engineering : The International Journal of Wind Power, 2013, vol. 37, issue. 1, p. 71-78.

[6]. K. Kleissl and C. T. Georgakis, "Bridge ice accretion and de- and anti-icing systems: A review", 7th Internation Cable Supported Bridge Operators Conference, 2010, p. 161-167.

[7]. P. Jonsson, "Intelligent networked sensor for increased road safety", in Department of information technology and media, 2011, Mid Sweden University: Ostersund, Sweden, p. 41.

[8]. N. D. Mulherin, "Atmospheric Icing and Tower Collapse in the United States", 7th International Workshop on Atmospheric Icing of Structures, 1996, Chicoutimi, Quebec, Canada: IWAIS.

Ice Detection Experimentation Setup Using Infrared and Active Heating

Taimur Rashid, Hassan A. Khawaja, K. Edvardsen
Department of Engineering and Safety
The Arctic University of Norway (UIT)
Tromsø, Norway
e-mail: taimur.rashid@uit.no

Abstract—**The paper shows the possible implementation of Infrared (IR) ice detection technique. The experimental setup is implemented keeping in view of the marine icing phenomena over the ships and offshore structures. The detection mechanism is unique from the passive IR detection by introducing the active heating concept. The intervention of the active heating information inside the IR ice detection system will be able to improve the system's detection capability and disseminate the valid information at user interface level. The experimentation shows valid detection of ice and no/ice conditions based on consistent temperature gradients.**

Keywords—icing; detection; infrared; heat; surface interface;

I. ICING AND INFRARED DETECTION

In the challenging environment such as below zero temperature conditions, ice accretion can occur at a rapid pace. This can adversely affect the marine operations in cold climate. Taking into account for such conditions, ice detection can be useful for the ice mitigation and removal upon the marine and offshore structures. Various techniques exist in the literature to detect the icing that exploit its physical or electromagnetic properties [1]. The parameters measured by these ice detectors includes the mass, rate and liquid water content [2]. Generally, the atmospheric icing is detected from most of these detectors. The other type of icing is marine icing that is a safety concern in marine operations inside the cold regions. Marine icing is different in nature from the atmospheric icing. It involves sea spray influence that is produced from the collision of the waves upon the structure and wind that shear the high wave crests [3, 4]. The subsequent sea spray generated by the collision of waves and its shearing travels in the air and freezes on impact with the ship superstructure or offshore structure elements. If this type of icing continues to occur for a longer duration, it can cause an increase in ice loading which could be hazardous if not mitigated in time. Such icing conditions are also hazardous for human operations. In this case, ice detection can be useful to assist the anti/de-icing process.

The techniques mentioned above for ice detection include point and area detection of ice. In the marine operations, remote detection of icing could be effective as it can assist the detection of a larger surface area. Remote monitoring of ice upon surfaces was tested in aviation industry where icing on aircraft wing was observed using infrared cameras [5]. The effectiveness of infrared application in icing for the marine environment needs to be investigated. Apart from the aviation industry, infrared remote monitoring is being used in various industrial applications where the temperature monitoring is critical on the larger surface area. Acquiring thermal signature from infrared devices gives the advantage to analyze temperature profiles of the complete system without any direct contact. Studies have shown that infrared cameras can be utilized to monitor the cold objects at low temperatures [5]. Recently, in the marine operations, specific infrared cameras are currently being used to detect the floating sea iceberg, which indicates the possible applicability of infrared devices in the marine environment.

In this paper, effort is being made to show the infrared experimentation setup for detection of marine icing. Lab-setup is explained taking into account of the anti/de-icing techniques used in ships and offshore structures in marine environment. Section-II explains the setup components including an infrared camera, heating elements, surface material, control and monitoring systems. Setup components details are not specified as the experimental setup for ice detection is preliminary in nature, therefore, can be modified for improvements. Section-III explains the experimental setup and section-IV shows the results and discussion regarding thermal gradients at ice/no-ice conditions. The paper concludes in section-V showing the technique's effectiveness towards ice detection in the marine environment.IR Thermography and Thermal Signature Detection at Low Temperatures

II. SETUP COMPONENTS

A. *Infra-Red (IR) Camera*

IR camera operates with the incident IR beam. IR light is electromagnetic radiation that has a longer wavelength as compared to the visible light. It has a spectral range starting from the edge of the visible red light from 0.74μm to 300μm. The infrared spectral band is generally sub-divided into four sub-bands; near infrared (NIR) (0.75–3μm), medium wavelength infrared (MWIR) (3–6μm), long wavelength infrared (LWIR) (6–15μm) and very long wavelength infrared (VLWIR) (15–1000μm) [6]. IR camera working principle is based on the thermography imaging. The major components of the IR camera are a lens, detector, video processing electronics and user interface control as shown in Figure 1. The IR camera operates with the incident beam of light focusing upon the detector by the lens. The detector contains the IR sensitive elements arranged in the array called focal plane array (FPA). These are IR sensitive elements and miniature in size (micro- meters). The number of elements inside the array determines the resolution of the IR imagery produced by the camera [7]. The processing electronics interprets the detector signals into the infrared imagery. The processing electronics also controls the parameters of the captured imagery. The sets of commands can be given to processing electronics via user interface. Currently available IR cameras generally include a user interface software to compute the parameters such as scene temperature, calibration, external trigger input and imagery recording. The calibration is often required to read out the correct temperature across the captured scene.

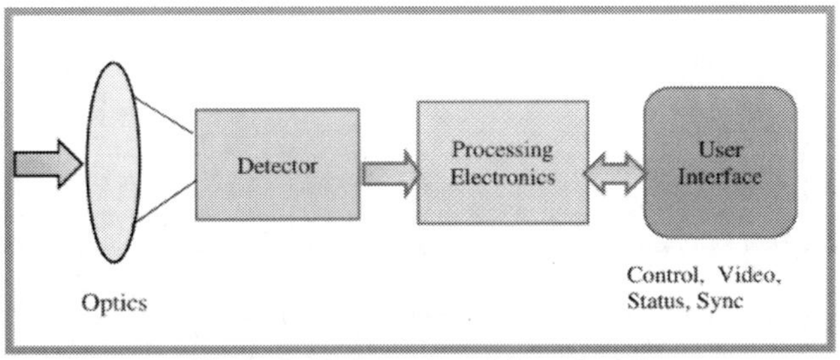

Figure 1. IR Camera working principle

Cold temperature scene can also be observed with the help of IR camera. The observation of icing surfaces from IR thermography has been reported in literature [8] but no significant literature is available of marine ice detection in cold regions. The application of IR thermography in ice detection for ships and offshore structures can be experimented to evaluate its capability.

B. *Heating Elements*

IR thermography for ice detection can be challenging when uniform scene temperature is observed. The thermographic profile of the cold object and the scene temperature might be the same in some cases that could lead false detection of ice. Furthermore, the reflectivity of the ice under certain conditions can indicate a false temperature captured by the IR detectors, which requires calibration. Normally calibration is done with the known objects temperature, which could be a difficult task to perform repetitively during the field operations in the cold harsh environment. The false detection problem from IR thermography can be minimized if the active heating mechanism is introduced underneath the platform or structure upon which ice is accreted. The heating elements will perform the major role in generating the known heat signature when the ice is accreted over it. The heating elements utilized in the experimentation setup could be electro thermal based with the strong heat generation capacity. The size of the heating elements should be minimum and compact so that they could be arranged in the form of arrays as discussed in section-III. Few examples of heating elements that could be tested as an active heating source for the experimentation are Peltier thermoelectric modules (Figure 2a) and Thermal resistive elements such as positive thermal coefficient of resistance (PTC) as shown in Figure 2b

Peltier thermoelectric modules are solid state devices based on thermoelectric heat pump theory as they behave like a heat pump and transfers the heat from one side of the device to the other side. As the modules withdraw the current, one side becomes immediately hot and another side becomes cold. The hot temperature can reach up to hundreds of degrees (C°); similarly, cold side acquires negative temperatures very quickly. On the other hand, the positive thermal coefficient of resistance (PTC) heaters works on the principle of resistive heating where resistance increases upon heating. PTC devices can provide the high-temperature range up to 150°C or more depend upon the type of resistive material used and current rating.

These elements discussed are commercially available in miniature sizes (few centimeter) and can be controlled with the DC or AC powered control circuitry. The control mechanism of these heating elements is significant for the experimentation that will be used with IR user interface capturing mechanism

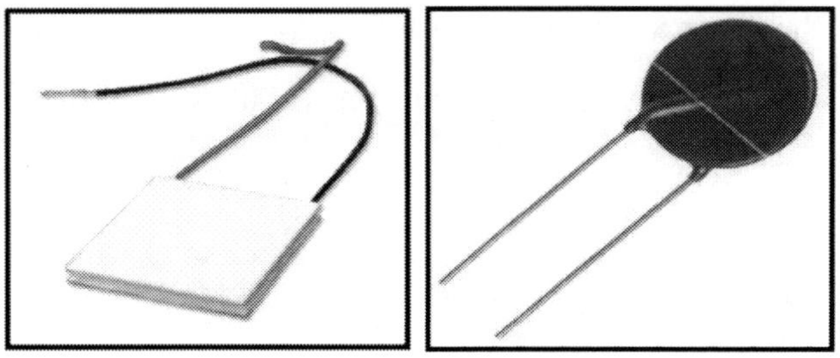

a. Peltier thermoelectric element [9] b. PTC thermal resistor element [10]

Figure 2. Heating elements

C. *Surface Interface*

The surface interface is the overlying material above the heating elements arrangement. The purpose of the surface interface is to supply heat through conduction. The heated elements underneath the surface transfer the heat to the icing layer accumulated on the overlying surface. Efficient conducting materials can be used as surface interface materials for the experimentation process. Metals for instance aluminium, iron, copper etc. can be considered as the interface materials.

D. *Control Module*

The control module consists of electronic circuitry used to control the heating elements. This module recognizes the input from the user interface and drives the heating elements through its digital output lines. The control module executes the image capturing based on producing the external trigger signal. This trigger signal drives the infrared camera to capture the image for that instance. The final imagery is displayed through the imaging interface for temperature profile recording. Thus heated elements on/off signals are generated by the control module that are in accordance with the IR imagery profile.

E. *User Interface*

The human interface in the experimentation process is the mutual interface of IR imagery analysis software and control module circuitry. The observation of the IR camera software will produce the thermal signature and temperature profiles of the icing. Control module will produce the operating cycles of the heating elements to produce the imaging profile. The resultant imaging is then analyzed to evaluate the captured scene.

III. EXPERIMENTAL SETUP

The experimental setup for marine ice detection comprises of the components discussed in the section-II. The IR camera of MWIR range is used at angle normal to the icing surface. This was done to avoid any possible reflections that could lead to false temperature detection. The IR resolution of the camera used in the experiment is 320 × 240 pixels with the temperature sensitivity of 0.05^0C. The distance of the IR camera from the icing surface was kept small (60 cm) such that the surface image fits into the camera frame. The reason behind was to keep the frame coordinates same for analysis and to avoid camera zoom during experimental observations on the user interface. Most of the commercially available IR cameras include the user interface package. The complete proposed setup is shown in Figure 3.

The active heating control in the IR ice detection is provided by the control module. The control module is responsible for controlling the power on and power off timings of the heated elements. The heating elements discussed can also be used as deicing agents. Integration of the camera's user interface with the control module helps to synchronize the captured scene with the control mechanism. The infrared energy of a certain temperature is released when control module drives the heating elements. The individual selection of the heated elements provides the flexibility to warm a particular area. This helps the IR energy to be captured at the desired locations. The IR signature captured can be evaluated in the IR user interface software to validate the presence of ice.

The operating mechanism of the experimental setup starts with the capturing of the IR frame without turning on the heating elements. Once the image has been captured the control module turn on the heating elements and second IR frame is captured. The images are saved and post processed to evaluate the results. The post processing of the images is performed with the patented software tool that is part of the user interface. The post processing included the frame calibration, temperature profile extraction and plotting the results.

The working principle of an IR camera is based on thermography imaging. The major components of the camera are lens, detector, video processing electronics and user interface control. The incident beam of light is focused by the lens upon the detector. The detector contains the IR sensitive elements arranged in the array called focal plane array (FPA). These are IR sensitive elements and miniature in size (micro-meters). The resolution of FPA determines the resolution of the IR imagery produced by the camera. Many IR cameras available have user interface to calculate the scene temperature along with imagery recording software. Calibration is often required to read out the correct temperature across the scene that is captured.

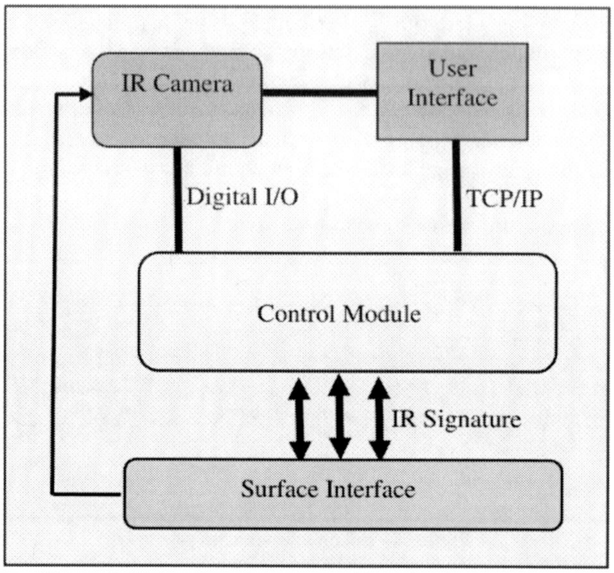

Figure 3. IR ice detection setup with active heat signature

IV. RESULTS AND DISCUSSION

The experimentation was performed to observe the infrared signature of pure ice and water droplets on a heated surface. These experiments were performed at room temperature. The heated elements were operated by the control module. The top of the surface interface was covered with pure ice. The pure ice sample was prepared in a round shape. The surface area of pure ice sample was $55cm^2$ with the thickness of 0.6 cm. This ice sample was placed on the heated area of approximately 64 cm^2. The heated elements were operated above 100^0C for a short period of time (20-30 seconds). The observations were made on the surface temperature from 23^0C to 115^0C. The duration to reach the peak temperature was approximately 25 seconds. The IR user interface was used to record infrared signatures of the ice sample. These isothermal profiles are shown in figure 4. The temperature profiles across the cross-sectional area of ice sample were observed from the isothermal images that is shown in the figure 5

The temperature profiles of the ice sample show consistent temperature recordings from 1.64^0C to 2.1^0C (figure 5) at the interface temperature of 23^0C, 80^0C, 110^0C and 115^0C. The presence of ice can be asserted with the temperature recordings around 0^0C. In the case of non-icing conditions above the surface interface, temperature profiles must be on the higher scale.

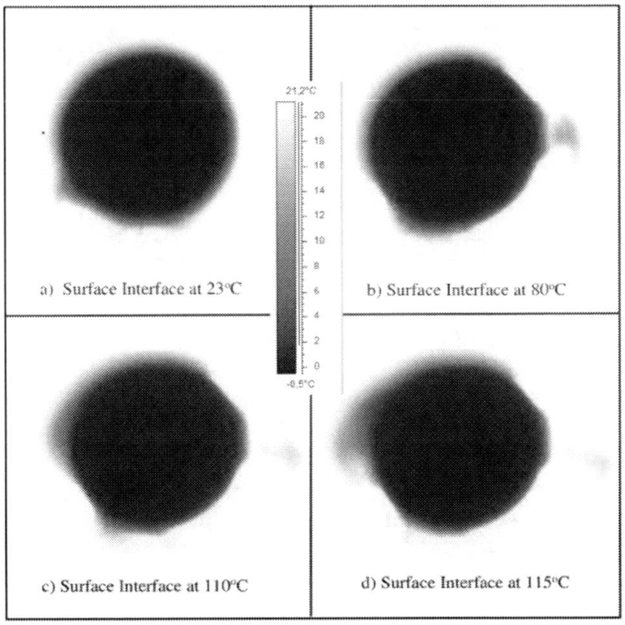

Figure 4. Pure ice iso-thermal signature on the surface interface

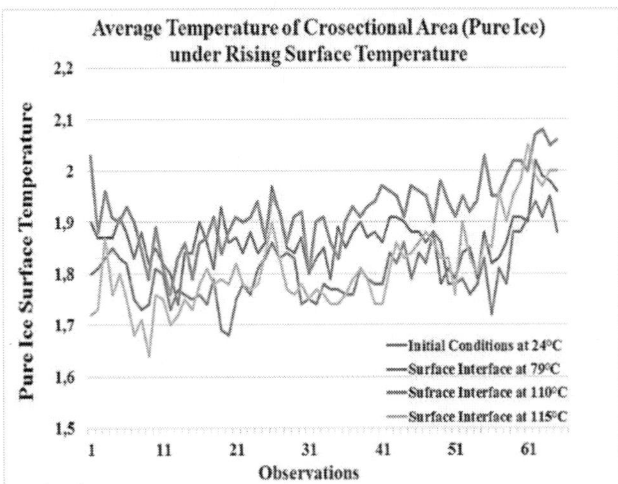

Figure 5. Pure ice cross sectional surface temperature over known heated interface

The other noticeable results were obtained by observing the water droplets of different sizes over the surface interface as shown in figure 6. The isothermal infrared signature shows the presence of droplets in contrast with the rest of the surface. These observations were recorded at the surface interface temperature of 23^{0}C, 38^{0}C, 55^{0}C and 80^{0}C. The average temperature recordings of the small and large water droplets were performed (figure 6). The water droplets temperature increased as expected and a significant difference in the temperature was observed between large and small water droplets (figure 6).

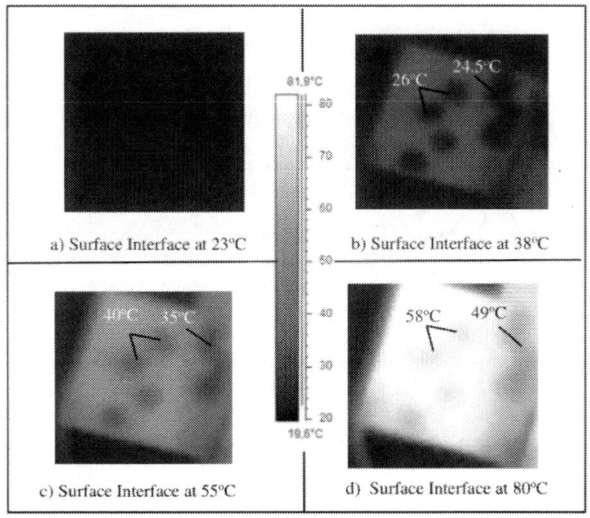

Figure 6. Water droplets isothermal signature on the surface interface

ACKNOWLEDGENMENTS

The work reported in this paper is funded by the MAROFF, project no. 195153/160 in collaboration with Faroe Petroleum. We would also like to acknowledge the support given by Prof. James Mercer at University of Tromsø.

REFERENCES

1. Fikke, S., Cost 727: atmospheric icing on structures. Measurements and data collection on icing: State of the Art, Publication of MeteoSwiss, 2006. 75(110): p. 1422-1381.
2. Rashid T., Mughal U. N., and Virk M. S., "Feasibility of Charge Transfer Based Atmospheric Ice Detection and Measurement," in International Conference on Sensor Technologies and Applications. 2014: p. 27-31.
3. Roebber P., and Mitten P., "Modelling and measurement of icing in Canadian waters," 1987: Atmospheric Environment Service.
4. Overland J., "Prediction of vessel icing," Journal of climate and applied meteorology, 1986. 25(12): p. 1793-1806.
5. Gregoris D., Yu S. and Teti F. "Multispectral imaging of ice," in Electrical and Computer Engineering, 2004. Canadian Conference on. 2004. IEEE. p. 2051-2056.
6. Stuart B., "Infrared spectroscopy," 2005: Wiley Online Library.
7. Rogalski A., "Infrared detectors: an overview," Infrared Physics & Technology, 2002. 43(3): p. 187-210.
8. Hori M., "In-situ measured spectral directional emissivity of snow and ice in the 8–14 μm atmospheric window," Remote Sensing of Environment, 2006. 100(4): p. 486-502.
9. P. F. U.K. Limited, Peltier Thermoelectric Modules. [cited 2015; Available from: http://uk.farnell.com/peltier-elements.
10. P. F. U.K. Limited, PTC Thermistirs. [cited 2015; Available from: http://uk.farnell.com/epcos/b59886c120a70 /ptcthermistor/dp/2144030.

Using AD5933 IC to Measure Dielectric Constant Variation of Atmospheric Ice

Umair N. Mughal, Beibei Shu
Department of Industrial Engineering, University of Tromsø
Narvik-8505, Norway
e-mail: umair.n.mughal@uit.no, beibei.shu@uit.no

Abstract — **AD5933 IC is a high precision impedance converter system. In this article, it is used for detection of an atmospheric icing event and to determine atmospheric ice type. A prototype circuit is developed and is tested using a microcontroller AtMega128 clock excitation frequency from 40Hz to 20kHz. The IC is calibrated using a 100kΩ resistor. The real and imaginary components of discrete fourier transform are recorded in order calculate the gain factor at each frequency increment. The unknown impedances are then calculated which are then utilized to calculate the complex dielectric constant of atmospheric ice at each frequency. The results are then compared with the experimental results of Stiles, Evans and Kuroiwa in order to detect an icing event and to determine its type. Results reflect that it is possible to use this approach for detection of an icing event, however it is difficult to determine icing type using this approach.**

Keywords - AD5933; Atmospheric Ice; Conductivity; Dielectric Constant; Dissipation Factor; Frequency Sweep.

I. INTRODUCTION

The aim of this article is to evaluate the usage of AD5933 Integrated Circuit (IC) to detect an atmospheric icing event and determine ice type. Using a pre-defined frequency range, this IC measure the real and imaginary components of discrete fourier transform of the load impedance. These components are recorded in order to calculate the gain factor at each frequency which is then utilized to determine the unknown impedances. In this experimental investigation, the load impedance is atmospheric ice. The calculated load impedances are utilized, to calculate capacitance of atmospheric ice at each excitation frequency. This capacitance measurement technique was highlighted in state of the art review by Mughal et. al. [1] and Homola et. al. [2], to be one of the many possible measurement techniques to detect atmospheric icing event, icing type and icing rate.

This article is divided in five sections. Section I is an introduction. Section II is the state of the art, which is further divided in three sections in order to understand atmospheric ice capacitance measurement technique using frequency sweep approach and application/construction of AD5933 IC. Section III is about the approach and architecture of the circuit developed to measure capacitance of atmospheric ice. Section IV describes the experimental results and discussions. Section V is the last section which includes conclusions and limitations to use this IC.

II. STATE OF THE ART

A. Capacitance Measurement Using Frequency Sweep:

Capacitive ice sensors generate an electric field to detect the presence of dielectric materials. An electric field radiates outward around the probe and a dielectric material in close proximity of the field affects the measured capacitance. Capacitance $C = C_0 \varepsilon_0 \varepsilon_r$ can be measured by the variation in relative permittivity or dielectric constant 'ε_r' or by the variation in electrode geometry 'C_0'. Where $C_0 = A/d$ where A is the area of the electrode and d is the distance between the electrodes, ε_0 is the permittivity of vacuum equal to $8.85x10^{12} F/m$

Water molecule is polar in nature due to electronegativity difference of 1.2 between hydrogen and oxygen. These polar molecules orient themselves with the electrical field. However, when the electrical field is removed they disorient themselves. Under the influence of electric field, polar molecule behave like a parallel combination of capacitor and resistor. The dielectric constant of these molecules $\varepsilon_r(\omega) = \varepsilon_r'(\omega) - j\varepsilon_r''(\omega)$ is a complex number, which is dependent upon the excitation frequency. Here ε_r' represents the amount of energy from the electric field, which is stored in the material and ε_r'' represents how lossy or dissipative a material is to the external electric field. This loss factor $\varepsilon_r''(\omega)$ includes the effects of both dissipation and conductivity. Also, the relative loss of the material is the ratio of energy lost to the energy stored and is defined as 'dissipation factor $D = tan\,\delta = \varepsilon_r''/\varepsilon_r'$. Polar materials generally have many dielectric mechanisms (atomic, electronic and dipolar) in different frequency domains associated with a cutoff frequency in each domain, which appears as a peak in $\varepsilon_r'' = \varepsilon_r''(\omega)$ (likewise $D = D(\omega)$) curve. The dipolar orientation is generally associated with the relaxation phenomenon, whereas the electronic and atomic polarization are associated with the resonance phenomenon. In the frequency domain analysis, the relaxation frequency 'f_c' is indicative of the relaxation time, $\tau_0 = 1/2\pi f_c$. This frequency can be detected by a peak by sweeping the excitation frequency and is generally unique for different materials. If we replace $\varepsilon(\omega \to 0) = \varepsilon_s$ and $\varepsilon(\omega \to \infty) = \varepsilon_\infty$, then by varying excitation frequencies, the dielectric constant of polar material can be analytically described by Debye relation, see (1) and Figure 1.

$$\varepsilon(\omega) = \varepsilon_\infty + \frac{\varepsilon_S - \varepsilon_\infty}{1 + j\omega\tau} \quad (1)$$

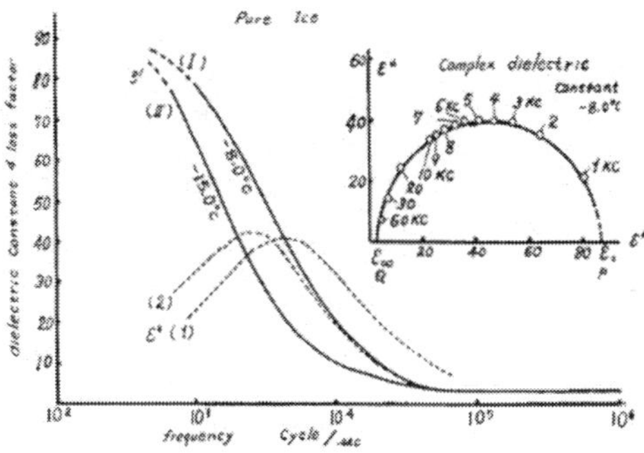

(a) ε_r variation of pure ice at two temperatures

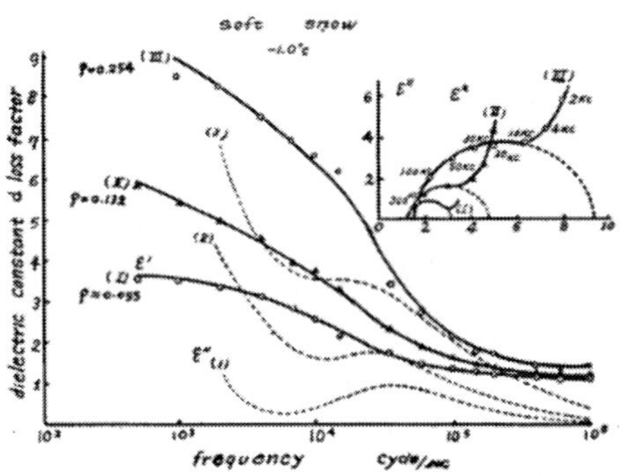

(b) ε_r variation of snow at three density ratio's

Figure 1. Visualization of Debye Relations [3]

B. Dielectric Constant of Atmospheric Ice

Figure 1a shows the dielectric constant variations of a sample of pure ice at two different temperatures (-8^0C and -15^0C). Both curves of $\varepsilon_r'(\omega)$ and $\varepsilon_r''(\omega)$ are shifting towards left as temperature was decreasing. The relaxation frequency 'f_c' was in the range of $1 \rightarrow 10$kHz where the value of $\varepsilon_r''(\omega)$ is in the range of $40 \rightarrow 50$. Also, Figure 1b shows the dielectric constant variations of three distinct samples of snow with density ratios $\rho = 0.095$, 0.132 and 0.254. Both curves of $\varepsilon_r'(\omega)$ and $\varepsilon_r''(\omega)$ are increasing in magnitude as the desity ratio's are increasing. The low frequency deviation of these curves from the ideal semi circle behavior (in Argand Diagram) is due to the conductivity of snow, which is increasing with increasing density ratio's. However, the relaxation frequency 'f_c' was not quite distinct but it lie in the range of $10 \rightarrow 100$kHz where the value of $\varepsilon_r''(\omega)$ are under 4 for all density ratio's. The application of the electrical properties to the measurement of ice thickness, temperature, crystal orientations are also presented in Evans [4]. It is mentioned in Sihvola et. al. [5] that for dry snow, the dielectric constant is determined by the density and for wet snow, the imaginary part and the increase of the real part due to liquid water have the same volumetric wetness dependence. In Sihvola et. al. [5], the results indicate that the complex dielectric constant is practically independent of the structure of snow. The static dielectric constants ε_{rs} of both polycrystalline and single crystals of ice have been carefully determined, Auty and Cole [6].

Furthermore, Weinstein [7] and Jarvinen [8] proposed two different capacitive based ice detection methods. In his patent [8], Jarvenin has proposed the use of AD5933 to detect icing event, icing type, ice thickness and icing rate, however no commercially available sensor is found to utilize this technique for measurement of atmospheric icing parameters.

C. AD5933 IC and its usage

AD5933 is a smallest and lowest power solution to measure the range of impedances using discrete fourier components. The general impedance measurement system can be seen in Figure 2. The system is excited by a range of frequencies in order to measure the output phase and impedance magnitude. This approach is called the frequency domain measurement technique [9].

In the block diagram from Figure 3, a direct digital synthesizer or DDS (AD9834) is used to generate a predefined frequency sweep to a tuning resolution of $0.1\text{Hz} \rightarrow 100\text{kHz}$. The output frequency is then filtered and amplified before being applied to the known impedance. Analog to digital converter (ADC) is then utilized to sample synchronously across all frequencies so as both the excitation and response waveform can be compared to allow full phase information. The data is then delivered to digital signal processing (DSP) block for further processing.

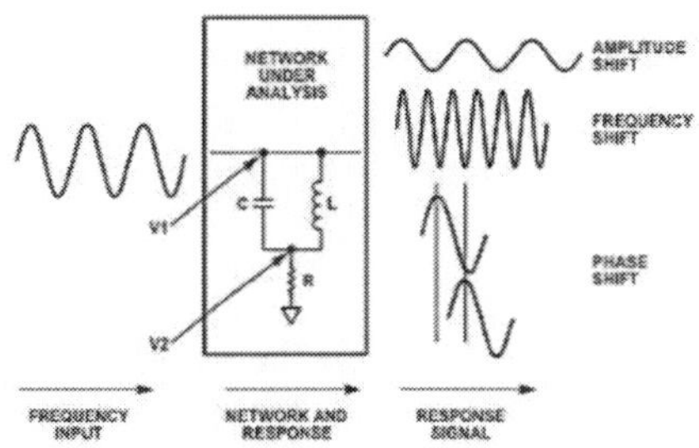

Figure 2. General Impedance Measurement System [10]

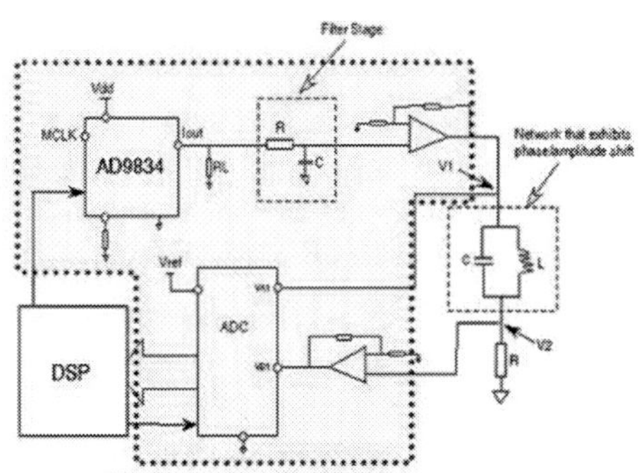

Figure 3. Integrated single chip solution [10]

AD5933 IC have been commercially utilized in impedance spectroscopy, proximity sensing, chemical analysis, bio medical analysis, human body impedance analysis and corrosion analysis. Norbotten B. J. [11] used AD5933 in the frequency range of $5 \rightarrow 100$kHz and measured human body impedance in the range of $0.1\text{k}\Omega \rightarrow 10\text{M}\Omega$. Similarly Pena A. A. [12] developed spectrometer for electrical bioimpedance using this IC. This IC has also been utilized for measuring blood glucose levels by Kamat et. al. [13].

III. Approach And Architecture

The frequency generator allows an external complex impedance to be excited with a known frequency. The frequency generator require three inputs, which are start frequency 'F_{START}', incremental frequency 'ΔF' and number of frequency increments 'N_{INCR}', see Figure 4.

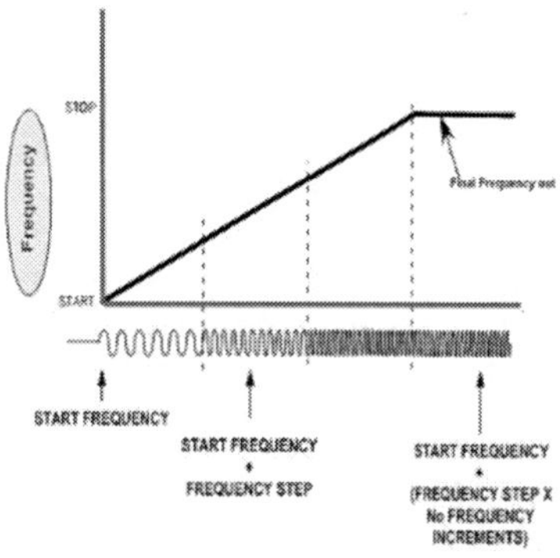

Figure 4. Frequency sweep characteristics

The microcontroller used to program and to implement the architecture was Atmega128 due to its memory. Also, this microcontroller had the flexibility to read/write on AD5933 IC's internal registers through I^2C interface. Nevertheless, the I^2C address of AD5933 was fixed by the manufacturer. In this experiment it was desired to sweep the frequency from $40Hz \rightarrow 20$kHz for a step of 40Hz. In order to meet this requirement, a changeable clock signal for AD5933 IC, was generated through Atmega128 timerl in Clock Timer Counter (CTC) mode, see Figure 5. In CTC mode the counter was cleared to zero, when the free running counter or a 16 bit register (TCNT1) matches either the output compare register OCR1A (WGM13:0 = 4 where WGM is wave generation mode) or the input capture register ICR1 (WGM13:0 = 12). The counter value (TCNT1) was increased until a compare match occurs with either OCR1A or ICR1, and then counter (TCNT1) was cleared, see Figure 6.

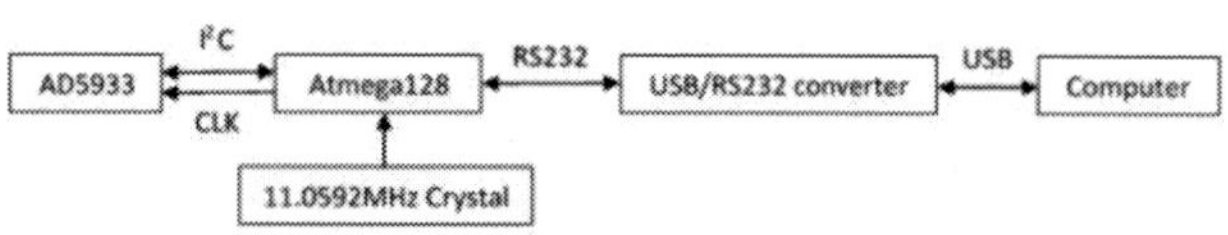

Figure 5. Block diagram for communication path

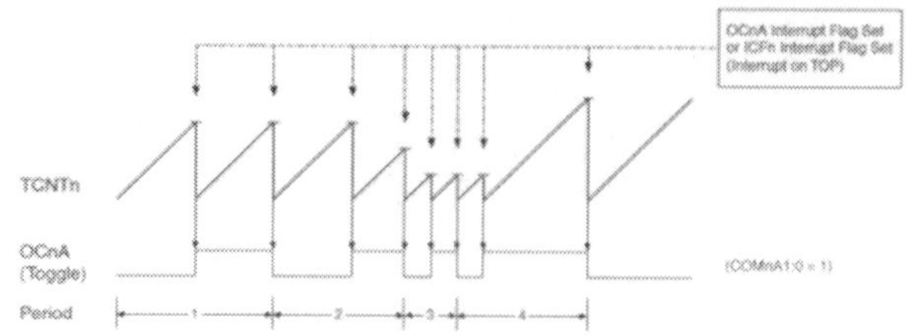

Figure 6. CTC mode, timing diagram

The function of timer1 over here was to generate frequencies, so that the CTC interrupat should be disabled to save CPU cycles. This Alf and Vegard RISC processor (AVR) timer was connected to general I/O Port. Then general I/O pin PD5 was converted to compare match output OC1A. After that OC1A pin function was set to toggle on compare match. Then the fuse bits were programmed to make clock division factor to 1 and set the timer1 clock source to no prescaling. Hence, the timer clock source was equal to crystal frequency, $clk_{I/O}$=11.0592MHz. The output frequency was f_{out}= $clk_{I/O}$/(2×OCR1A). OCR1A was a 16-bits register, which ranged from 1 to 65535 therefore the range of output frequency could be was $clk_{I/O}$/(2×1) to $clk_{I/O}$/(2×65535), that is, from 5.5296MHz to 84Hz. Therefore when the system was running, the only requirement was to change the value of OCR1A to change the output frequency. Therefore using an internal clock source, which was 16.776MHz, the AD5933 chip could measure the impedance spectrum in the required frequency range of 1 kHz–100kHz. However, using external clock source (as applied in this work), which was generated by AVR, the frequency range can go lower than 1 kHz.

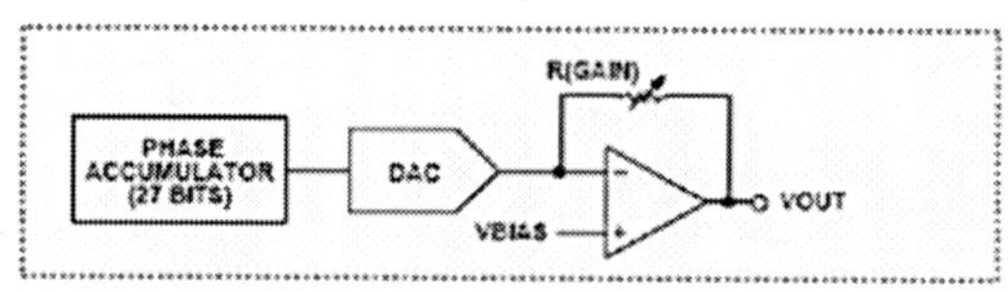

(a). Transmit Stage

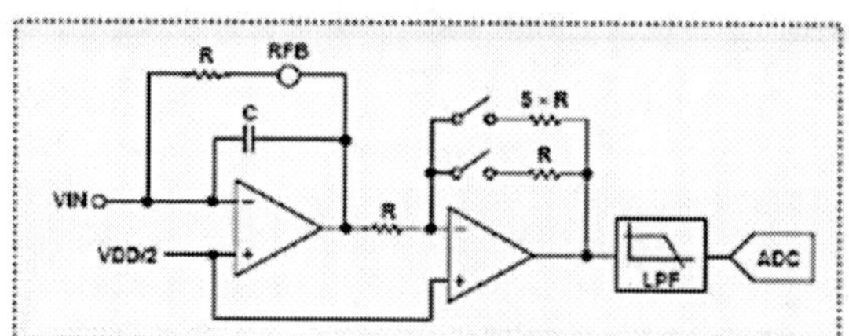

(b). Receive Stage

Figure 7. Transmit Stage and Receive Stage of AD5933 [10]

This IC worked in two stages, which are transmit stage and receive stage. The transmit stage of the AD5933 was made up of a 27 bit phase accumulator DDS core, which provided the output excitation signal at a particular frequency, see Figure 7a. The input to the phase accumulator was taken from the contents of the start frequency register

(Ram locations 82h, 83h and 84h). Although the phase accumulator offers 27bits of resolution, the start frequency register had the 3 most significant bits (MSBs) sets to 0 internally; therefore it became possible to program only the lower 24bits of the start frequency register. The frequency resolution 0.1Hz could be achieved. The frequency resolution was programmed via a 24 bit word loaded serially over the I^2C interface to the frequency increment register. The last input was number of increments.

The receive stage comprised of a current to voltage amplified, followed by a programmable gain amplifier (PGA), an anti aliasing filter, and an ADC, see Figure 7b. The unknown impedance was connected between the V_{OUT} and V_{IN} pins. The first stage current to voltage amplifier sat the V_{IN} pin as a virtual ground with a DC value of $V_{DD}/2$. The signal current developed across the unknown impedance was then flowed into the V_{IN} pin, which, developed a voltage signal at the output of the current to voltage converter.

The gain of the current to voltage amplifier was determined by selecting a feedback resistor of $Z_{calibrated} = 100k\Omega$ connected between rectified feedback (RFB) and V_{IN}. The aim was to maintain the signal within the linear range of ADC (0V to 3.3V analog positive supply voltage or AVDD). The gain setting was set to one. The signal was then sent through a low pass filter and was presented to the input of the 12bit, 1 mega samples per second (MSPS) ADC.

The response signal from the impedance was sampled by the on-board ADC and discrete fourier transform (DFT) processed by an on-board DSP engine. Thle DFT algorithm returned real 'R' and imaginary 'I' data-word at each frequency point along the frequency sweep. Using these 'R' and 'I', magnitude 'M' and phase 'φ' were calculated using (2) and (3). Therefore $M_{calibrated}$ and $\varphi_{calibrated}$ were measured using $R_{calibrated}$ and $I_{calibrated}$. Atmospheric ice was then placed on the electrode for which $M_{unknown}$ and $\varphi_{unknown}$ were measured using $R_{unknown}$ and $I_{unknowm}$.

$$M = \sqrt{R^2 + I^2}, \quad (2)$$

$$\varphi = tan^{-1}(I/R). \quad (3)$$

It was also necessary to ensure that the signal was always maintained within the linear range of the ADC over the impedance range of interest. Before measuring the unknown impedance, the calibration must be done. In calibration stage, the manufacturer mentioned that a gain factor needs to be calculated. The gain factor 'GF' could be calculated using,

$$GF = \frac{1}{Z_{calibrated} \times M_{calibrated}}. \quad (4)$$

However, in this analysis, there was no need to calculate the gain factor due to the reason that in the measuring stage, the unknown impedance '$Z_{calibrated}$' and its unknown phase were calculated using,

$$Z_{unknown} = \frac{Z_{calibrated} \times M_{calibrated}}{M_{unknown}} \quad (5)$$

$$\emptyset_{unknown} = atan\left(\frac{I_{unknown}}{R_{unknown}}\right) - atan\left(\frac{I_{calibrated}}{R_{calibrated}}\right) \quad (6)$$

As capacitance $C = 1/2\pi jfZ$, therefore using (5) and (6) in complex dielectric constant equation, we derive,

$$\varepsilon_r' - j\varepsilon_r'' = \frac{1}{2\pi jfC_0\varepsilon_0 Z_{unknown} exp(\emptyset_{unknown})} \quad (7)$$

Equation (7) is then further utilized to determine the dielectric constant of the unknown sample of atmospheric ice.

IV. Experimental Results and Discussions

Using (7), the results of ε_r' and ε_r'' were obtained by writing a simple algorithm in MatLab. The experimentations were done in the Cold Climate Chamber of UiT Campus Narvik, using the following samples at the respective temperatures,

i. Glaze ice frozen on the electrode plate at a temperature of -16°C,
ii. Glaze ice frozen on the electrode plate at a temperature of -20°C,
iii. Glaze ice frozen on the electrode plate at a temperature of -24°C,
iv. Natural Snow from ground outside university campus at a temperature of -3°C.
v. Normal tap water at a temperature of 26°C,

The results of glaze ice at three different temperatures can be seen in Figure 8. This figure indicates there was no prominent peak observed in the dielectric constant variation (ε_r'' = imaginary part) with the variation in frequency (Figure 8a), hence it was not possible to compare the results of Stiles [3] and Kuroiwa [14]. Both curves of $\varepsilon_r'(\omega)$ and $\varepsilon_r''(\omega)$ were shifting towards left as temperature was decreasing. However, the capacitance phase ($atan(\varepsilon_r''/\varepsilon_r')$) or dissipation factor ($\varepsilon_r''/\varepsilon_r'$) reflect an observable trend. In the frequency range of $1 \rightarrow 10$kHz (relaxation frequency 'f_c'), the variation in the phase is prominent (Figure 8b). This value of f_c was found in agreement with the experimental results of Stiles (Figure 1). It was also found that the average value of this phase reached a relative maximum of 20^0 by decreasing the temperature from $-16^0C \rightarrow -24^0C$, hence more capacitance. The results were however very noisy possibly due to some harmonics from the microcontroller and reasonably high conductance of the sample. In another test, the results were compared with the natural occurring snow, collected from outside the university campus and water samples. The results are shown in Figure 9. These results also indicated the same trend in the dielectric constant variation (ε_r'' = imaginary part) with frequency (Figure 9a), hence it was not possible to determine the relaxation due to dominated noise. Similarly, it was found that the phase of the capacitance ($atan(\varepsilon_r''/\varepsilon_r')$) reflect observable trend for samples of glaze ice, snow and water (Figure 9b).

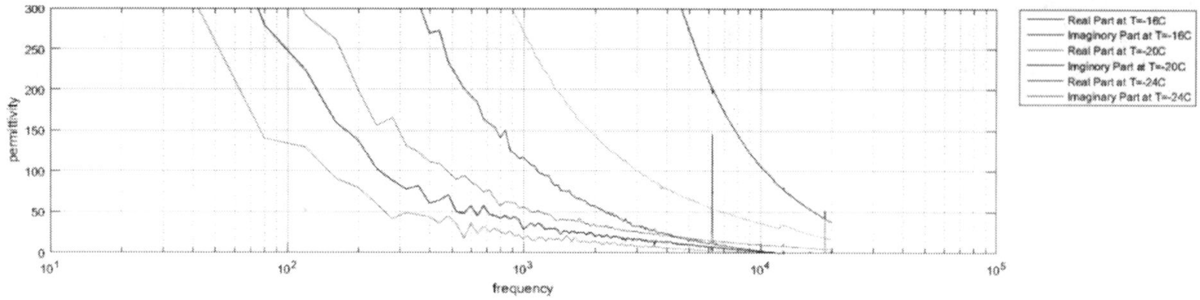

(a). Dielectric constant ($\varepsilon_r' = real, \varepsilon_r'' = imaginary$) variation with frequency

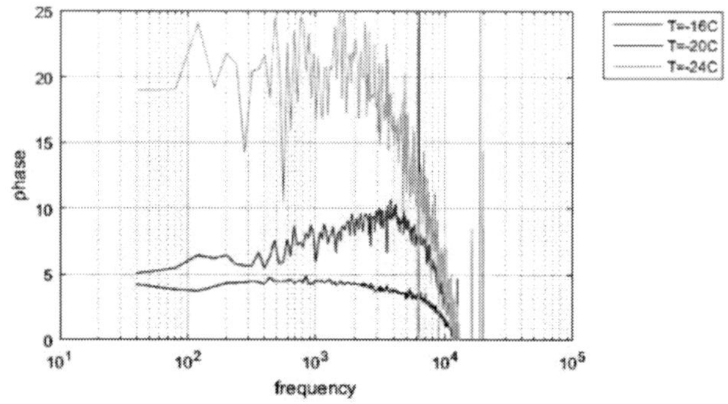

(b). Dielectric constant phase (atan($\varepsilon_r''/\varepsilon_r'$))

Figure 8. Dielectric constant variation with excitation frequency for Glaze Ice frozen on the electrode plate at temperatures -16°C, -20°C and -24°C [15]

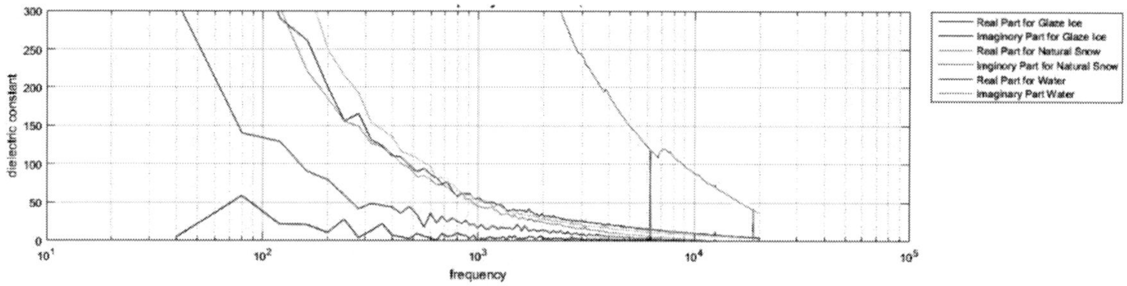

(a). Dielectric constant ($\varepsilon_r' = real, \varepsilon_r'' = imaginary$) variation with frequency

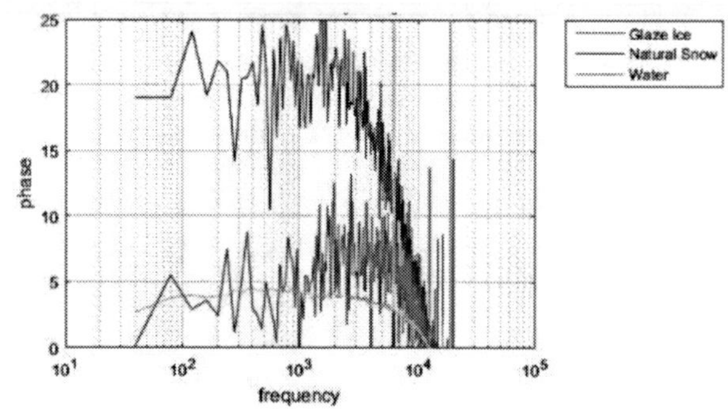

(b). Dielectric constant phase (atan($\varepsilon_r''/\varepsilon_r'$))

Figure 9. Dielectric constant variation with excitation frequency for glaze ice at -24°C, natural snow at -4°C and water sample at 24°C [15]

V. Conclusion and Future Work

AD5933 IC works upon the frequency domain capacitance measurement technique [9]. It was possible to use the dissipation factor for detecting an icing event using the approach utilized in this experimental study. Most of the existing experimental study [3] [4] [14], by sweeping the frequency to determine the dielectric variation in different type of atmospheric ice, are laboratory based. However, the aim in this article was to evaluate the usage of AD5933 IC to detect an atmospheric icing event and determine ice type. It was found that the scope to utilize the excitation frequency from microcontroller clock for AD5933 IC is limited. A lot of noise was observed in the values of complex dielectric constant due to this and values were found possibly due to unwanted harmonics. It was therefore not possible to compare these values with the experimental values of Stiles and Ulaby [3], Evans [4] and Kuroiwa [14]. It was found that that the average value of this phase reached a relative maximum of 20^0 by decreasing the temperature from $-16^0C \rightarrow -24^0$, hence more capacitance. Nevertheless, by recording the dissipation factor / phase value, it was found possible to at least detect an icing event. Also due to reasonably high conductivity of ice, the complex dielectric constant was continuously reducing even at same environmental conditions, however the dissipation factor remained stable for longer range of frequencies.

For future experimentations, it will be useful to improve the outputs of AD5933 IC for measuring atmospheric icing paramaters by utilizing the methods as described by Leonid [16].

Acknowledgment

The work was funded by Research Council of Norway Project No. 195153 (ColdTech RT3), Norwegian Centre for International Cooperation in Education Project No. HNP-2014/10023 and WindCoE (Nordic Wind Energy Centre) project funded within Interreg IVA Botnia-Atlantica, as part of European Territorial Cooperation (ETC).

References

[1] U. N. Mughal, M. S. Virk, and M. Y. Mustafa, "State of the Art Review of Atmospheric Icing Sensors," *Sensors and Transducers*, vol. 198, pp. 2-15, 2016.

[2] M. C. Homola, P. J. Nicklasson, and P. A. Sundsbo, "Ice sensors for wind turbines," *Cold Regions Science and Technology*, vol. 46, pp. 125-131, 2006.

[3] W. H. Stiles and F. T. Ulaby, "Dielectric properties of snow," *Journal of Geophysical Research*, vol. 85, pp. 91-103, 1981.

[4] S. Evans, "Dielectric properties of ice and snow - a review," *Journal of Glaciology*, vol. 5, pp. 773-792, 1965.

[5] A. Sihvola, E. Nyfors, and M. Tiuri, "Mixing formulae and experimental results for the dielectric constant of snow," *Journal of Glaciology*, vol. 31, pp. 163-170, 1985.

[6] R. P. Auty and R. H. Cole, "Dielectric Properties of Ice and Solid D_2O," *Journal of Chemical Physics*, vol. 20, pp. 1309-1314, 1952.

[7] L. M. Weinstein, "Ice Sensor," 1988.

[8] P. O. Jarvinen, "Total impedience and complex dielectric property ice detection system," 2008.

[9] K. Kao, *Dielectric Phenomena in Solids*, 2004.

[10] A. Devices. (2016, March 14th). *AD5933 Impedance to Digital Converter*. Available: http://dkc1.digikey.com/us/en/TOD/ADI/AD5933/AD5933.html

[11] B. J. Nordbotten, "Bioimpedance Using the Integrated Circuit AD5933," Master of Science, Department of Physics, University of Oslo, 2008.

[12] A. A. Pena, "A Feasibility Study of the Suitability of an AD5933 based spectrometer for EBI Applications," Electronic Instrumentation, University of Boras, 2009.

[13] D. K. Kamat, B. Dhanashri, and P. M. Patil, "Blood Glucose Measurement Using Bioimpedance Technique," *Advance in Electronics*, vol. 2014, 2014.

[14] D. Kuroiwa, "The dielectric property of snow," *Union Geodesique et Geophysique International* vol. Association Internationale of Hdrologie Scientifique, Assemblee generale de Rome,, pp. 52-63, 1956.

[15] U. N. Mughal, B. Shu, and T. Rashid, "Proof of Concept of Atmospheric Icing Sensor to detect icing, determine icing type and measure melting rate," *Submitted in IEEE Transactions on Dielectrics and Electical Insulation, Paper ID 6048*, 2016.

[16] L. Matsiev, "Improving Performance and Versatility of Systems Based on Single-Frequency DFT Detectors Such as AD5933," *Electronics*, vol. 4, pp. 1-34, 2015.

A Framework for Connectivity Monitoring in Wireless Sensor Networks

Daniel Pfleger, Ulrich Schmid
Institute of Computer Engineering
Vienna University of Technology
Vienna, Austria
Email: {dpfleger, s}@ecs.tuwien.ac.at

Abstract—**We present an overview of the features and the architecture of a framework for long-term monitoring of the communication topology of a synchronous wireless sensor network (WSN). Our framework, a prototype of which has been implemented for Atmel RZ200 motes running TinyOS, locally records the complete connectivity information for every node in every round, and disseminates this information to one or more root nodes that act as data sinks for monitoring information. Postprocessing tools allow to query the recorded communication graphs, in order to, e.g., verify structural properties like the presence of multiple strongly connected components. We demonstrate the utility of our framework by means of an experimental evaluation of the coverage of a recently introduced adversarial network model for directed dynamic networks. Our measurement results reveal that it has a very good coverage in several small-scale WSN deployments.**

Keywords–Wireless Sensor Networks; Monitoring; Network Topology.

I. INTRODUCTION

The design and analysis of algorithms and protocols for dynamic networks [1] has always been a very active area in networking and distributed computing research. In this research, many "abstract" network models, both adversarial and probabilistic, have been defined and used for validating the correctness and performance of network protocols.

One example of an adversarial model is *T-interval connectivity* [2], where one assumes that the communication topology may vary arbitrarily over time, except that a subgraph that spans all n nodes in the system must be stable in every sliding window of duration T. The advantage of an adversarial model is that it allows the design of protocols that *guarantee* certain properties (provided the assumptions of the model hold). Probabilistic models, on the other hand, are typically based on random graphs, which ensure certain basic network properties such as connectivity or k-connectivity with some (high) probability. Clearly, protocols designed atop of such models can only provide probabilistic guarantees.

Given the wealth of protocol- and algorithm-related research that is based on such models, surprisingly little can be said about their validity in real-world networks (see Section II). In particular, an adversarial model, e.g., based on T-interval connectivity [2] or the eventual occurrence of certain strongly connected components [3][4] in the communication graphs immediately raises the question of whether these are reasonable assumptions in a real dynamic network or not.

There are two fundamentally different approaches for addressing this question: (i) Analytic or simulation-based *coverage analysis* and (ii) *monitoring* of real networks. Coverage analysis relies on a detailed low-level model of the underlying communication network, and verifies either analytically or via simulations whether the communication graphs generated by the underlying model exhibit the required properties with sufficiently high probability. The main disadvantages of this approach are the critical dependency on the appropriateness of the underlying network model (= inherent coverage) and its inability to incorporate engineering details like protocol stack implementations, etc.

Obviously, monitoring experiments do not suffer from these deficiencies. However, unless one is content with very limited information, a dedicated (and typically fairly complex) measurement infrastructure is required. Surprisingly, despite the substantial body of existing experimental research on various types of wireless networks, we were unable to find an existing infrastructure that facilitates long-term monitoring of topology-related properties in evolving communication graphs. In this paper, we present a suitable framework for comprehensive topology monitoring in wireless sensor networks that does not need a special infrastructure, and demonstrate its utility by validating a recently introduced adversarial network model [5].

Detailed Contributions: Please also refer to our technical report [6], since lacking space did not allow us to include all the findings in this paper.

(1) We present an overview of the features and the architecture of a framework for the long-term communication topology monitoring in synchronous dynamic networks, which has been implemented for Atmel RZ200 wireless sensor network motes running TinyOS. In a synchronous computation, one (conceptually) assumes that all nodes execute in a sequence of perfectly synchronized *rounds* $r = 1, 2, \dots$, each consisting of (i) the broadcast of a message, (ii) the reception of all messages from the neighbors, and (iii) some local computation that also involves received messages. Our framework locally records the complete connectivity information for every node (i.e., the set of nodes from which an application message has been successfully received) in every round and disseminates this information multi-hop to one or more root nodes that act as data sinks for monitoring information. The root nodes forward this monitoring data, via a dedicated LAN, to a PC that fuses this data to construct the complete directed communication graph for every round. Postprocessing tools allow to query the recorded communication graphs in order to verify any desired graph property.

(2) We demonstrate the utility of our prototype implementation by means of the experimental evaluation of the coverage of an adversarial network model introduced in [5] in small-scale WSNs. Essentially, the model aims at dynamic networks

that may behave arbitrarily (even partition) during some finite initial period, after which the system remains reasonably well-connected sufficiently long. The network assumption $\Diamond\texttt{STABLE}(D)$ (see Definition 3) has a tunable parameter D, which is related to network stability. We evaluate the coverage of $\Diamond\texttt{STABLE}(D)$, i.e., the likelihood that it actually holds in every execution, in several WSN deployments that differ in node density, fatness of the deployment area, and interference level. Our results reveal a very good coverage in the considered settings, provided D is chosen appropriately.

Paper organization. We start with the description of the general features, architecture and operating principle of our framework in Section III. Section IV describes details of our implementation, Section V outlines the user interface, including some features of the currently available postprocessing tool. Section VI presents the purpose and results of our sample experiments. Some conclusions and directions of further work in Section VII complete our paper.

II. Overview of Related Work

Theoretical analyses based on random graphs, simulations, and measurements of real systems are all abundant in the existing literature, see, e.g., [7] for an overview.

Due to lacking space, we will restrict our attention to (a subset of) existing measurement approaches here; further references can be found in [6]. There are many open testbeds [8] , which provide a powerful infrastructure for dedicated experiments. Unfortunately, however, the (statistical) data provided in existing experimental evaluations typically address the properties of individual links [9] or system-wide properties like throughput [7][10] and other end-to-end performance characteristics [11]. By contrast, we are interested in detailed structural properties of not necessarily bidirectional communication graphs.

Existing approaches for experimentally exploring network topologies use active probing or passive monitoring, and may or may not require support from intermediate nodes. However, the inferable topology information is usually quite restricted, typically to network cardinality [12] or capacity [13]. Moreover, the topology of the underlying network is often limited. For example, the approach described in [14] uses the data correlation caused by intermediate network coding for inferring tree or DAG topologies. By contrast, [15] uses active probing with traceroute data, and primarily addresses problems caused by anonymous/non-cooperative intermediate nodes and the resulting uncertainties in topology inference. Pure network tomography approaches infer the network topology solely from data available at end nodes, typically using statistical approaches [16][17].

There is also a substantial body of work on connectivity monitoring in wireless sensor networks. Both active probing [18][19], where (a subset of) the network nodes query their neighborhood and forward connectivity data to some sink node, and passive techniques using data available at end-nodes only [20], as in network tomography approaches [21], can be employed here. Typical approaches using the latter assume that the WSN topology is a convergecast tree, where all nodes periodically send their data to a sink, using data aggregation. The topology is then reconstructed from the data received at the sink.

All these solutions provide, with varying accuracy, (part of) the entire topology. Moreover, they typically assume the existence of a bidirectional spanning tree for routing purposes. We are not aware of approaches that can infer sub-graph properties such as, for example, the presence of a rooted spanning tree or a strongly connected component, in sparsely connected communication graphs.

III. Framework Description

As already stated in Section I, the goal of our framework is to continuously monitor the evolution of the possibly sparsely connected, directed communication graph of a synchronous wireless sensor network over time. Per-node-recorded connectivity data is disseminated to certain special nodes ("root motes") that act as data sinks. The latter forward the data to a PC, where it can be analyzed and visualized.

In this section, we describe the general features, architecture and operating principle of our framework. Implementation-related details are provided in the subsequent section.

A. Required features

The design of our framework started out from several goals:
(1) **Synchronous applications**: We target synchronous WSNs, where the WSN nodes (called *motes* in the sequel) execute a round-based algorithm (which requires an underlying time synchronization mechanism).

(2) **Long-term monitoring**: We need to monitor the evolution of the entire communication graph of a synchronous WSN over days and more (which rules out to store the complete monitoring data locally at the motes).

(3) **Standard motes**: We do not impose any dedicated monitoring hardware infrastructure at our motes (which requires monitoring data dissemination to use the wireless interface only).

(4) **Partitionable directed communication graphs**: We must allow the WSN to possibly partition, for an arbitrary time (which precludes the existence of an underlying spanning tree for routing the monitoring data to a single sink).

(5) **Message loss**: We cannot a priori guarantee reliable delivery of all messages containing monitoring data (which requires selective retransmission).

(6) **User-supplied application**: It must be possible to plug-in a user-supplied round-based application algorithm (which requires a message-passing interface that also allows to specify transmission scheduling policies and transmission powers).

(7) **Fault-injection**: It must be possible to exercise some control over the network topology, e.g., for testing purposes (which requires to actively inhibit the application-level communication between given pairs of sender and receiver motes).

B. System architecture

In order to meet the above requirements, our framework consists of four different components depicted in Figure 1. The central part is the *monitoring network* itself, which consists of the WSN *motes* that both execute the synchronous application and the (low-level) monitoring infrastructure. The collected connectivity data is disseminated to a *monitoring PC*, which collects and integrates the information from all the motes in order to reconstruct the communication graph for every round.

This data dissemination is actually a two-step process: First, the per-mote recorded data is disseminated via multi-hop communication to some special *root mote*, which acts both as the primary data sink and as a root for time synchronization via the *Flooding Time Synchronization Protocol* (FTSP) [22] of the motes. For WSNs that may partition, our framework supports multiple root motes. Every root mote is serially connected to a dedicated *forwarding PC* component, which finally forwards all the data received from the serial interface to the monitoring PC component via LAN and vice versa. In other words, root motes and forwarding PC component act as "WSN-UART" and "UART-LAN" gateways, respectively.

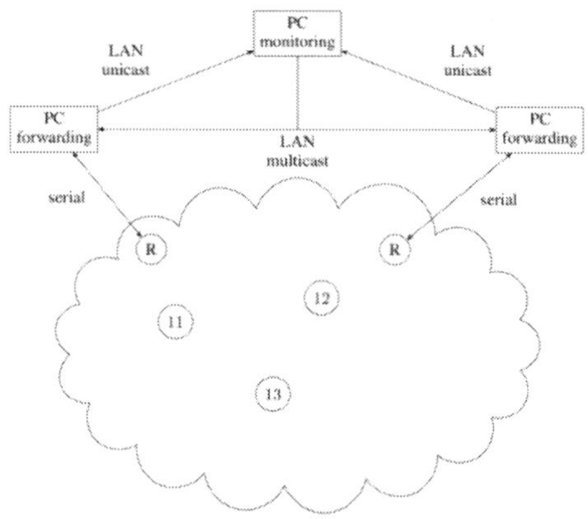

Figure 1: Overview of the framework's general structure. The framework consists of monitoring Motes (numbered), Root Motes (labeled with "R"), forwarding PC components and a monitoring PC instance.

In more detail, the components perform the following tasks:

Motes: The motes execute an user-supplied synchronous distributed algorithm that makes up the WSN application software. It has to use a single-hop broadcast to send an *application message* to all other motes in the WSN in every round. The monitoring infrastructure on every mote records from whom it successfully received a message in a round, and disseminates this data by broadcasting *report messages* via a suitable data collection protocol (described in Section IV-A) subsequently.

Root motes and forwarding PC: Each root mote is connected to an instance of the forwarding PC component and works as a WSN-UART-Gateway: Every report messages received from a mote via the wireless interface is forwarded via the serial interface. Vice versa, all control messages received from the forwarding PC component are sent to the motes using the radio interface.

In addition, the root motes are also root nodes for time synchronization via FTSP [22]. A detailed description of the time synchronization mechanism is given in Section IV-B.

Monitoring PC: Each instance of the forwarding PC component is connected to a single dedicated monitoring PC via a (wireless) Ethernet connection. Besides exercising all the framework setup and monitoring control tasks, it primarily gathers and integrates the per-node connectivity data contained in forwarded report messages and stores it in the file system for post-processing. Since report messages may be lost before they reach any root mote, the monitoring PC also checks the received connectivity information for missing data and actively requests retransmission of single report messages if needed. A detailed description of this messaging protocol can be found in Section IV-A.

C. General operating principle

Thanks to the time synchronization mechanism described in Section IV-B, our monitoring framework operates in a repeated sequence of three consecutive lockstep-synchronous *phases* sketched in Figure 2:

Phase 1 — record per-mote connectivity information: At the beginning of this phase, which actually represents a single round of the application algorithm, every mote broadcasts an application message generated by the user-supplied algorithm. It is sent via the single-hop broadcast service provided by our framework. To restrict the heavy mutual interference caused by simultaneous broadcasting of all motes, a suitable transmission schedule (+ power control) can be applied here.

During Phase 1, each node records the sender of every successfully received message (for the current round). The duration of Phase 1 must be chosen appropriately to ensure that every receiver can indeed receive and process the message from every sender. Thus, the set of motes a message has been received from by the end of Phase 1 reflects the in-edges of the communication graph ending at the receiver mote. Figure 2 (left) shows an example.

Phase 2 — disseminate collected data: When Phase 1 ends, every mote sends a *report message* containing its connectivity data, i.e., the set of motes it received a message from, to one or more root motes. Figure 2 (middle) shows an example.

Actually, since the diameter of the WSN may be large, a custom *multi-hop data collection* protocol is used for this purpose. As described in detail in Section IV-A, it uses a combination of flooding and local caching, in conjunction with a suitably long duration of Phase 2. Moreover, in order to circumvent the collisions resulting from simultaneous broadcasting of report messages, a suitable transmission schedule is used at the beginning of Phase 2.

Phase 3 — request and retransmission of missing report messages: When Phase 2 has terminated, the monitoring PC checks the received report messages for completeness and, if needed, sends messages requesting the retransmission of lost messages. Note that request messages are sent by the monitoring PC sequentially, so no transmission scheduling is necessary here. These *request messages* are in fact disseminated via a custom *multi-hop messaging* protocol (also described in Section IV-A), which uses the local caching of report messages to possibly speed-up the response time: Any

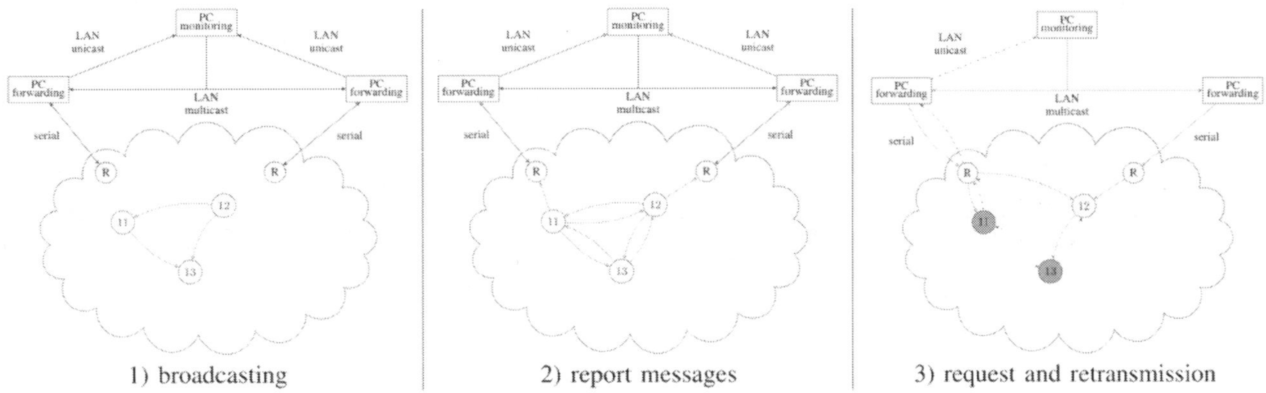

Figure 2: Our framework works in three consecutive lockstep-synchronous phases. Phase 1 (left): Recording of connectivity data. Phase 2 (middle): Disseminate connectivity data to monitoring PC. Phase 3 (right): request retransmission of missing data.

mote that has the required report message in its cache can answer the request. An example is shown in Figure 2 (right).

IV. Framework Implementation

In this section, we provide an overview of the prototype implementation of our framework, which has been developed for Atmel RZ200 motes running TinyOS. In particular, we elaborate on our custom multihop protocols, on time synchronization, and on the fault-injection capabilities provided by our implementation.

A. Multihop protocols

As already mentioned in Section III-C, our framework must implement two multi-hop data dissemination protocols for monitoring data:

(i) **Multi-hop data collection**: In Phase 2, each node sends a report message containing its connectivity data to the monitoring PC.
(ii) **Multi-hop messaging**: Since report messages may be lost in (i), the monitoring PC checks the received data for completeness and, if needed, requests the retransmission of missing report messages.

Existing routing and data collection protocols, such as the *Dynamic Manet On-demand Protocol* [23] (creating a unicast route) and the *Collection Tree Protocol* [24] (collecting data at a dedicated root node) require communication graphs that contain a reasonably stable spanning tree with bidirectional links between neighbors. Moreover, they need some sort of routing table and are hence expensive regarding RAM-usage. Since we could not afford this assumption due to our possibly sparsely connected, directed communication graphs, we had to develop a custom flooding protocol, augmented with local caching, as the basis of our multi-hop protocols. Our flooding protocol relies on several low-level facilities, which we will describe next.

Data encoding. Since our framework shall support large networks, despite small message sizes, a compact encoding of our monitoring data is needed. We implemented this by using a single bit to identify each node: Each node's ID corresponds to a single bit within an array holding the connectivity data recorded by a node, the so-called *monitor array*. If some bit is zero at the end of Phase 1, no application message has been received from the corresponding node in this round.

Message headers. Since flooding protocols are prone to sending messages to an excessively large number of nodes, possibly even resulting in cycles, we use a message header containing the following data: Besides *source* and *destination address*, it contains a unique *message ID* (sequence number) for each source address. Note that the pair of source address and message ID unambiguously identifies every message. To limit the spreading of a message, a *hop count* field, working as a time-to-live counter, is used.

Local caches. Every mote is equipped with two (small) caches, a *report-cache* (holding report messages) and a *header-cache* (holding headers of messages that are sent via the flooding protocol). Each is organized as a FIFO-buffer augmented with reordering abilities to minimize RAM-usage: A message/-header to be added is always appended to the tail of the FIFO-buffer. If a copy of the newly added message/header is already present in the buffer, the copy is deleted first. If the buffer is (still) full, the message/header at its head is deleted first. Obviously, these rules guarantee that (i) messages/headers cached earlier are dropped before later ones, and (ii) that the same message/header is never cached more than once.

Our custom **flooding protocol**, a variant of which is used both in the multi-hop data collection and in the multi-hop messaging protocol, combines the above low-level facilities to avoid cyclic sending of messages. The primary mechanism employed for this purpose is the usage of the unique message header combined with the local header-caches: First, the originator of a report or request message to be flooded broadcasts the message, with an appropriately initialized message header. Each time a node sends or forwards a message, it caches the message's header in the header-cache. Before a message is forwarded, the node checks whether the (unique!) message's header is already stored in cache. If so, the message is dropped, otherwise it is indeed forwarded by broadcasting it. Figure 3 depicts an exemplary scenario.

We can now describe the operation of our two multi-hop protocols:

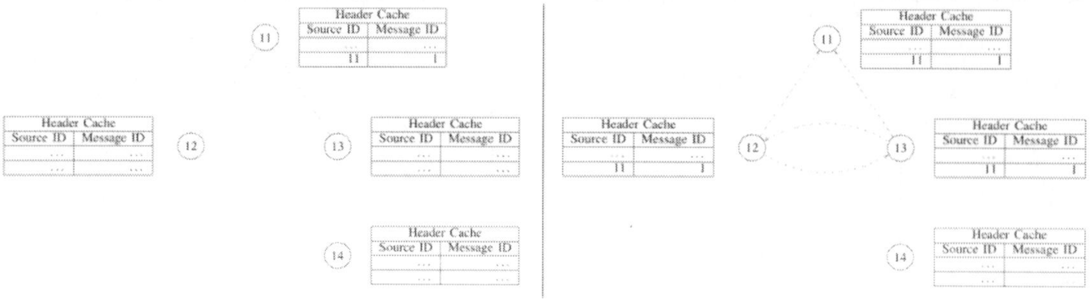

Figure 3: Our custom flooding protocol uses a header-cache at each node to avoid cyclic sending. As nodes 11 and 12 already sent the message at the left, their header-caches contain the message (11, 1). Thus they discard the message (red, dashed arrows); only node 14 accepts it (green, solid arrow).

(i) **Multi-hop data collection**: Recall that, in Phase 2, each node sends a *report message* containing its monitor array to the monitoring PC by means of this protocol. To accomplish this, the node uses a variant of our flooding protocol to reach at least one root mote: It addition to the above basic mechanism for avoiding cyclic message sending, it caches every sent or forwarded report message in a dedicated *report-cache* in order to support retransmissions (see next item).

(ii) **Multi-hop messaging**: Recall that, at the beginning of Phase 3, the monitoring PC checks the received monitoring data for possibly missing report messages. To initiate the retransmission of such missing report messages, the monitoring PC uses this protocol. It requests every root mote to disseminate the same *request message* using another variant of our flooding protocol: When receiving a request message, a node also searches its report-cache for the requested report message. If the message is found, the report message is re-sent via the multi-hop data collection protocol. If the report message is not found in the report-cache, the request message is forwarded following the standard rules to avoid cyclic sending.

Extensive tests, also using the fault-injection capabilities presented in Section IV-C, revealed that these protocols implement a very robust, fast and reasonably communication-efficient approach for convergecasting information from all nodes in the WSN to the monitoring PC, provided the relevant parameters, namely, phase durations, transmission staggering time and initial hop count, are adequately chosen.

B. Time synchronization

As mentioned in Section III-C, our round-based synchronous setting makes it mandatory to implement a common global time at all motes. In our framework, global time is defined by a 32 bit timestamp with a granularity of 1 millisecond. Every round has fixed duration R, called *round time*, measured in milliseconds; round $k \geqslant 0$ is hence started at global time $t^k_{start} = kR$ at every mote.

Due to the heterogeneous system architecture of our framework (recall Figure 1), the time synchronization mechanism consists of multiple parts:

(1) **Synchronizing the PCs**: As the forwarding and monitoring PCs are interconnected via Ethernet, we use the standard *Network Time Protocol* (NTP) to synchronize those.

(2) **Synchronizing the motes**: Since the motes do not understand NTP, they are using the *Flooding Time Synchronization Protocol* [22] (FTSP). Like NTP, it achieves a typical synchronization precision in the one millisecond range. FTSP uses a single master mote (called the *FTSP-root*) as the primary time-source for all other (reachable) motes.

(3) **Synchronizing the root motes to the forwarding PCs** As we are using two different protocols for time synchronization, we had to find a solution where both protocols are synchronizing to the same global time. As root motes do not execute the WSN application but just act as data sinks, our implementation (i) synchronizes every root mote to NTP time and (ii) forces every FTSP-root to be one of the root motes.

Since the junction between NTP and FTSP is the USB link between the pairs of forwarding PC and associated root mote, (i) is easily achieved by letting each forwarding PC periodically send its 32 bit NTP-timestamp to its connected root mote. If such a root mote is also working as an FTSP-root, it calculates the difference between NTP-time and FTSP global time and, if non-zero, adjusts the latter accordingly. All the other motes will hence effectively receive NTP-time from the FTSP-root and synchronize themselves to this time via FTSP.

In order to also achieve (ii), all root motes are configured with *unique node identifiers* (UIDs) *less* than the UIDs or ordinary motes. Since the FTSP-root is elected by all reachable motes dynamically as the mote with the minimum ID, this ensures that FTSP-roots will always be root motes (unless none of those was reachable, of course).

C. Fault-injection capabilities

To both facilitate testing of our implementation and advanced fault-injection experiments, we implemented a simple feature for dynamically enabling/disabling individual directed links between pairs of motes.

Each mote maintains a per-mote *blacklist array* for this purpose. Similar to the monitor array presented in Section IV-A, each bit in this array corresponds to a single sender mote: At the reception of a message, the mote checks whether the bit corresponding to the sender is set; if this is the case, the message is discarded and neither reported as having been received nor delivered to the application.

The monitoring PC maintains a blacklist array for each mote. If it is instructed by the user, via the experimental control user interface described in Section V-B, to enable resp. disable the link from x to y, it sets resp. clears the bit corresponding to x in the blacklist array dedicated for node y. It then sends a *fault injection message* holding the (updated) monitoring PC's copy of node y's blacklist array to node y, which is then updating its own copy. Note that the fault injection messages are also sent by means of our flooding protocol, following the rules to avoid cyclic sending.

V. Application Interface and Postprocessing

In this section, we provide a glimpse of how to use our framework: We survey some features that need to be configured prior to compilation, describe how to interact with the running system via the user interface provided by the monitoring PC, and list some features of our postprocessing tool.

A. System configuration

The first step setting up an experiment, is to choose certain system-wide parameters (via configuration C-Macros) before compiling and flashing the software to the motes (and forwarding PCs). Among these are upper bounds on the number of (root) motes and cache sizes, which are of course limited by the typically low RAM size.

The parameters for our flooding protocols are particularly important w.r.t. data completeness. Some of these are the initial hop count, durations of the Phases and the transmission staggering time for Phase 2. The latter also determine the substantial monitoring time overhead (i.e., the slow-down of the application's execution). Our postprocessing tool provides some meta-data that can be used to validate the chosen parameters, see Section V-C.

As mentioned before, it is possible to apply a user-supplied round-based algorithm on top of the Phase 1. Our framework hence provides an interface, which comprises functions for broadcasting/receiving messages and a *start-round* event, signalling the start of the current round and delivering the set of messages that have been received in the current round. Our interface also supplies the application with *signal-to-interference-plus-noise* (SINR) information here, However, in our prototype implementation, this data is void since the RZ200 motes do not support this feature. In response to the start-round event, the applied algorithm may compose the content of the next round's application message, as well as (optionally) select the transmission power and a staggering time for transmission scheduling. The actual broadcast is then handled, at the appropriate time, by our framwork.

B. Interactive setup and control

The user can control the experiments by means of a simple user interface provided by the monitoring PC, which reads and processes a number of commands from *stdin*:

- *start*: Once the start command has been read from *stdin*, a *start message* is flooded that causes the motes to (synchronously) start their monitoring activity.

```
start
block 11,13
wait 60000
free 11,13
```

Figure 4: Exemplary test script, which (i) starts monitoring, (ii) blocks the connections from 11 to 13, and (iii) frees this blocking after 10 minutes.

- *block* x, y resp. *free* x, y: These commands address the motes' fault-injection capabilities and block resp. free the application messages from node x to node y.
- *wait* x: Wait x milliseconds until the next line is read from *stdin*. This command allows the creation of test scripts: Using a textfile, one can easily block and free connections automatically at predefined times (which must of course be reflected in the monitoring data recorded). An exemplary script can be found in Figure 4.

C. Postprocessing tools

Once the connectivity data is stored (in a textfile) in the file system of the monitoring PC, one can apply arbitrary tools for postprocessing the collected data. The main feature of our custom postprocessing tool, which has been developed (in HTML/PHP) with answering the validation question of Section VI in mind, is to compute the sets of motes in *strongly connected components* (SCCs), using *Tarjan's* algorithm [25]. Recall that a strongly connected component is a component where every node is reachable from every other node.

Once the data has been processed one may use various features of our tool.

- A CSV-file holding the adjancency matrices for each round can be created.
- For any round, one can visualize the connectivity graph, as well as its contraction to SCCs.
- For any round and every mote, the FTSP-root's ID used for time synchronization and the root mote that delivered the report message to the monitoring PC, along with the message's hop count, can be printed. This data allows to detect inadequate hop count settings and/or needs for a revised placement of root motes, thus can be used to validate the configuration.
- As will be detailed in Section VI-A, our main interest lies in the stability of SCCs consisting of the same set of motes, i.e., the number of rounds that they persist. For this purpose, all the SCCs existing in a recorded data file can be listed over time, along with the first and the last round and its duration.

VI. A Case Study: Validating an Adversarial Network Model

In this section, we will provide the results of an experimental validation of the adversarial model introduced in [5] using our framework.

A. Validation question

The adversarial model of [5] assumes that every sequence of directed communication graphs $\mathcal{G}^1, \mathcal{G}^2, \ldots$ present in round

$1, 2, \ldots$ satisfies the graph properties summarized in Definition 3. We will now introduce the core concepts needed for defining those. Due to space constraints, we will replace some formal definitions by informal ones where possible.

Given the communication graph $\mathcal{G}$ of a round, a *root component* R is the set of nodes of a strongly connected component $\mathcal{R}$ in $\mathcal{G}$ without in-edges from nodes outside $\mathcal{R}$. Note that every graph has at least one root component. A root component R that exists in every graph of a (not necessarily consecutive) graph sequence $(\mathcal{G}^r)_{r=a}^{a+d-1} = \mathcal{G}^a, \ldots, \mathcal{G}^{a+d-1}$ is called a *common root*. Note carefully that the *interconnect topology* of the nodes in a common root R may be different in every $\mathcal{G}^i$. The term vertex-stable root component has hence been coined for common roots in [3][4].

One can show that a root component that is common in a sufficiently long graph sequence $\mathcal{G}^a, \ldots, \mathcal{G}^{a+d-1}$ guarantees multi-hop communication between *all* nodes in R. Moreover, if R happens to be the only root, termed *single root*, information from every node in R reaches all nodes in the entire network. This is captured by the following definition:

Definition 1 (Dynamic diameter D): A network has dynamic (network) diameter D, if for every graph sequence that contains a subsequence $\mathcal{G}^{r_1}, \ldots, \mathcal{G}^{r_D}$ of D not necessarily consecutive R-single-rooted communication graphs, it holds that information from every node in R from (the end of) round $r_1 - 1$ reaches all nodes in the network by (the end of) round r_D.

The following definition captures "the" central graph property used in [5]. It requires that a root that is common in a sequence of at least $D + 1$ rounds is single in a consecutive subsequence of at least $D + 1$ rounds:

Definition 2: We say that a graph sequence $(\mathcal{G}^r)_{r=\alpha}^{\alpha+d}$ has an $\mathtt{ECS}(D+1)$*-common root* ("embedded $D+1$-consecutive single common root") R, if (i) $(\mathcal{G}^r)_{r=\alpha}^{\alpha+d}$ has a common root R and (ii) $(\mathcal{G}^r)_{r=\alpha'}^{\alpha'+D} \subseteq (\mathcal{G}^r)_{r=\alpha}^{\alpha+d}$ has a single root R.

The graph property $\Diamond\mathtt{STABLE}(D)$ to be validated by our experiments is the following, see also [5, Def. 12]:

Definition 3 (Message adversary $\Diamond\mathtt{STABLE}(D)$): In every graph sequence $\mathcal{G}^1, \mathcal{G}^2, \ldots$ present in round $1, 2, \ldots,$ the conjunction of the following three properties must hold:

(i) The first root component R that is common for at least $D+1$ consecutive rounds is a $\mathtt{ECS}(D+1)$-common root.

(ii) At least one $\mathtt{ECS}(D+1)$-common root R' (possibly $R' \neq R$) occurs eventually, which re-appears as a single root in at least D not necessarily consecutive later rounds.

(iii) The dynamic diameter is D.

Our validation experiments evaluate, for every deployment and every $D = 1, 2, 3, \ldots,$ the coverage of $\Diamond\mathtt{STABLE}(D)$ and the statistics of two important stabilization time parameters. The (experimental) *coverage* $\mathrm{Cov}(D)$ (abbreviated Cov if D is clear from the context) of $\Diamond\mathtt{STABLE}(D)$ is defined as the number of testruns where $\Diamond\mathtt{STABLE}(D)$ holds over the number of all testruns. Note that this coverage definition is conservative, as it also counts testruns as failed where $\Diamond\mathtt{STABLE}(D)$ could have been satisfied eventually if the testrun had been continued (we very rarely encountered this situation for $D < 10$ in our experiments, though).

Given a testrun, let the *stabilization time* $r_{\mathrm{sr}}(D)$ be the round where the first $\mathtt{ECS}(D+1)$-common root R starts to become single (Def. 3.(i)); r_{sr} delimits the end of the initial ("chaotic") period of system operation. Similarly, let $r_{\mathrm{fi}}(D)$ be the round where the D-th single occurrence of R' (Def. 3.(ii)) happens; r_{fi} gives the (earliest) termination time of any consensus algorithm [5] in this testrun. In addition to Cov, we will also provide the averages of r_{sr} and r_{fi}, $\mathrm{Avg}\, r_{\mathrm{sr}}$ resp. $\mathrm{Avg}\, r_{\mathrm{fi}}$, in all testruns where $\Diamond\mathtt{STABLE}(D)$, for some given D, holds.

B. Experimental Setup

To validate the coverage of the graph property given in Definition 3 experimentally, we set up four different scenarios and monitored the connectivity over time in multiple testruns. Our different scenarios were obtained by varying two main parameters, namely, deployment area and the transmission scheduling, in a WSN consisting of 20 motes.

Deployment Area. For Deployment 1, we used the rooms of our institute, where there are many obstacles and walls between the single motes and substantial interference due to WiFi accesspoints, etc. The node density is relatively high and the expected area of good radio coverage is reasonably fat. By contrast, for Deployment 2, we spread the same number of motes (more or less) in line of sight of each other on the rooftop of our building, where the interference level is considerably lower. The resulting area of good radio coverage is less fat and less dense (only 1/3 of Deployment 1). In both of our deployments, the resulting network diameter turned out to be in the range of $[2, 7]$.

Transmission Scheduling. If all the motes send their application message simultaneously at the beginning of the round, the SINR at every receiver is quite low, whereas a proper transmission scheduling where every mote has its unique time slot for transmission results in a much better SINR. Transmission scheduling is hence crucial for the network's connectivity. Therefore, we decided to use transmission scheduling as our experiments' second parameter: n ("no") means no transmission scheduling, t means transmission staggering with a dedicated 20 millisecond slot for every mote.

When we subsequently write Scenario 1n, for example, we mean Deployment 1 without transmission scheduling.

System Settings and Configuration. In all our experiments, we used a single root mote placed in the network's center. The header-cache was chosen to store up to 64 message headers, while the report-cache was able to hold up to 128 report messages, sent via our multi-hop protocol that used an initial hop count of 5. The monitoring PC requested the retransmission of missing report messages during 10 phases following the original round before it gave up.

C. Validation Experiments

Scenario 1t: Institute using transmission staggering. As transmission staggering leads to (more or less) stable reception conditions for each mote's application message in each round, the topology did not change much during the testruns. As a result, we observed relatively long sequences where a single common root exists in each of our twelve testruns, which took from 89 to 224 application rounds.

Results. As shown in Table I (left column), for $D \in [4, 17]$, $\mathrm{Cov}(D) = 100\%$ since $\Diamond\mathtt{STABLE}(D)$ held in each of our testruns. Depending on D, $\mathrm{Avg}\, r_{\mathrm{sr}}$ ranges from 4 and 48 and $\mathrm{Avg}\, r_{\mathrm{fi}}$ ranges from 12 to 215.

Scenario 2t: Rooftop using transmission staggering. As in Scenario 1t, the use of transmission staggering led to relatively long sequences of single common roots. We conducted twelve testruns that took from 24 up to 231 application rounds.

Results. As shown in Table I (right column), $\mathrm{Cov}(D) = 100\%$ for any $D \in [4, 8]$. In those testruns, $\mathrm{Avg}\, r_{\mathrm{sr}}$, resp. $\mathrm{Avg}\, r_{\mathrm{fi}}$, ranges from 9 to 69, resp. from 15 to 181, depending on D.

TABLE I: EVALUATION RESULTS FOR SCENARIOS 1t AND 2t.

Scenario 1t			
D	Cov	Avg r_{sr}	Avg r_{fi}
3	0.667	4	12
4	1.000	4	13
...			
17	1.000	23	59
18	0.917	25	62
19	0.833	29	68
...			

Scenario 2t			
D	Cov	Avg r_{sr}	Avg r_{fi}
3	0.500	9	15
4	1.000	14	23
...			
8	1.000	24	42
9	0.917	34	54
10	0.750	34	55
...			

Scenario 1n: Institute without transmission staggering. As expected, letting all motes send their application messages (almost) simultaneously causes a much higher variability of the communication topology over time. As a consequence, we observed much shorter periods of rounds were a common root exists in our twelve testruns, which took from 89 to 303 application rounds.

Results. As shown in Table II (left column), $\mathrm{Cov}(D) = 66.67\%$ for $D = 4$. $\mathrm{Avg}\, r_{\mathrm{sr}}$ is tendentially increasing from 12 up to 135, $\mathrm{Avg}\, r_{\mathrm{fi}}$ is within a range of $[19, 191]$. We encountered 4 testruns, where $\Diamond\mathtt{STABLE}(D)$ was neither satisfied nor violated for any value of $D \geqslant 4$. As already hinted in the definition of $\mathrm{Cov}(D)$, $\Diamond\mathtt{STABLE}(D)$ might have been satisfied eventually, for these values of D, if these testruns had been continued. Not counting these testruns, the resulting coverage $\mathrm{Cov}(D) = 100\%$ for $D = 4$.

Scenario 2n: Rooftop without transmission staggering. As in Scenario 1n only short periods with a common root component existed. For this scenario, we conducted twelve testruns comprising between 75 and 266 application rounds.

Results. As shown in Table II (right column), $\mathrm{Cov}(4) = 83.33\%$ with $\mathrm{Avg}\, r_{\mathrm{sr}} = 48$ and $\mathrm{Avg}\, r_{\mathrm{fi}} = 60$. As in Scenario 1n, we encountered three testruns where $\Diamond\mathtt{STABLE}(D)$ was neither satisfied nor violated for any value of $D \geqslant 4$. Not counting these testruns, $\mathrm{Cov}(4)$ is again 100%.

D. Discussion

Comparing the results of the four scenarios presented in Section VI-C leads to a number of interesting insights.

Most importantly, we observed for no testrun a violation of properties (i) and (iii) of $\Diamond\mathtt{STABLE}(D)$ for any choice of $D \geqslant 4$. For every individual scenario where staggering was turned on, there is also a range for D that results in 100% experimental coverage of all properties of $\Diamond\mathtt{STABLE}(D)$ (see below) for any fixed value of D taken from this range. In the scenarios where no transmission staggering was used, we encountered some testruns where $\Diamond\mathtt{STABLE}(D)$ might still have been satisfied eventually for $D \geqslant 4$. In those testruns where we could validate $\Diamond\mathtt{STABLE}(D)$, $D = 4$ resulted in 100% coverage.

TABLE II: EVALUATION RESULTS FOR SCENARIOS 1n AND 2n.

Scenario 1n			
D	Cov	Avg r_{sr}	Avg r_{fi}
3	0.250	12	19
4	0.667	13	22
5	0.583	13	23
...			
9	0.583	61	81

Scenario 2n			
D	Cov	Avg r_{sr}	Avg r_{fi}
3	0.083	13	22
4	0.833	47	60
5	0.500	65	81
6	0.417	65	85
7	0.167	75	97

For each testrun $\Diamond\mathtt{STABLE}(2)$ was violated On the other hand, there was no testrun that violated condition (i) or (iii) of $\Diamond\mathtt{STABLE}(D)$ for any $D \geqslant 4$.

Figure 5 shows how D influences the coverage of $\Diamond\mathtt{STABLE}(D)$ for Deployment 1 and 2, irrespectively of the transmission scheduling. Recall that the area covered by the former is only about one third of the latter, fatter, and experiences more background interference. Interestingly, while the coverage of $\Diamond\mathtt{STABLE}(D)$ in Deployment 1 is better for (nearly) all values of D, for $D = 4$ the coverage is higher at Deployment 2.

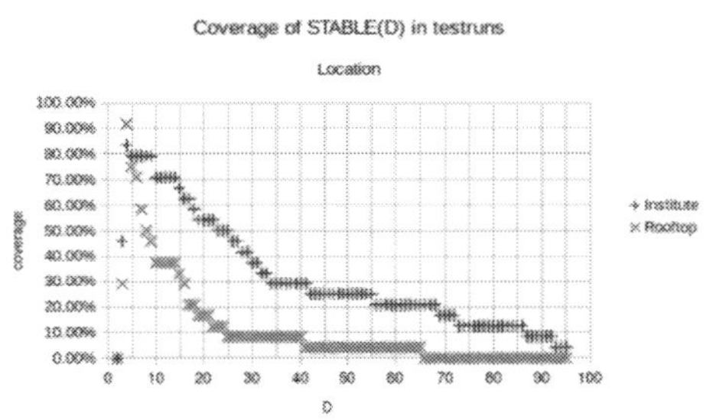

Figure 5: Coverage depending on deployment area

Figure 6 confirms the (expected) strong influence of transmission staggering on $\mathrm{Cov}(D)$, irrespectively of the deployment. It is apparent that the coverage of $\Diamond\mathtt{STABLE}(D)$ is uniformly much higher with transmission staggering than without. $\mathrm{Cov}(D) = 100\%$ for $D \in [3, 8]$ for the former, while it does not achieve 100% for any value of D in the latter case.

Overall, we can conclude that the adversarial model proposed in [5] has a very good coverage in all our deployments, provided D is appropriately chosen. In more detail:

- $\Diamond\mathtt{STABLE}(D)$ very likely holds for some D in the range of the actual average per-round network diameter. For smaller values of D, the coverage of $\Diamond\mathtt{STABLE}(D)$ drops.
- Since in none of our testruns properties (i) and (iii) of $\Diamond\mathtt{STABLE}(D)$ were violated for $D \geqslant 4$, it stands to reason that the fulfillment of $\Diamond\mathtt{STABLE}(D)$ for even larger D may be only a matter of time.

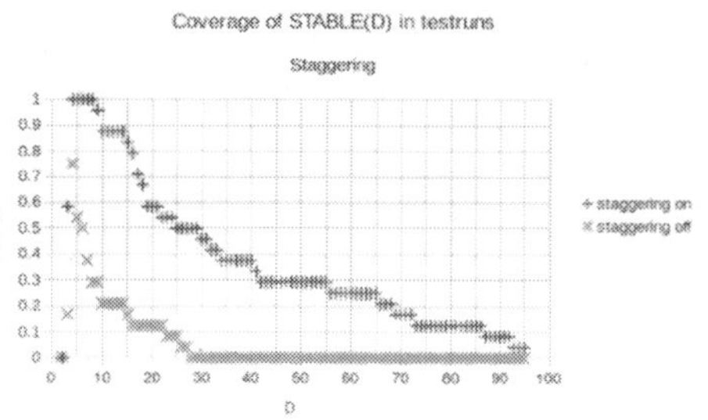

Figure 6: Coverage depending on transmission staggering

- A stable ECS($D+1$) root does not need to exist from the very beginning of the network's life. In fact, our observations confirm the hypothesis of [5] that one has to account for an initial "chaos-period" and that the network only eventually becomes reasonably stable.

VII. Conclusion

We provided an overview of the system architecture and the internal workings of a framework for long-term monitoring of the communication topology of synchronous wireless sensor networks consisting of memory-constrained wireless motes. We discussed and solved various issues, such as finding a suitable flooding protocol, adequate synchronization, data collection, and post-processing. Finally, we employed our framework in order to validate a network property introduced in [5] and found that it has a reasonable assumption coverage.

Part of our future work in this area will be devoted to decreasing the time overhead caused by our monitoring framework, to replace statically configured system parameters by on-line ones, and to adapt/scale-up the framework to other testbeds. In addition, we are working on improving the multi-hop protocols used in our framework and establish network conditions, which are sufficient for guaranteeing monitoring data completeness.

Acknowledgement

This work has been supported the Austrian Science Fund (FWF) projects P28182 (ADynNet) and S11405 (RiSE).

References

[1] F. Kuhn and R. Oshman, "Dynamic networks: Models and algorithms," *SIGACT News*, vol. 42(1), pp. 82–96, 2011.

[2] F. Kuhn, N. A. Lynch, and R. Oshman, "Distributed computation in dynamic networks," in *STOC*, pp. 513–522, 2010.

[3] M. Biely, P. Robinson, and U. Schmid, "Agreement in directed dynamic networks," in *Proceedings 19th International Colloquium on Structural Information and Communication Complexity (SIROCCO'12)*, LNCS 7355, pp. 73–84, Springer-Verlag, 2012.

[4] M. Biely, P. Robinson, U. Schmid, M. Schwar z, and K. Winkler, "Gracefully degrading consensus and k-set agreement in directed dynamic networks," in *Revised selected papers Third International Conference on Networked Systems (NETYS'15)*, Springer LNCS 9466, (Agadir, Morocco), pp. 109–124, Springer International Publishing, 2015.

[5] M. Schwarz, K. Winkler, and U. Schmid, "Fast consensus under eventually stabilizing message adversaries," in *Proceedings of the 17th International Conference on Distributed Computing and Networking*, ICDCN '16, (New York, NY, USA), pp. 7:1–7:10, ACM, 2016.

[6] D. Pfleger and U. Schmid, "A framework for connectivity monitoring in wireless sensor networks," Research Report TUW-241107, Technische Universität Wien, Institut für Technische Informatik, Treitlstr. 1-3/182-2, 1040 Vienna, Austria, 2015. http://publik.tuwien.ac.at/files/PubDat_241107.pdf [retrieved: June, 2016].

[7] C. Newport, D. Kotz, Y. Yuan, R. S. Gray, J. Liu, and C. Elliott, "Experimental Evaluation of Wireless Simulation Assumptions," *SIMULATION: Transactions of The Society for Modeling and Simulation International*, vol. 83, pp. 643–661, Sept. 2007.

[8] A.-S. Tonneau, N. Mitton, and J. Vandaele, "A survey on (mobile) wireless sensor network experimentation testbeds," in *Proceedings of the 2014 IEEE International Conference on Distributed Computing in Sensor Systems*, DCOSS '14, (Washington, DC, USA), pp. 263–268, IEEE Computer Society, 2014.

[9] K. Srinivasan, P. Dutta, A. Tavakoli, and P. Levis, "An empirical study of low-power wireless," *ACM Trans. Sen. Netw.*, vol. 6, pp. 16:1–16:49, Mar. 2010.

[10] A. Cerpa, J. L. Wong, M. Potkonjak, and D. Estrin, "Temporal properties of low power wireless links: Modeling and implications on multi-hop routing," in *Proceedings of the 6th ACM International Symposium on Mobile Ad Hoc Networking and Computing*, MobiHoc '05, (New York, NY, USA), pp. 414–425, ACM, 2005.

[11] L. Mottola, G. P. Picco, M. Ceriotti, c. Gună, and A. L. Murphy, "Not all wireless sensor networks are created equal: A comparative study on tunnels," *ACM Trans. Sen. Netw.*, vol. 7, pp. 15:1–15:33, Sept. 2010.

[12] H. B. Acharya and M. G. Gouda, "On the hardness of topology inference," in *ICDCN*, pp. 251–262, 2011.

[13] A. Bestavros, J. W. Byers, and K. A. Harfoush, "Inference and labeling of metric-induced network topologies," *IEEE Transactions on Parallel and Distributed Systems*, vol. 16, no. 11, pp. 1053–1065, 2005.

[14] P. Sattari, C. Fragouli, and A. Markopoulou, "Active topology inference using network coding," *Physical Communication*, vol. 6, pp. 142–163, 2013.

[15] Y. A. Pignolet, S. Schmid, and G. Trédan, "Misleading stars: what cannot be measured in the internet?," *Distributed Computing*, vol. 26, no. 4, pp. 209–222, 2013.

[16] R. Castro, M. Coates, G. Liang, R. Nowak, and B. Yu, "Network tomography: Recent developments," *Statistical Science*, vol. 19, pp. 499–517, 08 2004.

[17] M. Coates, A. O. Hero III, R. Nowak, and B. Yu, "Internet tomography," *Signal Processing Magazine, IEEE*, vol. 19, no. 3, pp. 47–65, 2002.

[18] B. Deb, S. Bhatnagar, and B. Nath, "Stream: Sensor topology retrieval at multiple resolutions," *Telecommunication Systems*, vol. 26, no. 2-4, pp. 285–320, 2004.

[19] M. Zhang, M. C. Chan, and A. L. Ananda, "Connectivity monitoring in wireless sensor networks," *Pervasive and Mobile Computing*, vol. 6, no. 1, pp. 112–127, 2010.

[20] Y. Liu, K. Liu, and M. Li, "Passive diagnosis for wireless sensor networks," *IEEE/ACM Trans. Netw.*, vol. 18, pp. 1132–1144, Aug. 2010.

[21] M. Keller, J. Beutel, and L. Thiele, "How was your journey?: Uncovering routing dynamics in deployed sensor networks with multi-hop network tomography," in *Proceedings of the 10th ACM Conference on Embedded Network Sensor Systems*, SenSys '12, (New York, NY, USA), pp. 15–28, ACM, 2012.

[22] M. Maròti, B. Kusy, G. Simon, and A. Lèdeczi, *The Flooding Time Synchronization Protocol*. Verderbilt University, Institute for Software Integrated Systems, Nov. 2004.

[23] R. Thouvenin, "Implementing and evaluating the dynamic manet on-demand protocol in wireless sensor networks," master's thesis, University of Aarhus, Department of Computer Science, 2007.

[24] O. Gnawali, R. Fonseca, K. Jamieson, D. Moss, and P. Levis, "Collection tree protocol," SenSys, pp. 1–14, 2009.

[25] R. Tarjan, "Depth-first search and linear graph algorithms," in *SIAM J. Computation*, vol. 1, pp. 114–121, Jan. 1972.

A New Formalisation for Wireless Sensor Network Adaptive Context-aware System: Application to an Environmental Use Case

Jie Sun, Gil De Sousa, Catherine Roussey, Jean-Pierre Chanet, François Pinet

Irstea, UR TSCF
9 avenue Blaise Pascal
CS 20085
F-63178 Aubière, France
Email: jie.sun@irstea.fr, gil.de-sousa@irstea.fr, catherine.roussey@irstea.fr
jean-pierre.chanet@irstea.fr, francois.pinet@irstea.fr

Kun-Mean Hou

LIMOS
Campus Universitaire des Cézeaux
1 rue de la Chebarde
TSA 60125 - CS 60026
F-63178 Aubière cedex, France
Email: kun-mean.hou@isima.fr

***Abstract*—Henceforth, new generations of Wireless Sensor Networks (WSN), as part of the Internet of Things (IoT), have to be able to adapt their behaviour to collect, from the study phenomenon (or feature of interest), quality data for long period of time. In this article, we propose a new formalisation for the design and the implementation of context-aware systems. To illustrate this whole proposal, an environmental use case, the study of flood events in a watershed, relying on a WSN for the data collection, is presented.**

Keywords–Context-aware system; formalisation; architecture; Wireless Sensor Network; Internet of Things; environment; phenomenon.

I. INTRODUCTION

The acquisition of heterogeneous data is essential in the era of IoT and Big Data that is just starting. These two research topics have application in numerous fields: industry, "smart home", "smart care", agriculture, environment, etc. WSN technology is now viewed as part of the IoT [1]. The increased use of WSN envisioned at the beginning of the 2000's [2], is now a reality as shown, for example, in environment [3] and agriculture [4]. In these applications, a WSN collects natural phenomenon observations (temperature, humidity, etc.) and sends them to a context-aware system, which may propose adaptation actions based on context. To build a full context adaptation service, information about wireless sensors themselves such as their energy levels are also required. Indeed, despite steady progress in hardware (the development of low energy communication modules for example), a wireless sensor still has scarce resources. It is the case for "scalar" WSN and it is even more for Wireless Multimedia Sensor Networks (WMSN) [5]. Thus, to better use these limited resources, all the components that are part of the data acquisition process have to work together in a cooperative way, from the component that collects raw data to the one that provides indicators to end users. Generally, these components are the wireless sensors, the gateway(s) and the remote Decision Support System (DSS). The acquisition and transmission frequencies required by the DSS, through the gateway, have to be consistent with the energy available at the level of the wireless sensors. For some alert applications such as fire prevention, data transmission is sometimes more important than the "survival" of a node of the network. Thus, all the components implied in the data acquisition process have to adapt their behaviours to the context in order to achieve the best performances. A WSN is also subject to unpredictable events that, without fast interventions, can threaten the stability of the whole system. The combination of the common decisions and actions is the issue addressed in this paper. More precisely, we propose a formalisation to define high level context which, integrated into an adaptive context-aware system, will be used to reduce the number of exchanged communication packets. Our formalisation proposes different reasoning steps in order to build the high level context. Section II presents the main existing concepts related to context-aware systems. Section III of the article explains our proposal of formalisation of context in order to build any context system based on WSN. Section IV shows its application with the design of a context-aware system dedicated to a complex environmental use case. Section V presents our implementation of this formalisation in order to develop a context-aware system and an adaptive context-aware one focused on the previous environmental use case. The second system adapts its behaviour to the context in order to limit packet exchanges. Section VI describes different context systems developed for the same purpose. The last section concludes this article.

II. CONTEXT-AWARE SYSTEM MAIN CONCEPTS

One of the most known and accepted definitions of context is given by [6] as *Context is any information that can be used to characterize the situation of an entity. An entity is a person, place, or object that is considered relevant to the interaction between a user and an application, including the user and applications themselves.* As indicated in this definition, context is focused on one entity. Several contexts can be defined, for example, the context of the user, the context of the device running the application, and so on. As explained in [7], different categories of context exist. **Low level context** corresponds to the raw data acquired by sensors or static data provided by users. **High level context** is computed from the low level one, with more informative data associated to the application and the user. Figure 1 presents the processes associated to an adaptive context-aware system when data are collected by a WSN. It could also be applied to sensor networks or other systems that generate raw data.

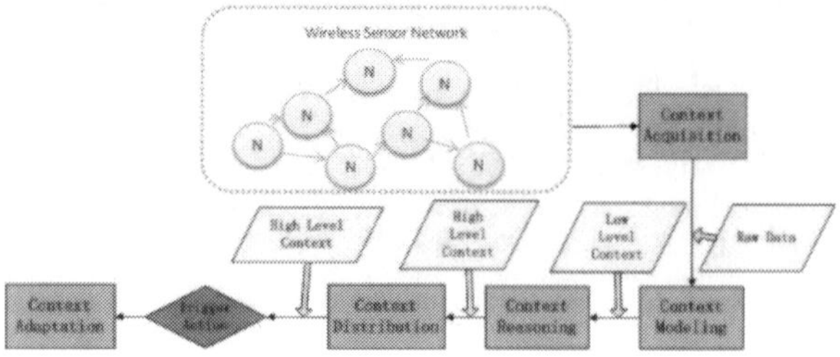

Figure 1. Context cycle of an application based on WSN

In an adaptive context-aware system, different processes are required:

- Context acquisition: collecting raw data and metadata that are useful to build the context.
- Context modeling: organisation of the collected data through a specific context data model. The process gives an interpretation to each raw data. For example, the value 24 becomes the measurement of the outdoor temperature in degree Celsius. This process builds the low level context. This process is also called annotation or tagging [7].
- Context reasoning: the high level context is computed or inferred from the low level one. This process can imply different approaches based on machine learning [8] or rule engine [9].
- Context distribution: diffusion of the high level context to the different consumers, for example, the end user or any system components that are able to adapt their actions according to the current context.
- Context adaptation: actions to adapt any system components according to context changes.

Notice that a context-aware system stops at the context distribution process and sends alert to the end users.

III. PROPOSED CONTEXT FORMALISATION

The work in [10] defines the concept of entity "state" as *a qualitative data which changes over times (summarizing a set of information)*. Based on this definition, we propose a new definition of "context" as *a set of entities characterized by their state, plus all information that can help to derive any state changes of these entities*. In our context-aware system formalisation, we add the definition of two classes of entities:

1) **observable entity**: entity that is directly observed by sensors.
2) **entity of interest**: entity whose characterisation is obtained from one or many other entities and required by the application.

We propose two new reasoning steps to create the high level context in the reasoning process, illustrated in Figure 2. Rules based reasoning is often used to deduce high-level context [7]. As far as we know, our works are the first to promote the division of rules in several reasoning steps in order to make the management of rules easier. Indeed, state of an entity of interest cannot be acquired directly based on low level context. Two levels of reasoning are presented to build the high level context:

- The low level context contains the sensor measurements stored in the context data model. The state of observable entities is inferred from the low level context as indicated by the dotted arc in Figure 2. The high level context contains the state of observable entities.
- The state of an entity of interest is inferred from the state of other entities. The high level context is enriched by the state of the entity of interest.

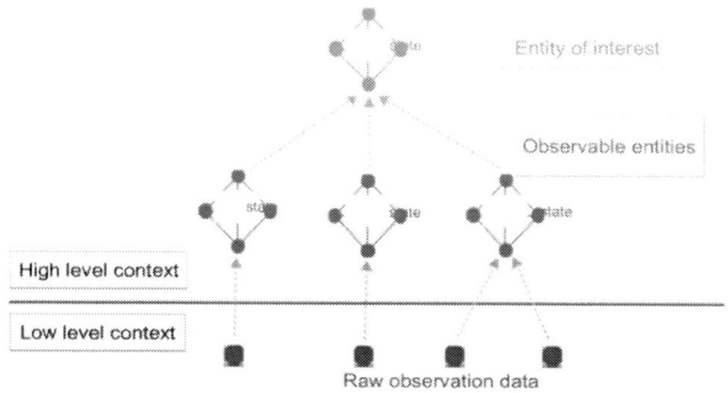

Figure 2. Classes of entities

If we take the example of a wireless sensor management application, we consider a wireless sensor as an entity of interest where one of its associated observable entities is its power supply (a battery). From this observable entity, a sensor measures a charge/an energy level as a raw data observation or low-level context. Based on capacity and charge values, we deduce the percentage of energy remaining in the battery. This percentage is represented by the variable *Energy*. Figure 3 presents an example of finite-state machine used to deduce the energy state (high, middle or low) of the battery which is included in the high level context.

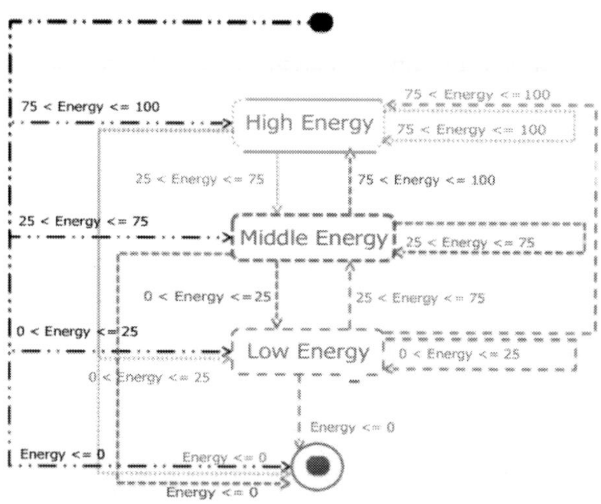

Figure 3. Example of wireless sensor energy finite-state machine

The number of states and entities depends on the application requirements. Any hardware component, such as memories of a wireless sensor, can be added in our context formalisation. It can also be applied to software such as the operating systems. The number of system failures or watchdog calls constitutes raw observation data to derive states of the associated observable entities. The state of a wireless sensor will then be deduced from all the considered (hardware and software) entity states. These different entities and their states enrich the context. However, the complexity of the deduction process increases with the number of relevant entities analysed. Providing entities and states in limited number is essential to have a highly dynamic context-aware system but this should not be at the expense of the quality of the final application decision. In the WSN topic, another possible use of this formalisation is for link quality evaluation application. This problem is well-known in routing protocols. Different metrics can be considered such as the available bandwidth, the latency, the available energy in the neighbourhood nodes and others [11]. The Quality of Service (QoS) of a link can be deduced from different observable entities such as the connected nodes and the bandwidth. Our context formalisation can be improved depending on the complexity of the application requirements. For example, a wireless sensor management application wants to evaluate if a wireless sensor can communicate. The states of the wireless sensor entity (the entity of interest) are "able to communicate" or "not able to communicate". Its state will be deduced from the link entity and the battery entity (enough energy to communicate). For a WSN management application, its entity of interest is the WSN. The state of the WSN could be computed from the states of all its wireless sensors (or nodes). Its connectivity state could be calculated from the QoS of all the links between its wireless sensors. At the end, the application can just need the states of the WSN, established from the states of all its nodes and of the gateway(s). Thus, we divide the context and the reasoning in several parts. Each part can be supported by different components of the context-aware system. If the two steps of the reasoning process is supported by two different components, the first component that deduces the state of an observable entity can communicate it to the second component. For performance reason, it would be better to communicate only the changing state events (with the associated value). In the following section, a context-aware system is built for an environmental use case. We experiment our formalization on it.

IV. ENVIRONMENTAL APPLICATION USE CASE

The considered environmental application is a watershed monitoring system which is able to send alert about flood risk. As shown in Figure 4, the application uses a WSN for data acquisition. This network is composed of wireless sensors, called "Water flow node", equipped with stream gauge measuring the water flow rate. One of these wireless sensors is located on the outlet of the watershed. The network contains also "Precipitation nodes" measuring the precipitation quantity. All the measurements are sent to a DSS. This DSS deduces the risk of the occurrence of a flood and send it to users. One of our assumptions is that the WSN has a star topology: each node communicates directly with the DSS, we do not introduce routing protocol constraints at this step.

In the application, we define four entities:

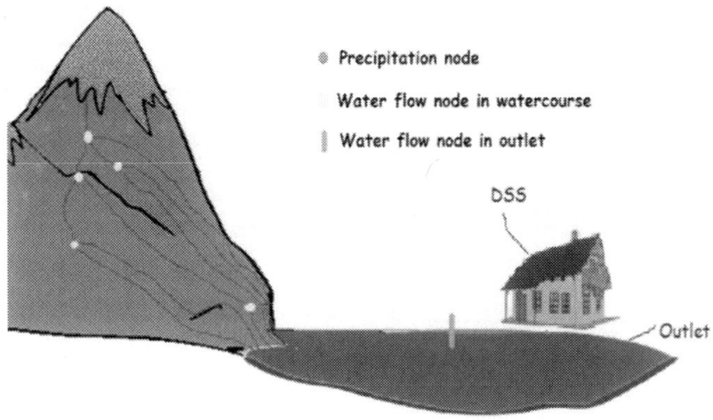

Figure 4. Example of watershed monitoring

1) the Precipitation entity which is an observable one. Its state is calculated from the data collected by the "Precipitation nodes" located at different points of the watershed. The Precipitation entity (P) has two states: high and low.
2) the WaterCourse entity which is an observable one. Its state is calculated from the data collected by the "water flow nodes" located at different points of the tributary stream (water courses). The WaterCourse (W) entity has two states: high and low.
3) the Outlet entity which is also an observable one. Its state is calculated from the data collected by the "water flow node" located on the outlet of the watershed. The Outlet entity (O) has two states: high and low.
4) the Flood entity is the entity of interest of the application. The flood entity is not an observable entity but its state depends on the states of all the observable entities. The Flood entity has four states "Normal", "Rain", "Risk", "Flood". "Normal" state means there is no risk. "Rain" state means that the watershed has received lot of precipitations, but there is no flood. "Risk" state means that flood is coming. "Flood" state means that the flood is there, the main river is overflowing. Application users want to know as soon as possible when a risk state is reached.

All the measurements are stored in the context data model in order to build the low level context. Several reasoning steps will be proposed in order to build the high level context of the Flood entity:

1) The precipitation measurements from the various "Precipitation nodes" are aggregated. One threshold should be set on the aggregation value in order to determine when the Precipitation entity moves from the low to the high state and vice versa.
2) The water flow measurements from the various stream gauges, which equip "Water flow nodes" located in the water courses, are aggregated. One threshold should be set on the aggregation value in order to determine when the WaterCourse entity moves from the low to the high state and vice versa.
3) Based on the measurements of the stream gauge that equips the "Water flow node" located at the Outlet,

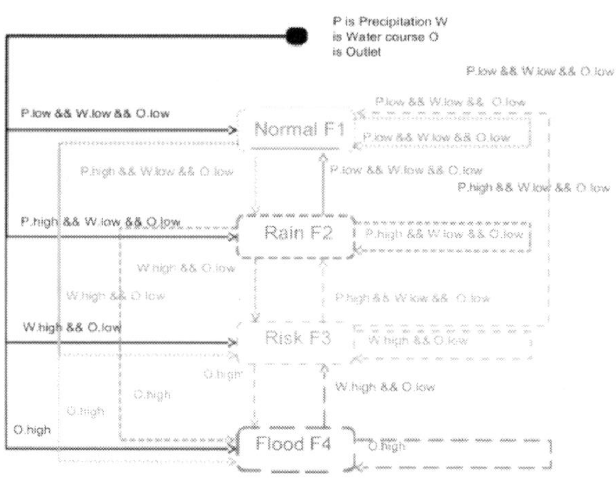

Figure 5. Example of flood finite-state machine

one threshold should be set in order to determine when the Outlet entity moves from the low to the high state and vice versa.

4) Figure 5 presents the finite-state machine that deduces the state of the Flood entity from the states of the three other observable entities. This diagram follows every step of the emergence of a flood. Usually, when a flood event occurs, the Flood entity will move from the "Normal (F1)" state to the "Rain (F2)" one, proceed to the "Risk (F3)" one and finish with the "Flood (F4)" one.

V. FORMALISATION USE IN SIMULATION

To implement our formalisation, we extend the simulation system based on the multi-agent system JADE (Java Agent DEvelopment Framework) [12] as introduced in [10]. JADE is implemented in Java. Three main features of JADE are:

1) **Agent communication**: exchange of messages between agents.
2) **Message content modeling by ontologies**: use of ontologies to model the exchanged message contents between agents.
3) **Integration with other tools**: possible use of tools like Jess rule engine [13] as a decision component of an agent.

However, current implementations based on JADE do not use different levels of reasoning. The work in [14] [15] only realize exchange of messages between agents. It does not care about the content of message modeling and other tools integration. In our simulation, we implement the features from Figure 6. We use ontologies to model the content of the messages exchanged between agents. Thus, we can build the low level context from observable entities (e.g. rainfall amount). Then, we can use Jess and a set of rules to infer the states of observable entities (e.g. Precipitation state) and build the high level context. The state of the entity of interest (e.g. Flood state) is also inferred by Jess and another set of rules from the state of the observable entities. Then the high level context is expanded. As mentioned in [7], the context modeling is often based on ontologies. Ontologies are defined by [16] as *an formal explicit specification of a shared conceptualization*. According to World Wide Web Consortium (W3C), ontologies are vocabularies that define the concepts and relationships used to describe and represent an area of concern. Thus, ontologies provide meaning to data (as data model do).

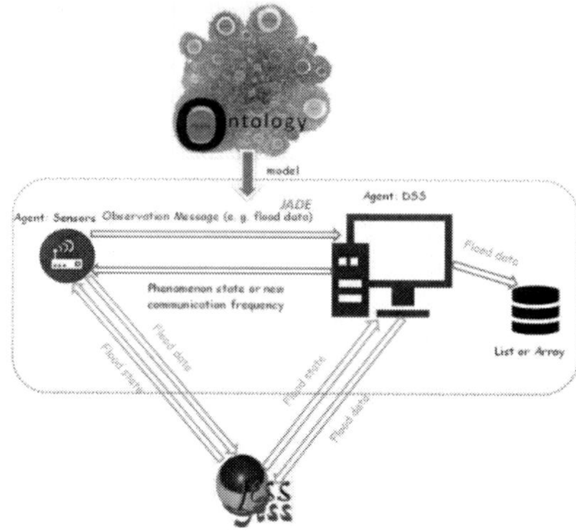

Figure 6. Simulation architecture

Our ontology is based on Semantic Sensor Network ontology (SSN) proposed by the W3C [17]. This ontology is a nucleus on which other ontologies can be connected, in order to develop a full context data model. The main concepts of SSN that we reused are "Sensor", "FeatureOfInterest", "Property", "Observation". Our observable entities or entity of interest are defined in SSN as "FeatureOfInterest". Possible entities can also come from some dedicated ontologies such as the Climate and Forecast ontology [18] or the SWEET ontology [19]. To describe time stamp, we reuse the Time ontology proposed by the W3C [20]. We use the QU ontology to define the unit [21]. To describe the state of our entities, we reuse the ontology proposed in [10].

```
(defrule floodState NormalF
1(declare (salience 10))
?p <- (pluvio {state        == low})
?w <- (WaterCourse {state== low})
?o <-(outlet{state          == low})
?f<- (flood)
=> ( modify ?f (state f1))
)
```

Figure 7. Rule deducing the Normal state of Flood entity

Concerning the reasoning process, we use the Jess rule-based engine [13] as indicated above. Jess is also implemented in Java language. We define several rules sets. Some are dedicated to infer the state of observable entity based on predefined thresholds and aggregation values. Others are dedicated to infer the state of the Flood entity. For example, the rule presented in Figure 7 deduces the state "Normal (F1)" of the Flood entity from states of observable entities.

We implement two systems where the DSS receives all the measurements and performs all the reasoning processes. These systems use the same WSN composed of heterogeneous wireless sensors to collect precipitation quantities, the water courses and the outlet flow rates. Figure 8 is a UML sequence diagram that presents the operating mode of "system 1", a context-aware one that send the Flood entity state to end user. Figure 8 presents the four processes of a context-aware system: context acquisition, context modeling, context reasoning and context distribution. The three different types of wireless sensors, previously mentioned, are represented by: "PrecipitationNode", "WaterCourseNode" (for the "water flow nodes" located in the tributary stream), "OutletNode" (for the "water flow node" located in the outlet). In "system 1", the acquisition and the transmission frequencies are equal.

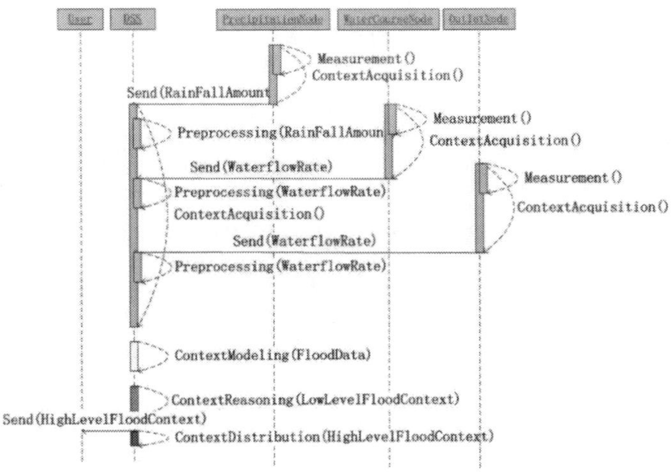

Figure 8. Sequence diagram of the Flood context-aware system (system 1)

Based on the previous system, we develop an adaptive context-aware one, "system 2", presented in Figure 9. The adaptation decision is implemented by the DSS. It deduces a new transmission frequency for each wireless sensor based on the Flood entity state.

Using our simulation architecture, we have compared these two systems at the level of the total amount of exchanged communication packets, using one-month data collected on a watershed, provided by [22]. Three "PrecipitationNodes", two "WaterCourseNodes" and one "OutletNode" are considered in our simulation. In JADE, we define as many agents as nodes. We also add a DSS agent. Each node agent acquires raw observation data and sends them to DSS. The sample frequency is of one measurement every minute. In the "system 2", the transmission frequency is modulated (calculated by the DSS) as shown in Figure 9. The table presented in Figure 10 shows how the transmission frequencies are computed based on the Flood entity state. The DSS agent processes the context modeling in order to build the low level context. It infers the high level context from the low level one using Jess rule engine. Figure 11 shows the obtained results. The nodes of the "system 1" has transmitted near 250000 packets. With the "system 2", the number of transmitted message is reduced to less than 100000 packets. In terms of the phenomenon monitoring quality, the two systems detect the same number of state changes.

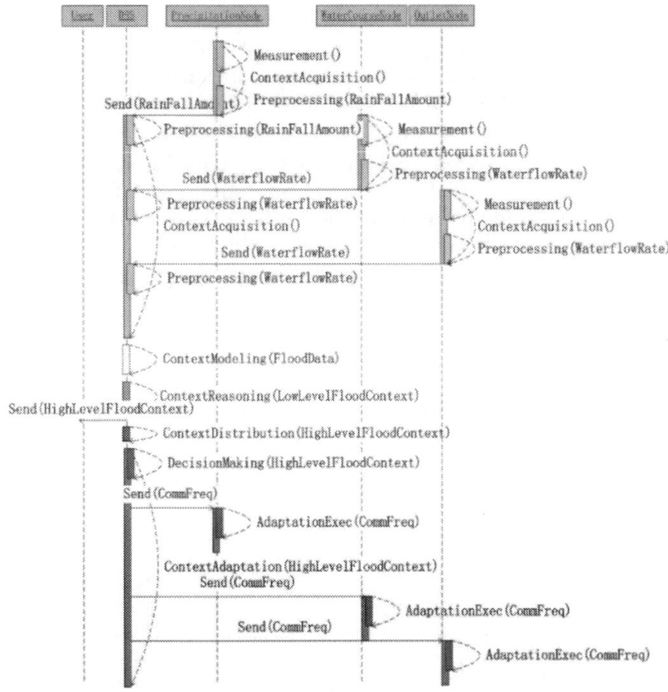

Figure 9. Sequence diagram of the Flood adaptive context-aware system (system 2)

Flood State	NORMAL	RAIN	RISK	FLOOD
Transmission Frequency	1/3*Acquisition Frequency	1/2*Acquisition Frequency	Acquisition Frequency	Acquisition Frequency

Figure 10. Table of transmission frequency based on Flood entity state

VI. RELATED WORK

No system of this type dedicated to flood monitoring was found. However, a context-aware system for water quality management exists. The InWaterSense project proposes a context-aware system to deduce the water quality of any water bodies (lake, river) [9] [23]. Their system is totally built using Semantic Web technologies. SSN ontology is used as a nucleus in order to build the context model. They also use the Jess rule based engine. Their rule format is based on SQWRL language. It is able to build aggregation value using rules. Thus, their rules merge the characteristics of observable entities and those of the entity of interest. Their rules infer the

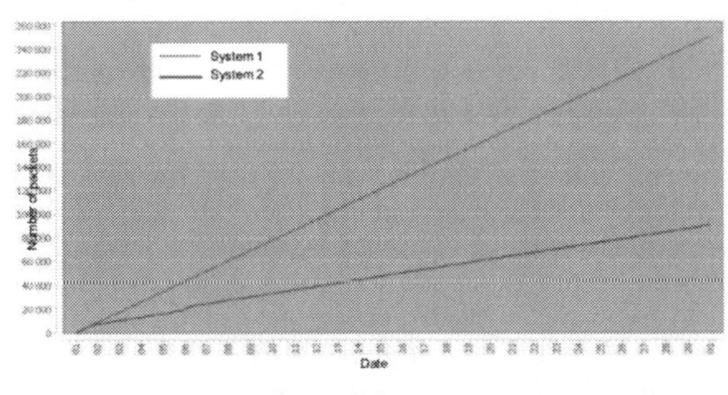

Figure 11. Number of exchanged communication packets

state of the water body without intermediate steps. Compared to our approach, their rules are much more difficult to manage due to their complexity. Our formalisation eases the reasoning process by splitting it into several steps: deduction of the states of observable entities; then, deduction of the state of the entity of interest.

The work of [24] proposes a WSN architecture called "Sepsen" in order to integrate, in nodes, several components: semantic annotator based on fragments of ontology, rule-based engine and a knowledge base that stores events. The goal is to decrease the number of event messages between sensors by classifying them as share, forward or discard event. The share events are sent to other sensor nodes to update their knowledge base. The forward events are sent to the gateway. The discarded events are removed. However, the semantic annotation is done manually. The rule indicates that a sensed value should be above a threshold in order to become a share or forward event. Using the PowerTOSSIM environment, the "Sepsen" architecture is applied on a simulation scenario showing the energy saving which this kind of approach can bring.

None of these systems uses the same formalisation based on observable entities, entity of interest and states. Thus, even if all these systems use a rule-based engine and ontologies, their rules are very complex and hard to maintain.

The Semsorgrid4Env project [25] wants to help coastal flood planning managers to make decisions during coastal flooding events. It proposes a mash-up application that integrates heterogeneous datasets: sensor data stream, historical database. The integration is made possible by a set of ontologies: SSN, SWEET, etc. In this project, the context is not modeled explicitly.

When dealing with complex phenomena like natural disasters, context-aware systems based on WSN become situation awareness system also based on WSN. In this type of system, the data management model is composed of different layers (sensor data, aggregation data, situation representation knowledge) [26]. Our formalisation can be integrated in the situation layer. In the work of [26], a situation is defined as the representation of a "structured part of the reality". It contains all the description of entities involved in the situation. Context is a point of view of one entity about the situation.

VII. Conclusion and Perspectives

In this article, we have proposed a new formalisation for the design and the implementation of context-aware systems. One of its advantages is that our approach can be used for multiple purposes. It can integrate both the monitoring of the studied phenomenon (feature of interest) and the management of the hardware and the software system used to observe it. More generally, it provides a unified way to deal with all the components/entities of an observation process. This formalisation can be used in different application topics related to agriculture, environment, "smart care", "smart home", industry. To illustrate its use, we have provided an environmental use case application: the study of flood events in a watershed. In the Irstea institute, we have different data related to this topic and we will continue the implementation and the experiment of our approach in this application field. A simulation architecture is provided to evaluate systems developed using our formalisation. This architecture is based on the ontology concept with the use of the multi-agent system JADE and the rule-based engine Jess. Different scenarios for this environmental application will be proposed in our future work taking into account different states and extended wireless sensors reasoning capabilities. Our application will also be implemented with tools suitable for the limited resources of wireless sensors.

Acknowledgment

This research is partly funded by the grant of the French Auvergne region, and now in the new Auvergne-Rhône-Alpes region (temporary name) and, the grant of the European Regional Development Fund (ERDF). The authors would like to thank the team of the Orgeval observatory for their help.

References

[1] L. Atzori, A. Iera, and G. Morabito, "The internet of things: A survey," Computer Networks, vol. 54, no. 15, 2010, pp. 2787 – 2805.

[2] I. F. Akyildiz, W. Su, Y. Sankarasubramaniam, and E. Cayirci, "Wireless sensor networks: a survey," Computer networks, vol. 38, no. 4, 2002, pp. 393–422.

[3] M. F. Othman and K. Shazali, "Wireless sensor network applications: A study in environment monitoring system," Procedia Engineering, vol. 41, 2012, pp. 1204 – 1210, international Symposium on Robotics and Intelligent Sensors 2012 (IRIS 2012).

[4] A. ur Rehman, A. Z. Abbasi, N. Islam, and Z. A. Shaikh, "A review of wireless sensors and networks' applications in agriculture," Computer Standards & Interfaces, vol. 36, no. 2, 2014, pp. 263 – 270.

[5] I. F. Akyildiz, T. Melodia, and K. R. Chowdhury, "A survey on wireless multimedia sensor networks," Computer Networks, vol. 51, 2007, pp. 921–960.

[6] A. K. Dey and G. D. Abowd, "Towards a better understanding of context and context-awareness," in Workshop on The What, Who, Where, When, and How of Context-Awareness, as part of the 2000 Conference on Human Factors in Computing Systems (CHI 2000), The Hague, The Netherlands, April 3, 2000, pp. 204 – 307.

[7] C. Perera, A. Zaslavsky, P. Christen, and D. Georgakopoulos, "Context aware computing for the internet of things: A survey," Communications Surveys Tutorials, IEEE, vol. 16, no. 1, 2014, pp. 414–454.

[8] C. Goumopoulos, B. O'Flynn, and A. Kameas, "Automated zone-specific irrigation with wireless sensor/actuator network and adaptable decision support," Computers and Electronics in Agriculture, vol. 105, 2014, pp. 20–33.

[9] E. Jajaga, L. Ahmedi, and F. Ahmedi, "An expert system for water quality monitoring based on ontology," in 9th Research Conference on Metadata and Semantics Research (MTSR) 2015, Manchester, UK, September 9-11, 2015, 2015, pp. 89–100.

[10] R. Bendadouche, C. Roussey, G. D. Sousa, J.-P. Chanet, and K.-M. Hou, "Extension of the semantic sensor network ontology for wireless sensor networks: The stimulus-wsnnode-communication pattern," in 5th International Workshop on Semantic Sensor Networks in conjunction with the 11th International Semantic Web Conference (ISWC), Boston, USA, November 2012, pp. 49–64.

[11] R. Draves, J. Padhye, and B. Zill, "Comparison of routing metrics for static multi-hop wireless networks," ACM SIGCOMM Computer Communication Review, vol. 34, no. 4, 2004, pp. 133–144.

[12] F. Bellifemine, A. Poggi, and G. Rimassa, "Jade–a fipa-compliant agent framework," in Proceedings of PAAM, vol. 99, no. 97-108. London, 1999, p. 33.

[13] E. Friedman-Hill, Jess in Action: Java Rule-Based Systems. Greenwich, CT, USA: Manning Publications Co., 2003.

[14] J. Subercaze and P. Maret, "Programming semantic agent for distributed knowledge management," in Semantic Agent Systems. Springer, 2011, pp. 47–65.

[15] T. Logenthiran, D. Srinivasan, and A. M. Khambadkone, "Multi-agent system for energy resource scheduling of integrated microgrids in a distributed system," Electric Power Systems Research, vol. 81, no. 1, 2011, pp. 138–148.

[16] R. Studer, V. Benjamins, and D. Fensel, "Knowledge engineering: Principles and methods," Data & Knowledge Engineering, vol. 25, no. 12, 1998, pp. 161 – 197.

[17] M. Compton et al., "The ssn ontology of the w3c semantic sensor network incubator group," Web Semantics: Science, Services and Agents on the World Wide Web, vol. 17, 2012, pp. 25 – 32.

[18] W. S. S. N. I. Group, "Climate and Forecast (CF) features," W3C, Tech. Rep., 2011, retrieved: 04, 2016. [Online]. Available: http://www.w3.org/2005/Incubator/ssn/ssnx/cf/cf-feature

[19] NASA, "Semantic Web for Earth and Environmental Terminology (SWEET)," Jet Propulsion Laboratory California Institute of Technology, Tech. Rep., 2016, retrieved: 04, 2016. [Online]. Available: https://sweet.jpl.nasa.gov/

[20] J. R. Hobbs and F. Pan, "Time Ontology in OWL, W3c Working Draft 27 September 2006," W3C, W3C Working Draft, sep 2006, retrieved: 04, 2016. [Online]. Available: https://www.w3.org/TR/owl-time/

[21] H. P. de Koning, N. Rouquette, R. Burkhart, H. Espinoza, and L. Lefort, "Library for Quantity Kinds and Units: schema, based on QUDV model OMG SysML(TM), Version 1.2," CSIRO, Tech. Rep., 2011, retrieved: 04, 2016. [Online]. Available: http://www.w3.org/2005/Incubator/ssn/ssnx/qu/qu

[22] G. Tallec, P. Ansart, A. Gurin, O. Delaigue, and A. Blanchouin, "Observatoire oracle," 2015. [Online]. Available: http://dx.doi.org/10.17180/OBS.ORACLE

[23] L. Ahmedi, E. Jajaga, and F. Ahmedi, "An ontology framework for water quality management," in Proceedings of the 6th International Conference on Semantic Sensor Networks (SSN), ser. CEUR Workshop Proceedings, vol. 1063. Sydney, Australia: CEUR-WS. org, Oct. 2013, pp. 35–50.

[24] M. K. Kasi, A. Hinze, C. Legg, and S. Jones, "SEPSen: semantic event processing at the sensor nodes for energy efficient wireless sensor networks," in Proceedings of the 6th ACM International Conference on Distributed Event-Based Systems. Berlin, Germany: ACM Press, 2012, pp. 119–122.

[25] A. J. G. Gray et al., "A Semantically Enabled Service Architecture for Mashups over Streaming and Stored Data," in The Semantic Web: Research and Applications, G. Antoniou, M. Grobelnik, E. Simperl, B. Parsia, D. Plexousakis, P. De Leenheer, and J. Pan, Eds., vol. 6644. Crete, Greece: Springer, 2011, pp. 300–314.

[26] M. Stocker, M. Rönkkö, and M. Kolehmainen, "Abstractions from Sensor Data with Complex Event Processing and Machine Learning," in IEMSs Conference Proceedings, vol. 2014. USA, California, San Diego: IEMS society, Jun. 2014, pp. 1273–1280.

Quality of Service and Energy Efficient Evaluation of Hierarchical and Flat Routing Protocols for Wireless Sensor Networks

Abdelbari Ben Yagouta, Bechir Ben Gouissem
Communication System Laboratory Sys'Com
National Engineering School of Tunis
University Tunis El Manar
Tunis, Tunisia
Emails: {abdelbari.benyagouta@gmail.com, bechir.gouissem@enit.rnu.tn}

***Abstract*—Wireless Sensor Network (WSN) is a network with limited power sensing devices with a communications infrastructure for monitoring physical or environmental conditions, such as temperature, sound, pressure, etc. Among the concerns of these networks is prolonging the lifetime by saving nodes energy. There are several protocols specially designed for WSNs based on energy consumption and network lifetime. However, many WSNs applications require QoS (Quality of Service) criteria, such as latency and throughput. In this paper, we will compare three routing protocols for wireless network sensors LEACH (Low Energy Adaptive Clustering Hierarchy), AODV (Ad hoc on demand Distance Vector) and LABILE (Link Quality-Based Lexical Routing) using Castalia simulator in terms of energy consumption, number of nodes alive and stability period, throughput and latency time of packets received by the base station under various conditions. The results prove that LEACH had the longest network stability period, consumes the least energy and had the least latency time, while the LABILE and AODV protocols have the highest throughput.**

Keywords-WSNs; Quality of Service; LEACH; AODV; LABILE.

I. INTRODUCTION

WSNs are a special case of Ad hoc networks [1], widely used in various applications such as, environmental monitoring, military surveillances, intelligent transportation, healthcare, etc. A WSN is a collection of large numbers of sensor nodes deployed in a geographical area to be controlled. Each sensor is limited in terms of processing power, wireless bandwidth, battery and storage capacity. In most WSNs applications, it is difficult even impossible to change or recharge power resources, which makes the energy consumption a major constraint of WSNs lifetime [2]. Since wireless communication requires significantly more power than processing tasks, energy conservation is crucial while designing network protocols for WSNs. Clustering approach is one of the best ways for reducing energy consumption of nodes. In these sensor nodes, rather than sending individually, first, the sensor nodes group themselves into clusters, and then an elected cluster head (CH) sends the aggregated data from all to the sink. Other than the power consumption criterion, real-time applications such as, military applications require QoS criteria like latency.

In typical WSNs applications, throughput is not significant as other parameters, because a sensor node sends small packets. But, the use of acoustic and imaging sensors requires significant throughput, as data must be streamed through the network. Thus, certain WSNs applications require maximizing throughput. In that context, distance-vector routing protocols based on calculating of direction and distance to any link in a network and multi-hop approach can ensure a great throughput.

In this work, we have compared three WSNs routing protocols; AODV and LABILE based on distance-vector and LEACH based on clustering approach. The source codes of these three routing protocols are developed for Omnet++/ Castalia simulator by GERCOM (research Group on Computer Network and Multimedia Communication) [3]. The comparison results show that, LEACH had the longest stability period, consumes least energy, and had the least latency time, while LABILE and AODV protocols have the highest throughput. The rest of the paper is organized as follows. In Section II, we review the related work in this field. Section III will provide an overview of the three routing protocols AODV, LABILE and LEACH. Section IV describes the common simulation settings used in different scenarios. Section V discusses the results and analysis; finally, we conclude the paper in Section VI.

II. RELATED WORK

Various comparative studies have been made between hierarchical and flat routing protocols for WSNs based on the energy saving criteria and network lifetime such as in [4]. In those studies, AODV, LEACH and LEACH-E routing protocols are compared for energy efficiency and network lifetime. The simulation results show that, under different simulation time, LEACH and LEACH-E protocols consume less energy than AODV. Indeed AODV has the least network lifetime. However, many WSNs applications have latency and throughput constraints like real-time application.

The particularity of this work is to compare hierarchical (LEACH) and flat routing protocols (AODV and LABILE) in terms of latency, throughput and energy consumption under different scenarios to determinate which type of routing protocols is more suitable for QoS constraints.

III. ROUTING PROTOCOLS FOR WSNS : AN OVERVIEW

WSNs routing protocols are classified according to their architecture or their operating principles into flat, location-based and hierarchical/cluster categories [5]. Flat routing protocols represent an appropriate solution for several applications, such as smart-homes, healthcare and environmental monitoring. Many applications employed in these scenarios have low tolerance for packet delay and loss. On the other hand, routing protocols based on clustering are an alternative to improve QoS and energy consumption for many applications [6], such as multimedia traffic [7]. The energy saving, throughput and packets transmission delay represent a great worry for WSNs, and a real compromise between flat and hierarchical routing protocols; so, for these reasons we have chosen to compare AODV and LABILE and LEACH.

A. AODV Routing Protocol

AODV protocol [8] was originally proposed in RFC 3965. In AODV, on-demand routes can be discovered, which decrease the overhead, by using pairs of Route Request (RREQ) and Route Reply (RREP) messages. However, the route selection process is only based on the minimal number of hops, which is not suitable for ensuring energy-efficiency and reliable data transmission. The deficiency of energy-efficiency mechanism results in energy holes and an uneven distribution of scarce network resources. Moreover, AODV only stores one possible route for a given destination node. This means that if a single route fails or is unavailable, a new route must be discovered, which requires more time and increases the delay or failure rate of data delivery.

B. LABILE Routing Protocol

LABILE [9] proposes a routing algorithm based on lexical structures and link quality evaluation. Using LQI, i.e., a metric provided by the physical layer of IEEE 802.15.4 standard, LABILE is able to evaluate the link quality. The LABILE proposal evaluates end-to-end link quality by classifying the possible values of LQI, determines a threshold value for link classification, where the lowest values of LQI (below the threshold) are considered bad, and represents links that are more susceptible to packet loss. During the route discovery process, all the bad links are counted, recorded and reported with the aid of an additional field in RREQ and RREP messages. The purpose of LABILE is to select routes with good link qualities. However, this behaviour implies that these routes have an exhaustive use, and lead to the premature death of these nodes. This is due to a lack of mechanisms for determining when there is a need to use alternative routes.

C. LEACH Routing Protocol

LEACH [10], is the first hierarchical cluster based routing protocol for WSNs, developed by W. R. Heinzelman et al. from MIT. It is based on the concept of rounds where each round consists of two phases: first, clusters set up phase and second a steady state phase.

1) Cluster set-up phase: In this phase, each node decides whether or not to become a CH for the current round r. This decision is made by the node n choosing a number between 0 and 1 randomly. If the number is less than a threshold T(n), the node becomes a CH for the current round [10].

2) Steady set-up phase: In the steady working stage, each member node of the cluster sends data to the corresponding CH during the allocated communication slot. After receiving all the data, the CH aggregates it and sends to the sink. In order to minimize the power consumption, the steady phase duration is kept far greater than the cluster constructing phase duration..

IV. SIMULATION SCENARIOS

In this work, we want to make a comparison between hierarchical and flat WSNs routing protocols in terms of energy consumption, packet latency and throughput. In order to achieve convincing results, we will simulate the chosen protocols several times in various scenarios. For simulation, we will use the OMNET++/Castalia simulator [11]. By using the "Throughput Test" application implemented in Castalia simulator, we suppose that all nodes have data to sending, have an initial energy of 10 joules and randomly placed in a 100 m x 100 m area.

Table I depicts the common simulation settings for all scenarios, with the last three parameters that contain (*) are specific to LEACH protocol.

TABLE I. GLOBAL SIMULATION PARAMETERS.

Parameters	Values
Routing protocols.	AODV, LABILE, LEACH.
Node deployment (topology)	Random
Number of Simulation Repetition	20
Sink Position (x, y, z)	(50 m, 120 m, 0 m)
Collision Model	Simple collision
Area	100 m x 100 m
Initial energy/node	10 Joules
Sink Initial Energy	100 Joules
TX output power	-5 dBm
Packet rate	1 packet/s
Node Buffer size	1000 bytes
Application name	Throughput Test
Path loss exponent	2.0 (Free Space)
Radio parameter file	CC2420.txt
Round length *	20s (Duration between two rounds)
Slot length *	0.2ms (TDMA slot dedicated to each node)
Routing percentage *	0.05 (Percentage of Cluster Head 5%)

V. RESULTS AND ANALYSIS

In this section, we will present results under different simulation scenarios by varying simulation time, node density and packet size. These results are analysed to demonstrate the performance of these protocols in terms of latency time, throughput and energy consumption.

A. *Energy consumption and network lifetime*

In this section, we have evaluated energy consumption and network lifetime for different scenarios described below.

*1) Time variation scenario:*In this scenario, we have simulated the protocols for different simulation times and analysed their performance in terms of energy consumption, network lifetime and network stability period. The parameters of this scenario are illustrated in Table II.

TABLE II. TIME VARIATION SCENARIO PARAMETERS.

Parameters	Values
Simulation time (s)	[20, 40, 60..600]
Number of nodes	100
Packet size (byte)	100

Figure 1 shows the variation of total consumed energy according to the simulation time. The graph depicts that LEACH consumes the least, while AODV and LABILE have the highest total energy consumption. It also shows that the nodes that use AODV and LABILE consumes all of their energy at time 150 s, while for LEACH it remains until time 470 s.

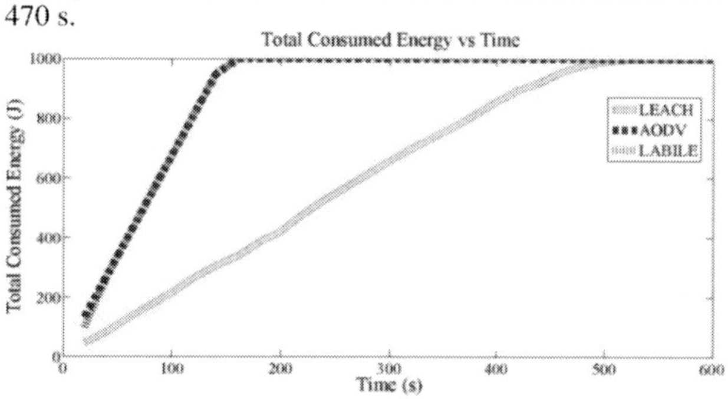

Figure 1. Total Consumed Energy vs Time.

From Figure 2, it is quite clear that by using LEACH the first node dies at time 435 s (stability period = 435 s) and the last at time 470 s. Nevertheless, with AODV and LABILE all nodes are dead between 145 s and 150 s (stability period = 145 s). Therefore, we can conclude that the nodes using LEACH consume less energy and subsequently the network has a long stability period. However, nodes using AODV and LABILE consume more energy and the network has a brief stability period relative to LEACH.

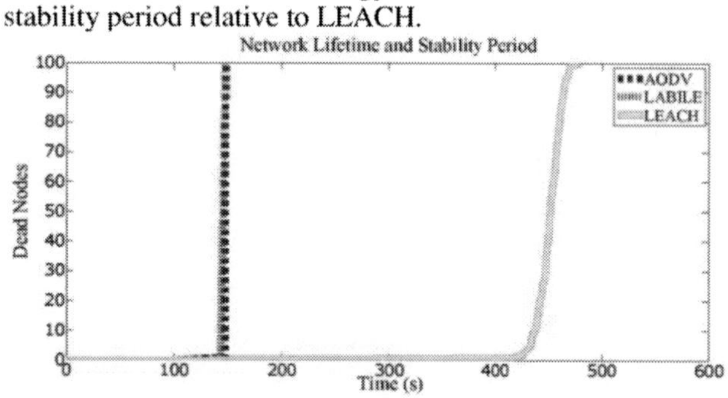

Figure 2. Network lifetime and Stability period.

So, due to the multi-hop routing technique used by flat routing protocols, energy consumption increases proportionally to the number of hops to reach the sink. Therefore, the nodes energy dissipates very quickly and the network stability period becomes short.

However with the hierarchical routing protocol that uses data aggregation; only the CHs nodes (only 5% of nodes) transmit data to the sink. Therefore, it retains the total energy of the network and increases the stability period.

2) Nodes density variation scenario: In this scenario, we have simulated the protocols for different numbers of nodes (100, 200, 300 and 400) and analysed their performance in terms of energy consumption. The parameters of this scenario are illustrated in Table III.

TABLE III. NODES DENSITY VARIATION SCENARIO PARAMETERS.

Parameters	Values
Simulation time (s)	20
Number of nodes	100, 200, 300, 400
Packet size (byte)	100

Figure 3 shows the variation of total consumed energy according to the number of nodes. The graph depicts that by increasing the number of nodes deployed, energy consumption also increases for the three routing protocols, but AODV and LABILE consume more energy than LEACH. With flat routing protocols, based on multi-hop routing, if we increase the density of nodes deployed, there will be as many of the nodes involved in the data transmission to the sink, so the energy consumption increases proportionally.

However, with hierarchical routing protocol, if we increase the node density the energy consumption increases obviously well, but with a lower slope than AODV and LABILE. These results are explained by the made where the number of nodes increases only the number of CHs increases (which are responsible for the data transmission to the sink).

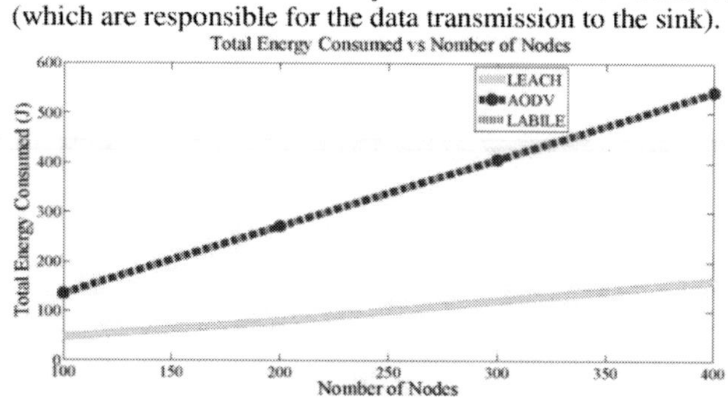

Figure 3. Total Consumed Energy vs Number of nodes.

3) Packet size variation scenario: In this scenario, we have simulated the protocols for different packet size (100, 200, 400, 600 and 800 bytes) and analysed their performance in terms of energy consumption. The parameters of this scenario are illustrated in Table IV.

TABLE IV. NODES DENSITY VARIATION SCENARIO PARAMETERS.

Parameters	Values
Simulation time (s)	20
Number of nodes	100
Packet size (byte)	100, 200, 400, 600, 800

Figure 4 shows the variation of total consumed energy according to the different packet size. The graph depicts that by increasing packet size energy consumption also increases for the three protocols but AODV and LABILE consume more energy than LEACH. For AODV and LABILE, by using multi-hop routing technique, by increasing packet size, nodes consume more energy to forward the packets from node to other until arriving to the sink. LABILE consumes less energy than AODV because it uses roads based on good link qualities selection technique. For LEACH, with the use of data aggregation, the CH eliminates data redundancy, which reduces the size of the transmitted packets to the sink. Therefore, the energy consumption increases proportionally with packet size, until it reaches the maximum data buffer size.

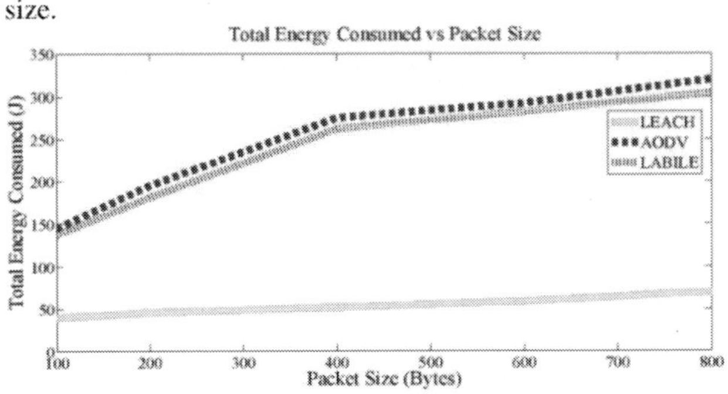

Figure 4. Total Consumed Energy vs Packet size.

B. Throughput

In this section, we have evaluated throughput (Total Data received by sink) for different scenarios described below.

*1) Time variation scenario:*In this scenario, we have simulated the protocols for different simulation times and analysed their performance in terms of total data received by the sink. The parameters of this scenario are illustrated in Table V.

TABLE V. TIME VARIATION SCENARIO PARAMETERS.

Parameters	Values
Simulation time (s)	[20, 40, 60..600]
Number of nodes	100
Packet size (byte)	100

Figure 5 shows the variation of total data received by the sink according to the simulation time variation. The graph depicts that by increasing the simulation time AODV and LABILE transmit more data to the sink than LEACH until it consumes all of her energy.

For these simulation results, we will compare the protocols, only during their stability period. LEACH has a low rate compared to other protocols because only CH sends data to the sink (5% of the total number of nodes). LABILE has a less rate than AODV because it sends the data only through the good quality links, so less traffic in the network and fewer packets transmitted to the sink.

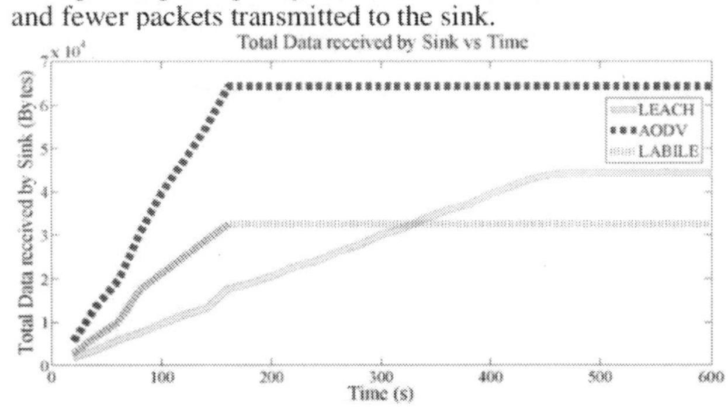

Figure 5. Total data received by the sink vs Time.

2) Nodes density variation scenario: In this scenario, we have simulated the protocols for different numbers of nodes (100, 200, 300 and 400) and analysed their performance in terms of throughput. The parameters of this scenario are illustrated in Table VI.

TABLE VI. NODES DENSITY VARIATION SCENARIO PARAMETERS.

Parameters	Values
Simulation time (s)	20
Number of nodes	100, 200, 300, 400
Packet size (byte)	100

Figure 6 shows the variation of total data received by sink according to the number of deployed nodes. The graph depicts that by increasing the number of deployed nodes AODV and LEACH are able to transmit more data to the base station unlike LABILE that transmits less. In this scenario, LABILE possesses a lower throughput than AODV and even as LEACH, because if we increase the number of nodes, the route selection algorithm takes a long time in the processing and in links quality selection phase. Therefore, fewer packets transmitted to the sink. LEACH throughput increases proportionately by increasing the numbers of nodes because the number of CH increases.

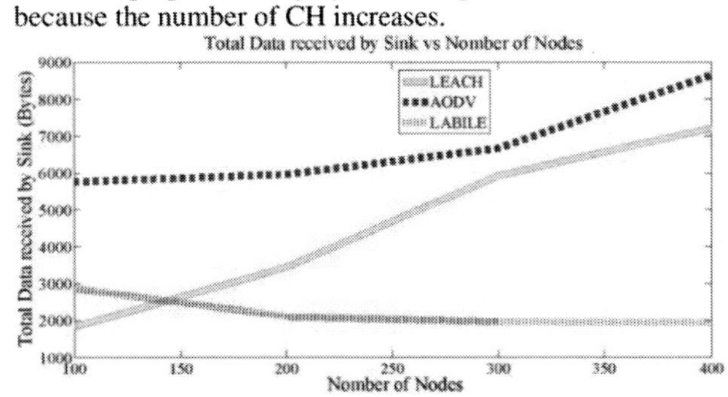

Figure 6. Total data received by the sink vs Number of nodes.

3) Packet size variation scenario: In this scenario, we have simulated the protocols for different packet size (100, 200, 400, 600 and 800 bytes) and analysed their performance in terms of total data received by the sink. The parameters of this scenario are illustrated in Table VII.

TABLE VII. PACKET SIZE VARIATION SCENARIO PARAMETERS.

Parameters	Values
Simulation time (s)	20
Number of nodes	100
Packet size (byte)	100, 200, 400, 600, 800

Figure 7 shows the variation of total data received by the sink according to the packet size. The graph depicts that by increasing the packets size, AODV and LABILE transmit data to the base station more than LEACH. AODV and LABILE provide better throughput for a packet size of 400 bytes. If the packet size exceeds 400 bytes, the buffer becomes overloaded and throughput decreases. For LEACH, throughput increases proportionately with the packet size until the size of 600 bytes because the CHs remove data redundancy in the packets. If the packet size exceeds 600 bytes, the buffer saturates.

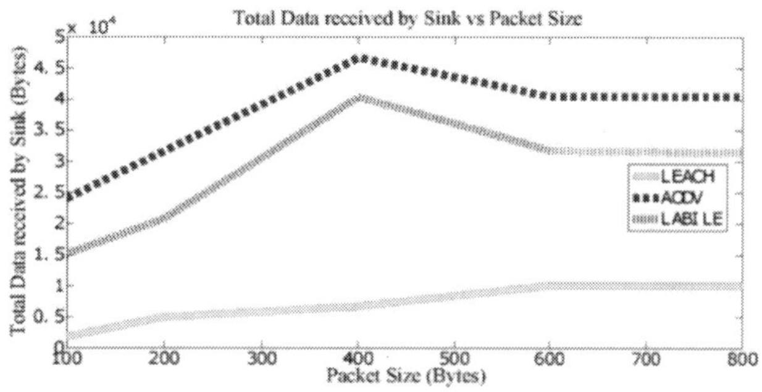

Figure 7. Total data received by the sink vs Packet size.

C. Throughput

In this section, we have evaluated packets latency time for different scenarios described below.

*1) Time variation scenario:*In this scenario, we have simulated the protocols for different simulation times and analysed their performance in terms of packets latency time. The parameters of this scenario are illustrated in Table VIII.

TABLE VIII. TIME VARIATION SCENARIO PARAMETERS.

Parameters	Values
Simulation time (s)	20, 40, 60, 80, 100
Number of nodes	100
Packet size (byte)	100

Figure 8 shows the variation of latency intervals of received packets according to the simulation time. The graph depicts that by increasing the simulation time LEACH sent 90% of data in the range of (0-20 ms) while AODV sent the majority of data with time greater than 200 ms and LABILE with uniform distribution between 0 and 200ms. Conversely, LEACH sends 90% of the data with a latency less than 20 ms, because the nodes send their data to the CH and the CH forward this data directly to the sink. AODV and LABILE send their packets with a larger latency because the packets are moving from node to node until they reach the sink.

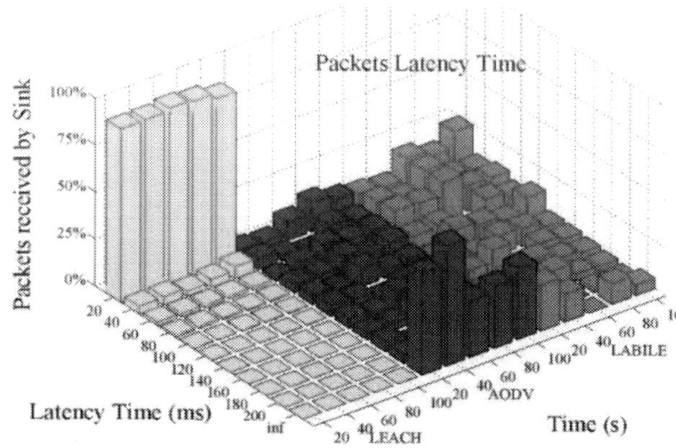

Figure 8. Packets latency time vs Time.

2) Nodes density variation scenario: In this scenario, we have simulated the protocols for different numbers of nodes and analysed their performance in terms of packets latency. The parameters of this scenario are illustrated in Table IX.

TABLE IX. NODES DENSITY VARIATION SCENARIO PARAMETERS.

Parameters	Values
Simulation time (s)	20
Number of nodes	100, 200, 300, 400
Packet size (byte)	100

Figure 9 shows the variation of latency intervals of received packets according to the number of deployed nodes.

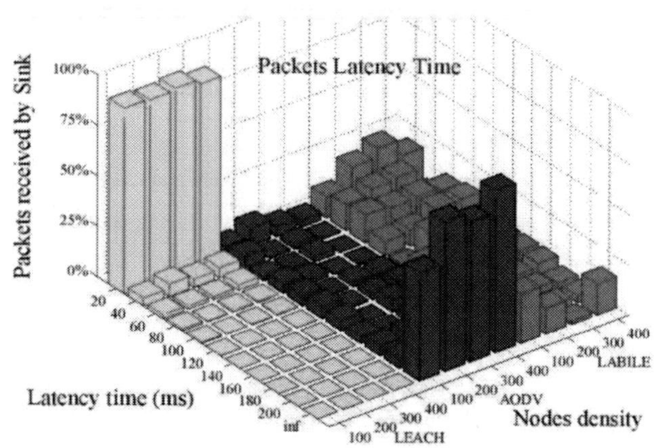

Figure 9. Packets latency time vs Number of nodes.

The graph depicts that by increasing the number of deployed nodes LEACH sent 90% of data in the range of (0-20 ms) while AODV sent 50% of data with time greater than 200 ms and LABILE with uniform distribution between 0 and 200 ms. For LEACH, if we increase the number of nodes, 90% of the packets always arrive at the sink with a latency less than 20 ms.

For flat routing protocols, if the number of nodes increases, the number of packets hops increases and the delay accumulates. With LABILE packets have less delay than AODV, due the mechanism of good links selection, which reduces the number of hops to the sink.

3) Packet size variation scenario: In this scenario, we have simulated the protocols for different packet size (100, 200, 400, 600 and 800 bytes) and analysed their performance in terms of packets latency time. The parameters of this scenario are illustrated in Table X.

TABLE X. PACKET SIZE VARIATION SCENARIO PARAMETERS.

Parameters	Values
Simulation time (s)	20
Number of nodes	100
Packet size (byte)	100, 200, 400, 600, 800

Figure 10 shows the variation of latency intervals of received packets according to the packet size. The graph depicts that by increasing the packet size, LEACH sent the majority of data in the range of (0-20 ms) while AODV sent 80% of data with time greater than 200 ms and LABILE sent 50% of data with uniform distribution between 0 and 200 ms. For flat routing protocols, if the packets size increases, the processing time and the packet forwarding delay increases and subsequently the packets arrives at the sink with over delay. For LEACH, if the packet size exceeds 600 bytes, the CHs take longer for data fusion and elimination of redundancy. By result, only 50% of data arrives with a latency of less than 20 ms.

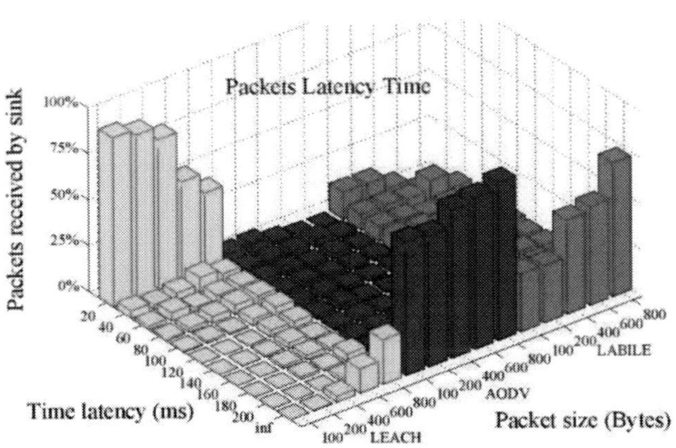

Figure 10. Packets latency time vs Packet size.

General Synthesis: For LEACH, with a 100 bytes packet size, 90% of the packets always arrive at the sink with a latency less than 20 ms, even with a density of 400 nodes / 100 m x 100 m. Even with a packet size of 400 bytes 75% of data arrives to the sink with a latency time less than 20 ms. So, we can conclude that LEACH protocol has the least delay to send data due to the data aggregation technique. Nevertheless, the LABILE and AODV protocols have the highest delay to send packets due the using of the multi-hop routing technique.

VI. CONCLUSION

In WSNs, a significant consideration has been given to the prolongation of node lifetime. Efficient utilization of energy is crucial for enhancing the node lifetime. Although wireless network sensors routing protocols like ad hoc on demand distance vector can be used, they usually do not focus on energy conservation, network lifetime prolongation of sensor nodes and delay to send data.

In this paper, we have evaluated three routing protocols for WSNs namely AODV, LABILE and LEACH using Castalia Simulator for energy consumption, network lifetime, throughput and latency time with reference to simulation time, number of deployed nodes and size of transmitted packets. Simulation results show that, under different conditions, LEACH protocol has least energy consumption and highest network lifetime compared to the LABILE and AODV protocols. The AODV and LABILE protocols have the least network lifetime because of high-energy consumption per node. This makes AODV and LABILE unsuitable for WSNs, where lifetime is a primary metric for evaluating the performance and LEACH protocol has become better for network lifetime.

Under different simulation conditions, the results show that LEACH protocol has the least throughput because of the use of data aggregation technique. Nevertheless, the LABILE and AODV protocols have the highest throughput and that from the multi-hop technique used by both routing protocols. This makes LEACH unsuitable for WSNs applications, where throughput is a primary metric for evaluating the performance likewise, AODV and LABILE become better for this type of applications. Under different scenarios, the results show that LEACH protocol has the least delay to send data due to the data fusion technique. Nevertheless, the LABILE and AODV protocols have the highest delay to send packets due to the using of multi-hop technique. This makes AODV and LABILE unsuitable for real-time WSNs applications, where latency time is a primary metric for evaluating the performance and LEACH become better for this type of applications.

ACKNOWLEDGMENT

The authors would like to thank the anonymous reviewers for their helpful comments. They would also like to thank the Editors for their generous comments and support during the review process.

REFERENCES

[1] C. M. Cordeiro, D. and P. Agrawal, "Ad Hoc and Sensor Networks: Theory and Applications, World Scientific Publication 2006", ISBN 981-256-681-3, ISBN 981-256-682-1.

[2] M. Zhang and S. Wang, "An Energy Efficient Dynamic Clustering Protocol based on Weight in Wireless Sensor Networks, Journal of Networks", vol. 6, no. 7, 2011, pp. 1057-1064.

[3] Sensor Network Routing Protocols, LEACH Clustering Protocol v0.2, AODV, and LABILE Codes Source, Available Online: www.gercom.ufpa.br/index.php?option=com_osdownloads&view=downloads&Itemid=346 (accessed on 9 June 2016).

[4] Jyoti Kashniyal and H. L. Mandoria, "Energy Efficiency Analysis between AODV, LEACH and LEACH-E using Castalia, International Journal of P2P Network Trends and Technology (IJPTT)", vol. 3, issue. 4, May 2013, pp. 240-244, ISSN:2249-2615.

[5] S. Ehsan and B. Hamdaoui, "A survey on energy-efficient routing techniques with QoS assurances for wireless multimedia sensor networks", IEEE Commun. Surv. Tutor. 2012, pp. 265-278.

[6] M. Becker, A. Gupta, M. Marot, and H. Singh, "Improving Clustering Techniques in Wireless Sensor Networks Using Thinning Process. In Proceedings of the International Conference on Performance Evaluation of Computer and Communication Systems: Milestones and Future Challenges", Lisbon, Portugal, December 2011, pp. 203-214.

[7] A. Hnini, A. Ezzati ; A. Hajami, "LEACH protocol for multimedia traffic with a variable-size packet. In Proceedings of Multimedia Computing and Systems (ICMCS), 2014 International Conference", Marrakech, Marocco, 14-16 April 2014, pp. 906-909.

[8] C. Perkins, E. Belding-Royer, and S. Das, "Ad hoc on Demand Distance Vector (AODV) Routing (RFC3561)", Available online: http://www.ietf.org/rfc/rfc3561.txt(accessed on 30 March 2016).

[9] M. Butt, et al. "Labile: Link Quality-Based Lexical Routing Metric for Reactive Routing Protocols in IEEE 802.15.4 Networks. In Proceedings of the 5th International Conference on Future Information Technology (FutureTech)", Busan, Korea, 2123 May 2010, pp. 16.

[10] W. R. Heinzelman, A. Chandrakasan, and H. Balakrishnan, "Energyefficient communication protocol for wireless microsensor networks, in Proceedings of the 33rd Annual Hawaii International Conference on System Sciences (HICSS-3300)", January 2000, p. 223.

[11] Castalia, "Wireless Sensor Networks Simulator", Available Online: https://castalia.forge.nicta.com.au/index.php/en/ (accessed on 5 April 2016).

A Preventing Schema to Determinate Structural Damage in Buildings Caused by Earthquakes Using a Platform Based in Wireless Sensor Networks

Laura M. Rodríguez Peralta, Eduardo Ismael-Hernández, Roberto López Caso, Lorna V. Rosas Téllez, Edna P. Santiago Vargas
Engineering Department
Universidad Popular Autónoma del Estado de Puebla - UPAEP
Puebla, México
e-mail: lauramargarita.rodriguez01@upaep.mx, eduardo.ismael@upaep.mx, roberto.lopez02@upaep.edu.mx, lornaveronica.rosas@upaep.mx, ednapatricia.santiago@upaep.edu.mx

Christian Pérez Aguilar
Faculty of Electronics,
Benemérita Universidad Autónoma de Puebla – BUAP
Puebla, México
e-mail: cbpa9@msn.com

Abstract—**This paper presents a proposal to develop and implement analytical and technology tools for estimating the level of vulnerability of existing buildings. The proposed platform includes the design and implementation of a comprehensive structural monitoring platform based on wireless sensor networks. This platform is a low cost instrument capable of providing the necessary information to implement methods of response analysis and consequently improve structural damage detection. With the development of the system, we will be able to obtain practical criteria and automated functions, in order to estimate seismic structural vulnerability of existing buildings in a preventive way.**

Keywords-structural vulnerability; seismic events; wireless sensor networks; acceleration sensors.

I. Introduction

Considering the negative impact of earthquakes on society (loss of life and property), the importance of mitigating the risk associated with this phenomenon is recognized around the world. A strategy for reducing the risk of earthquakes involves buildings that can withstand the effects of the earthquakes [1]. To reduce the consequences or the amount of damage caused by these events, earthquake engineering provides criteria, methods, and tools for structural designs of such infrastructure. Additionally, earthquake engineering includes testing, maintenance, and reinforcement on existing buildings. The margins of uncertainty that affect our ability to predict and characterize seismic intensity level are very high. This uncertainty affects our understanding of the relationship between the actual properties of the constructions (gravitational loads, stiffness and mechanical properties of the structure), and the assumed values in the structural design process. The above forces deal rigorously with these concepts within a framework based on probability analysis applied to seismic risk estimation.

New buildings are generally designed and built following the aforementioned design criteria. However, for existing buildings there are several factors that can affect their performance against seismic events, namely: the age of the building, the absence of a structural maintenance program, the presence of damage due to past earthquakes, among others.

Therefore, the development and implementation of methods and tools for the structural vulnerability assessment can be considered as useful strategy to reduce the costs associated with losses in existing buildings due to earthquakes [2]. For this purpose, methods for damage detection and structural monitoring systems based on sensors have been proposed and developed recently. These systems have been focused mainly on structural health monitoring of bridges, tall buildings, dams and critical infrastructure [3]. Most of these systems use wired sensors instead of wireless sensors; this can hinder their deployment, especially in historical buildings. Another identified problem is related to the difficulty for end users to interpret and analyze information obtained from monitoring. In addition, the investment required to implement and operate these systems in most cases is very high, which limits their use to smaller buildings and public buildings such as hospitals, school buildings, etc. In developing countries, it is very difficult to implement these types of systems because of their cost. For this reason, it is important to develop low-cost monitoring systems in order to estimate the structural vulnerability and deploy them on buildings such as schools, hospitals, among others.

This paper is organized as follows. Section II includes a descriptions of related work. Section III presents the SAVER Web-based monitoring platform and a detailed description of the structural vulnerability module. Section IV briefly presents the SAVER sensor node. Section V presents the modeling and deployment of an application example of the SAVER project. Finally, section VI provides some conclusions and future work perspectives.

II. Related Works

Structural Health Monitoring (SHM) systems are emerging tools to help engineers improve the safety and maintainability of critical and conventional structures. SHM combines a variety of sensing technologies with an embedded measurement controller to capture, log, and analyze real-time data. SHM systems are designed to reliably monitor and test the health and performance of structures. Most of the existing solutions of SHM systems around the world employ movement-sensing devices, like accelerometers, but the majority studies use wired networks. In addition, most of them are used for detecting only one parameter correlated with the damage level and this is typically the inter-story drift. This parameter is enough to evaluate the performance given the occurrence of an earthquake; it means that is useful for evaluating the post-earthquake condition. But the problem arises when we need to evaluate the performance or vulnerability condition before an earthquake. In this case we need more information and the drift is not enough, because we also need to generate a model and obtaining the non-linear response for the structural system.

On the other hand, in the literature we can find some studies that apply to Wireless Sensor Networks (WSNs) for structural health monitoring. Among these, we find the work of Kim [4]. In this project, Mica2 motes [5] are used to determine the structural health of the Golden Gate Bridge located in San Francisco CA. Other works are focused on the structural health monitoring of offshore wind turbines [6]. However, most studies are oriented to the monitoring of large structures, i.e., bridges [7][8], dams, etc. This allows us to claim that currently there are few efforts to monitor and determine the structural vulnerability of buildings. Furthermore, many of the existing systems are focused on determining the health status of the buildings during an earthquake event with considerable intensity.These systems are very useful for a post-seismic evaluation conditions, security and stability. Given the great advantages of having a structural monitoring system to determine some dynamic properties that have strong correlation with the structural responses, it is necessary to make efforts for the development of such systems.

The use of WSNs have brought several advantages in structural monitoring and the establishment of structural health compared to conventional methods where computers connected to accelerometers are used. In conventional methods, it is necessary to install cables through the structure; disturbing its normal operation and generating maintenance cost. Other disadvantages are low efficiency, high cost, inflexibility and disturbance. Another problem is the high equipment and wiring installation and maintenance cost. Compared with conventional methods, WSNs provide the same functionality at a much lower price and more flexible monitoring. Other advantages are high efficiency, flexibility, reliability, and scalability. WSNs are not easy to be disturbed by operation equipment and can facilitate efficient distributed data processing and real time damage detection [8].

The cost of a conventional system with a computer and a force-balanced accelerometer is about USD 20000 per sampling point. The estimated cost of the proposed system, in this work is less than USD 200 per point. In WSNs, no wiring is required; making installation and maintenance much easier and inexpensive. More so, the use of WSNs allows SAVER platform to be deployed and operate even if the building is in operation. It does not cause further visual impact due to its small size, low power consumption, and installation flexibility. The advantage of structural health monitoring based on WSNs can be extended if the Micro-Electro-Mechanical Systems (MEMS) acceleration sensor type is used. The MEMS accelerometer is a silicon chip, which is very compact in size, low power consumption, and cheap. Without MEMS, a small WSN, even low-power and low-cost accelerometer, would be degraded.

Thus, the Structural Analysis of Vulnerabilities of Buildings through Wireless Sensor Networks (SAVER) project aims at gathering information to establish the structural vulnerability level of buildings. Such information will be used in decision making for two schemes: prevention programs, and post-seismic evaluation. As mentioned before, knowing the structural vulnerability or seismic risk level of a specific building could be useful for the owner, because he or she can implement retrofit strategies on the building in order to recover its structural health condition and avoiding possible collapse, structural damage or injuries from users in case of a future earthquake.

The SAVER platform will be able to monitor and display information in real-time. It will determine, from the implementation of several methods, for estimating seismic response and damage detection, the level of structural vulnerability of buildings. A complete description of SAVER project's architecture can be found in [9].

III. Web Based WSN Monitoring Platform

In addition, our platform will offer several services that will notify users about potential risks of the structure through alarms, email and SMS. Besides, it will have a Web based monitoring platform and a mobile app for Android and IOS. Also, this platform will generate graphs, reports and statistics. Some preliminary results of the SAVER project was published in [9].

The SAVER Web-based platform provides a building's structural vulnerability analysis, of the different sensors inside each building. These reports provide information like the power supply and the time capture of each parameter [10].

The preliminary results of the SAVER project are presented in this section. These results principally involve the assembly, setup and configuration of a wireless sensor network including the sensor node.

The details of the results obtained so far are described in the following sections.

A. Database description

For proper operation, nine main tables are handled, which have the necessary information to control the sensors parameters: *Building, Sensor Acceleration, Sensor*

TempHum, Node, Cluster, Seism, Acceleration Amplitude, User and *Scenarios*.

For each building, we store its structure information, its features, its location, as well as the location of the nodes inside it. Also we store data of clusters, where a cluster is composed by a set of nodes. It is important to note that a building can be cover by one or more clusters. Each node contains four kinds of sensors: one of them is an Acceleration Sensor which records three-axial acceleration movement (longitudinal, transversal and vertical), Temperature, Humidity Sensors that record the ambient temperature and humidity, respectively, and a GPS sensor.

This data is used to establish when an earthquake occurs by overcoming the condition of an acceleration threshold and after this happens; we store the date, time, maximum amplitude, and the acceleration and frequency amplitude for each axis. All of these are used to calculate the Fourier spectrum in terms of frequency (Figure 1).

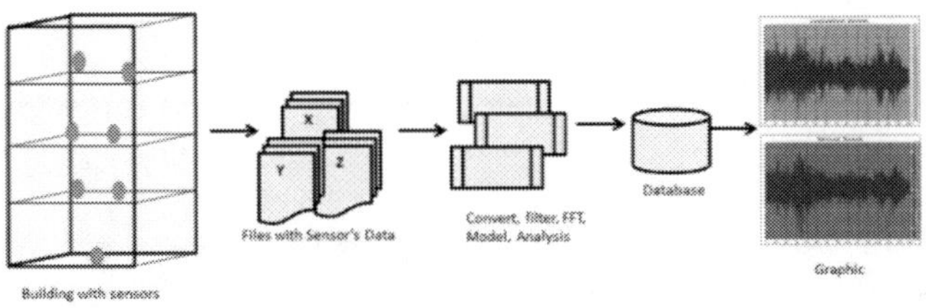

Figure 1. Flow of the process.

The description of the tables is detailed as following:

- *SensorAcceleration*: It stores the longitudinal, transversal and vertical records from Acceleration Sensor.
- *Sensor TempHum*: It stores the temperature and humidity that occurs in the environment at a specific time.
- *Node*: It stores the ID of each node, as well as the Acceleration Sensor ID, the Temperature and Humidity Sensor ID, the cluster where the node belongs and the localization where the node is placed on the building.
- *Cluster*: Here, the cluster ID and its location are stored.
- *Building*: Here we can store the building´s geometry, blueprint per floor in which is showed the location of each node, name, use, address, state, country, latitude, longitude, topography, foundation type, building support type of "x" and "y" axis.
- *Acceleration Amplitude*: It contains many acceleration amplitudes and Fourier spectrum of the records.
- *User*: It stores the username, password, type of user, name, last name, telephone and email of the system users.
- *Scenarios*: It stores pictures of the building, floor and room where the sensors are placed.

The SAVER database design is shown in Figure 2.

The "Home" section includes a brief description of the project, while the "Building" section is able to display the plans and basic information of each building (Figure 3). The WSN section shows the topology of the network, including its description and real-time location of each sensor inside the building. The Structural Vulnerability System (SVS) section will provide the generation of vulnerability reports, in order to consult the building's structural health and establish its possible rehabilitation strategies. As an example, Figure 4 shows the graphs of the longitudinal, transverse and vertical ambient vibration records captured each 0.005 seconds at UPAEP High School.

B. *Structural Vulnerability module*

To evaluate the structural vulnerability we can use a diagram as the shown in Figure 5. This procedure was originally proposed by Rodríguez Peralta et al. [9] and shows the process to establish the structural vulnerability level. This level will be associated with a structural damage parameter, u. In structural engineering is very well known that damage level can be estimated using a function defined as:

$$d(u) = 1 - \exp(-au^m) \qquad (1)$$

In this equation, a and m are parameters to be determined according with the structural system features (for example if the structural system includes frames, walls or a combination of this sub-systems); u is the local deformation of interest, normalized with respect to its peak value at failure (total loss). The damage function for the structural system is obtained as function of the corresponding inter-story distortion (drift). In this way, the parameter u is related to the lateral displacement. The damage function is continuous, for that reason the damage levels are given by an interval of values. The advantage of our approach is that the lateral displacement u can be determined considering two criteria: 1) using actual seismic records (as similar existing systems work for giving a post-event structural health condition); and 2) using ambient vibration records (that it is the novelty in this project). For that reason, in this paper we focus on the second criterion, details for the former can be found in [9].

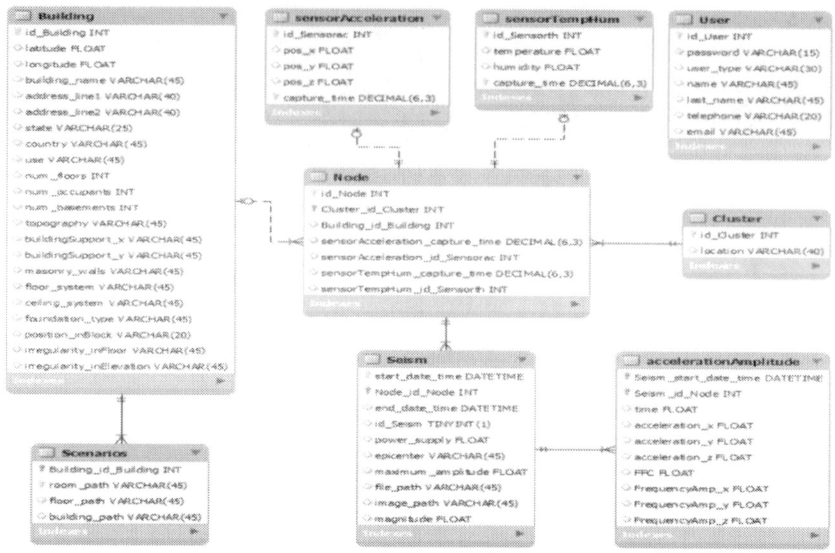

Figure 2. SAVER Database schema.

The second approach, based on ambient vibration records, can be used to perform modal analysis and generates simplified structural models. These models are necessary for carry out the non-linear analysis and getting the parameter u. The approach considers several steps, which are described in the follow (Figure 5). i) First, it is necessary to synchronize the signals with a common time reference and carry out the polarization procedure according to the sensor´s orientation and the reference system. ii) The baseline correction of the original records also is needed. iii) In order to eliminate the undesirable components of frequency a signal filtering procedure is recommended for this, we can use a Butterworth filter. iv) For the ambient vibration records, previously corrected in three directions, we can apply the Fast Fourier Transform (FFT), in order to obtain the Amplitude Fourier Spectra. v) With this information (Amplitude Fourier Spectra) we can estimate the transfer functions, as well as the vibration periods and modal shapes (modal analysis). vi) The vibration period and the modal shapes can be used for generating a Simplified Reference System (SRS) using the criteria proposed by Ismael-Hernández et al. [11]. The SRS has dynamic properties that represent the behavior of the building, however, it is necessary to introduce the corresponding transform response factors. These factors are also defined in [11]. In order to obtain the non-linear response of the SRS, in terms of lateral displacement, an adequate hysteresis model will be adopted. vii) The non-linear responses can be related with a specified seismic scenario, in this step the accelerogram (actual or synthetic) is defined. viii) The non-linear response analysis on the SRS is carried out and the parameter u is estimated. ix) The damage function, given by Equation 1, is evaluated considering the u value. x) Finally, the damage level is established and classified. It is important to mention that we can use the second approach to verify the structural health condition for future seismic scenarios, thus SAVER project aims to evaluate the vulnerability previous the occurrence of an earthquake. So far, no similar system with this capability exists.

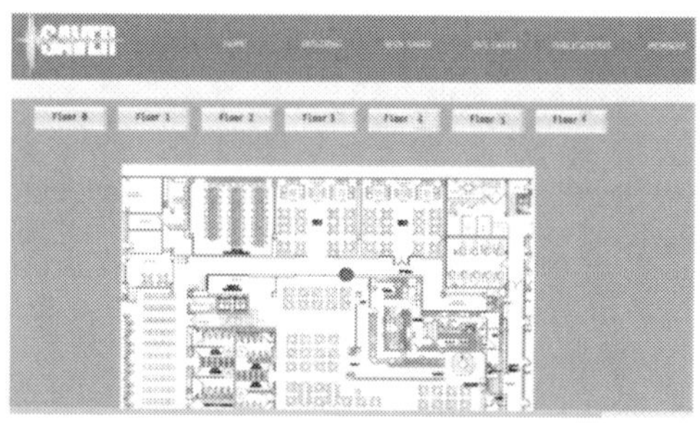

Figure 3. Section "Building".

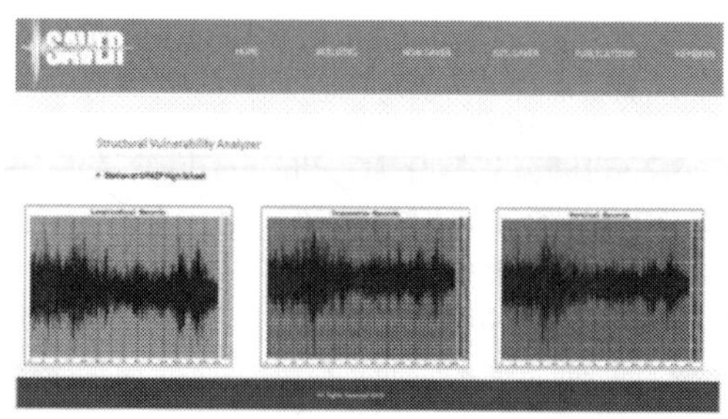

Figure 4. Section "SVS".

IV. SAVER SENSOR NODE

The sensor node is responsible for the acquisition and transmission of data for further analysis and interpretation. The node gets Acceleration (vibration) in the three axes (X, Y and Z) from the surface where the node is mounted.

The measurement signals are sent to a Microcontroller where they are processed. This is in order to interpret and to make necessary adjustments to the data. Then, the data is sent via radio-frequency devices to other sensor nodes.

The data acquired for the sensor is 12 bits information that include acceleration in 3 axes and internal temperature.

A. Prototype

The SAVER prototype consists of an Arduino UNO micro-controller that is attached with a Xbee shield. The Uno is a microcontroller board based on the ATmega328P. It has 14 digital input/output pins, 6 analog inputs, a USB connection, a power jack, an ICSP header and a reset button [12]. The micro-controller is attached with a Pololu module that contains a LSM303D accelerometer, voltage regulator, and a temperature sensor. The radio is a Xbee pro S2B operating in 2.4GHz [13], based on the range regulated by NOM-121-SCT1-2009 in the Mexican territory. To communicate with the sensor, we use SPI and Zigbee protocol.

Figure 5. Activities diagram to evaluate the Structural Vulnerability Level.

The LSM303D is a 3D digital linear acceleration sensor and a 3D digital magnetic sensor. The LSM303D includes an I2C serial bus interface that supports 100 kHz and 400 kHz in SPI serial standard interface. The measurement ranges are ± 2, 4, 6, 8, 16 g, for SAVER node the specific range is ±2g with a sensitivity of 0.061 mg/LSB. The energy demand of the LSM303D is 300 μA with a linear acceleration sensitivity change consumption vs. temperature of ±0.01% °C tested based on 25°C. The module has two advantages for the node. The first is the internal temperature sensor that gives the information every period of time and the second is the self-test option. When self-test is activated, the device output level is given by the algebraic sum of the signals produced by the acceleration acting on the sensor and by the electrostatic test-force [14]. The frequency programmed for the sensor is 100 samples per second according to seismic requirements.

In Figure 6, the final prototype is shown and includes one accelerometer and a temperature/humidity sensor.

The node was tested via PYTHON interface to log the collected data in a .txt file and to graph the force applied to each axis. With a baud rate of 9600 bauds-per-second (bps), the Arduino board acquires data in binary and then processes it to transform in g data. The resolution used was ±2 g with and Analog-Digital Converter (ADC) of 16 bits, meaning it is expected a number within ±32,767, which are max/min absolute values of the sensor. Figure 7 shows the PYTHON interface and the acquired data.

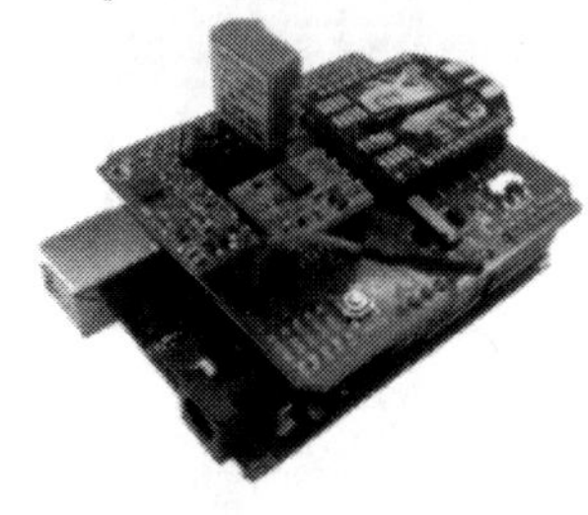

Figure 6. Final prototype of SAVER sensor node.

POINT	X AXIS	Y AXIS	Z AXIS
1	37	1623	14962
2	40	1628	14961
3	25	1640	14960
4	45	1621	14962
5	27	1662	14962
6	30	1627	14963
7	47	1603	14962
8	29	1618	14962
9	25	1665	14961
10	36	1622	14962
11	45	1676	14960
12	57	1625	14962
13	28	1627	14959
14	39	1660	14960
15	38	1614	14962
16	21	1640	14962
17	22	1625	14962
18	44	1652	14962
19	21	1653	14962
20	32	1652	14960
21	44	1665	14962
22	38	1628	14962
23	39	1649	14961
24	61	1645	14962
25	36	1640	14962

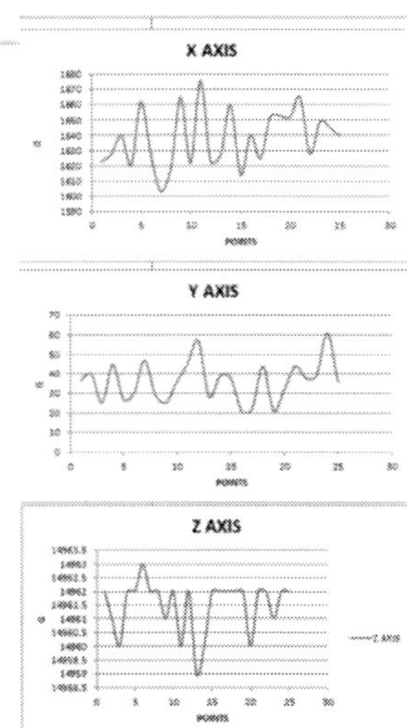

Figure 7. PYTHON Interface and Acquired Data from SAVER Sensor node.

Free Digi software, XCTU [15] is used to configure the radio devices.

In the test presented herein, devices are in factory defaults. The working cluster is presented in Figure 8.

Figure 9 shows the data obtained in each of the elements of the network. Data is observed using the serial monitor Arduino IDE. LSM303D accelerometers are connected to the End Devices. Those components obtain values corresponding to the X, Y, Z axes. Window COM4 shows the data obtained from an end device. This data is sent to the router (window COM6), which will forward it to the coordinator. Due to the coordinator is set in API mode, values obtained for it are represented in hexadecimal format. They are displayed in the window COM8. Ech column contains data of X, Y, Z axis respectively, and the Router address.

V. WSN Deployment in a Building

The expected results, in SAVER project, intend to give the basis for the analysis of buildings and gather instrumental data that can provide the necessary information to implement methods of vulnerability analysis and therefore, to estimate the seismic risk of buildings, such as hospitals or schools.

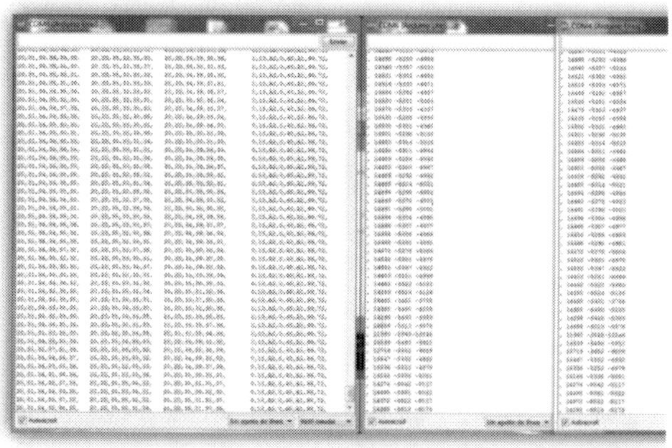

Figure 8. Data from the Coordinator, Router and End Device (Sensor Node) displayed on the Serial Monitor Software Arduino IDE.

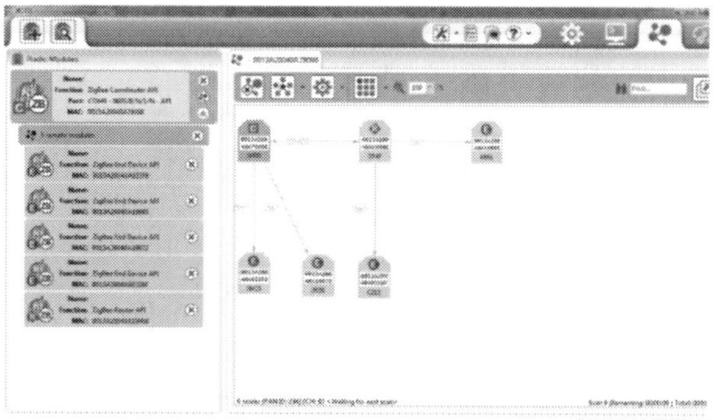

Figure 9. Cluster including: 1 Coordinator, 1 Router and 4 Sensor Nodes.

SAVER project will be validated in the building T that is located in the Central Campus of UPAEP University, Puebla City Mexico, and was built in 2007. The plan of the building has a rectangular geometry with dimensions 24 x 35 m. The building has six levels with a height of 3.15 m each one; the total height is around 19 m. The building does not have regular configuration in plan and elevation; because it presents openings and overturning along its height. The use of the building is mixed, there are two restaurants, twelve lecture rooms, a computer room, three meeting rooms, and several office areas and twelve classrooms. The structural system is based on steel resisting-moment frames (columns and beams). Some columns have circular cross sections and the other have squared cross section. The beams are based on W standard shapes. The floor systems are based on thin composite steel-concrete with 0.12 m thickness. The non-structural elements (internal walls) are based on drywalls with 0.10 m thickness. The external walls are based on masonry with 0.15 m thickness. The predominant material on the facade is glass. Figure 10 shows a view of the WSN in building T.

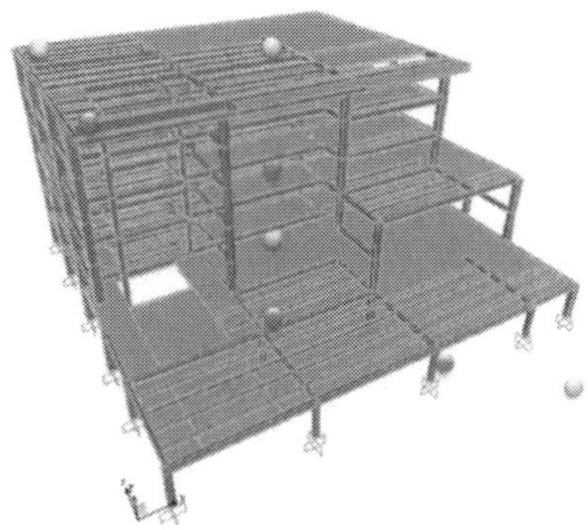

Figure 10. Lateral view of the WSN in the building T.

Ambient vibration records in three points were obtained on the building, P01 and P02, which correspond to the geometric centroid and the corner at the roof of the building, respectively; P03 corresponds to the geometric centroid at the ground floor of the building. For each point four records were taken considering 15 minutes. A tri-axial forced balanced accelerometer (Kinemetrics Basalt Accelerometer) was used as an instrument for obtaining the records (Figure 11). In this stage of our study we only present the modal analysis using the Basalt Accelerometer, we are working to implement our sensors in order to present a comparison between them.

The procedure for modal analysis presented in Figure 11 is summarized in the following lines. Frequencies and periods were determined for the first three modes: longitudinal (L), transversal (T) and rotational (R). For this, a computer program GEOPSY [16] was used in order to obtain the Amplitude Fourier Spectrum (AFS) for each record, in this way, the horizontal components of the movement (longitudinal and transversal) are only considered for computing the spectral ratios. The procedure for each of the mode is described below. Longitudinal mode (L), the numerator corresponds to the AFS in the longitudinal component obtained in the geometrical centroid at the roof level, and the denominator corresponds to the AFS in the longitudinal component obtained in the geometrical centroid at the ground floor. A similar procedure was used for transversal and rotational modes.

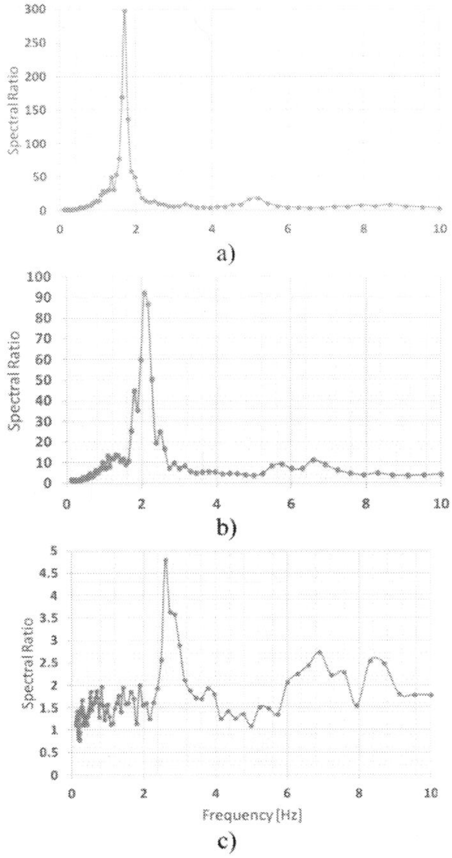

Figure 11. Spectral ratios estimated for the building using ambient vibration and a forced balanced accelerometer; a) Longitudinal mode, b) Transversal mode, and c) Rotational mode.

VI. Conclusion and Future Work

This paper presented the SAVER project. This multidisciplinary project proposes a monitoring platform that aims at estimating the structural vulnerability and preliminary seismic risk level of buildings through wireless sensor networks. This platform will offer a low-cost technology for monitoring and determining the structural health of buildings. The preliminary results of SAVER project, that have been obtained so far, were presented. In particular, (i) the SAVER architecture, (ii) the sensor node, (iii) Web platform, and (iv) the structural vulnerabilities analyzer module. This project provides two main advantages comparing to commercial solutions: (i) a low-cost, not intrusive, and flexible monitoring system, and (ii) a platform to estimate the structural vulnerability and risk level. This has paramount importance since this platform will provide useful tools and information to increase knowledge and reduce uncertainty about the buildings' performance and behavior to seismic events. Thus, with this platform we can mitigate seismic risk in buildings.

Finally, the following steps (in short-term) of this research that are intended to carry out are:

- Test mBed boards to compare manageability with the sensors.
- Compare and implement different accelerometers sensors and test humidity in locations where SAVER nodes will be located.
- Implement SAVER sensor network and test under worst-case scenario conditions.
- In relation to the Structural Vulnerabilities Analyzer module is intended to extend its functionality and implement the transfer functions between the sensor nodes. Likewise, we intend to implement the remaining modules SAVER platform. Develop and implement the models using simplified reference systems.

Acknowledgment

We would like to express my special thanks of gratitude to Alejandro E. Jarero Mora, Fernando Coyopol, who have collaborated in the SAVER Project. We also appreciate the support given by Consejo Nacional de Ciencia y Tecnología (CONACyT-FOINS) through the project number 249071.

References

[1] L. Esteva, "Basis for the formulation of seismic design criteria", (In Spanish), Publication 182, Institute of Engineering, National University of Mexico, 1968.

[2] E. Ismael-Hernández, D. I. Mora-Pino, A. Herrera-Bautista, J. A. Herrera-Hernández, M. A. Spíndola-Palacios, and M. Abhinava-Krishna, "Structural reliability for school buildings in seismic regions of Mexico using ambient vibration", Proc. 50 SE-EEE, International Conference on Earthquake Engineering, Skopje, Macedonia, Paper ID 200, 8 pages, 2013.

[3] S. Ivanovic, M. Trifunac and M. Torovska, "Ambient vibration test of structures - a review", ISET Journal of Earthquake Technology 37:407, 37:4, pp. 165-197, 2000.

[4] S. Kim, "Wireless Sensor Networks for Structural Health Monitoring", Master of Science in Computer Science, University of California at Berkeley, Department of Electrical Engineering and Computer Sciences, 2005.

[5] UC Berkeley, "Hardware Designs", [retrieved: July, 2016], from http://www.tinyos.net/scoop/special/hardware

[6] Ping Wang, Yan Yan, Gui Yun Tian, Omar Bouzid, and Zhiguo Ding, "Investigation of Wireless Sensor Networks for Structural Health Monitoring," Journal of Sensors, vol. 2012, Article ID 156329, 7 pages, 2012. doi:10.1155/2012/156329.

[7] K. C. Jeongyeup Paek, "A Wireless Sensor Network for Structural Health Monitoring: Performance and Experience", Embedded Networked Sensors, EmNetS-II, The Second IEEE Workshop on on Embedded Networked Sensors, pp. 1-10, Sydney, Australia, 2005.

[8] Guang-Dong Zhou and Ting-Hua Yi, "Recent Developments on Wireless Sensor Nerworks Technology for Bridge Health Monitoring", Mathematical problems in Engineering, V. 2013, article ID 947867, Hindawi Publishing Corporation, 2013.

[9] L. M. Rodríguez Peralta, E. Ismael Hernández, S. A. Cardeña Moreno, D. Martínez Jiménez, and A. E. Muñoz Guarneros, "Towards to a platform of monitoring based in WSN to estimate the structural health of buildings", Second European Conference on Earthquake Engineering and Seismology (2ECEES), Istanbul, Turkey, August, 2014, pp. 24-29.

[10] Structural Analysis of VulnerabilitiEs of buildings through wiReless sensor networks – SAVER, [retrieved: July, 2016], http://saver-buildings.com/

[11] E. Ismael-Hernández, O. Díaz-López and L. Esteva, "Seismic vulnerability analysis for optimum design of multistory reinforced concrete buildings", Proc. 13th World Conference on Earthquake Engineering, Vancouver, Canada. Paper 514. August, 2004.

[12] Arduino UNO, [retrieved: July, 2016], https://www.arduino.cc/en/Main/ArduinoBoardUno.

[13] XBee®/XBee-PRO® ZB RF Modules, Digi International Inc., [retrieved: July, 2016], https://www.adafruit.com/datasheets/XBee%20ZB%20User%20Manual.pdf

[14] STMicroelectronics, "LSM303D, Ultra-compact high-performance eCompass module: 3D accelerometer and 3D magnetometer", [retrieved: July,. 2016], http://www.st.com/Web/en/resource/technical/document/datasheet/DM00057547.pdf

[15] Digi International, "X-CTU (XCTU) software", [retrieved: July, 2016], http://www.digi.com/support/kbase/kbaseresultdetl?id=2125

[16] Wathelet M., (2005), "Geopsy Project", Europena Project NERIES.

Smart Services Through Smart Item Agent

Jiří Tengler, Juraj Fabuš, Peter Kolarovszki, Viktória Fabušová
The Faculty of Operation and Economics of Transport and Communications
University of Žilina
Žilina, Slovak republic
e-mail: {jiri.tengler,juraj.fabus,peter.kolarovszki,viktoria.fabusova}@fpedas.uniza.sk

Abstract—**This work deals with the realization of smart item agent, which is equipped with motion, vibration, acceleration, temperature, humidity sensors and a tracking module through GPS (Global Position System). The main reason for choosing this solution was to reduce crash delivery problems and increase the quality of services. These two problems are very interesting for postal or logistics providers. Item agent collects data during transport in the logistics process of the selected organization. The output is a summary of the data used to monitor the quality and identification of the different services that are provided to the selected type of items. The configuration is an intelligent agent addressed as follows: The heart of the agent is a programmable integrated circuit, which takes care of collecting and storing information from the sensors mentioned above. Part of the agent may also be a GSM (Global System for Mobile Communications) module, which allows us to track the shipment in real time, but at the cost of lower battery life cycle agent. The collected data will be used to improve the organization of its services and the ability to identify the failure of the service at a specific point in the logistics chain through smart sensor package. The results of our research are represented by the solution (smart agent) and also the methodology for diagnosing the quality of services in conjunction with postal or logistics operator needs.**

Keywords-postal sector; postal package; MCU; smart sensors; IoT.

I. INTRODUCTION

Quality in the field of postal services could be defined as a file of used properties of service taking into account the fact that the service would be performed according to standards and requests of customers. That is one reason why postal operators perform quality monitoring of their services [1][2].

Quality monitoring in postal services in terms of letter mails is indeed nothing special for most of postal operators nowadays. The entire process of quality monitoring deals with move tracking of selected tested postal mails at the same time in recording of their respective time stamps at the time of passing through particular transfer points. This process can be performed either by the use of barcodes technology, or more frequently, by the use of RFID technology (Radio-Frequency Identification). However, this process is performed at a large scale for postal letter mails only due to adherence of various national as well as international standards. Thus, these measurements give only information including the time and place of passage of postal correspondence. This information is sufficient for the service "delivery of correspondence" [3][4].

Besides postal letter mails that have continuous gradual decrease of volumes, there is also another group of postal products that, unlike letter mails, have managed to achieve growing tendencies – postal parcels. With its nature, this service in question allows to transport various commodities and goods of various sizes, etc. The question is what kind of other quality parameter could be considered for this service, except for those already assessed for postal letter mails. The subject of postal letter mails service is a delivery of content (mostly papers) to addressee of respective postal mail. Once the content of a letter is readable, a quality fact can be taken into account. In case of postal parcels service, it is a little bit different. The subject of postal parcels service is transport of respective product, meaning also non-paper form. If a content of a mail is article with respective function, grade and quality, let us assume that these properties should not distinguish between dispatching and delivery to final addressee. Based on a real-life experience, it is not always the case. Extensive analysis revealed potential causes of damage or loss of postal parcels [5][6]. There are several reasons for potential damage of postal parcels:

a. Inadequate packed mail (improper cover, filling, in the case of multipart goods to their poor attachment),
b. Inadequate placing of mail into transport or manipulation unit (in a real case, this means bad storing of postal parcels in postal crates, truck or even into a mailing rate),
c. Inadequate manipulation of mail (loading and unloading of the mailing, moving postal parcel through sorting system),
d. Inadequate selection of transport route (poor choice of transport communication in poor condition etc.),
e. and more [7][8].

These activities could eventually impose impairment of content, reduction of mail, reduction of functionality, grade or quality of content. The detection of the exact point of any inaccuracy occurrence is very complex, as these are detected just after their final delivery to addressee. Even though we could detect, in which phase of transport process the inadequacy in question had been made, it is not obvious which activities had preceded to it. As it has already been said, the postal service package is used for transporting various goods. From this, we can conclude that each specific item should be packaged specifically for the transport path and specifically transported. For example, glass must be transported so as not to be broken or foods, flowers, etc. should be transported in such a package, to prevent overheating and super cooling due to the weather and similar cases. It would be advantageous to have a tool that could record negative influence on the content of transported parcels. That is why this research was started, which subsequently was referred to as Smart agent.

Therefore, a question could be raised if it is suitable to perform quality monitoring also for postal parcels, allowing by its own nature a capture of more relevant data than just points and time of pass-over of postal mail through postal transport network [9][10].

In the second section, we briefly discuss about the current state of usage of smart sensors in the postal sector and we have provided a reason for the realization of the solution. In the third section, we specify the requirements and present the logical design of smart agent. The fourth section is devoted to describing the parcel shipping process for the selected postal operator. An inseparable part of this section is a design methodology for measuring of this operator. In the fifth section, we describe the measurement process itself through smart agent. The sixth section is devoted to the interpretation of the measurement results. In the final section, we highlight the value of the whole issue and suggest other possible steps.

II. Analysis of Current Situtation

There is currently a large number of technical solutions that enable logging and also forward data captured via smart sensors. These solutions are then useful in many areas of human life [11].

In our paper, we are primarily interested in the area of the postal sector. These solutions are of course applicable where it is relevant or necessary to collect this data. There is a small number of postal operators using smart sensors in their activities. A large group of the above-mentioned postal operators uses smart sensors for mapping or monitoring of their processes. A further group of postal operators uses smart sensors as an additional service for their transportation services. These are mainly packages or even transport units. The reason for developing our own solution lies in poorly scalable and modifiable commercial solution for our particular area of interest. Another reason was the involvement of students in problem solving of selected postal operator with whom we have cooperated in the development of the device.

III. Concept of Smart Agent

The current development of information-communication technologies allows to apply an electronics of minimal dimensions even into the field where we could hardly imagine to be applied in past. As a proof, let us use the application of RFID technology into almost all the fields of human activity. We can say that the whole concept of its essence is increasingly approaching the issue of Internet of Things (IoT), or a subset of it called internet processes (IoPro – Internet of Processes). In essence, this philosophy deals with the interaction of the reporting entity with different influences captured through intelligent sensors. So, not only it allows tracking the subject and the influences acting on it, but it does to some extent capture and portray the processes associated with it.

The result of our attempts has been a realization of a small electronic equipment that would be put into the postal parcel, whereby the measurement would be performed likewise at postal letter mails by use of testing parcel. Indeed, fields of application can be eventually much wider, either for postal operator or final user of respective postal service. Despite the great potential of this device, it is planned to be used only on repeated testing of specific parts of postal transportation network of postal operators. This situation affects the price for the components of the device. The purchase price ranges from 16 to 35 Euros, using components with online and offline versions.

The foundation of our equipment is energy-efficient integrated circuits, which are connected with intelligent sensors. Connected storage media were used for data storage and battery power with sufficient capacity were considered [12].

The basic components of the smart agent:

- The energy control unit MCU (microcontroller or Micro Control Unit),
- Intelligent sensors (humidity, gyroscope, acceleration, temperature)
- External storage memory,
- Battery power.

Additional components:

- GSM module (Global System for Mobile Communications),
- GPS module (Global Positioning System),
- Intelligent sensors (falls, stresses).

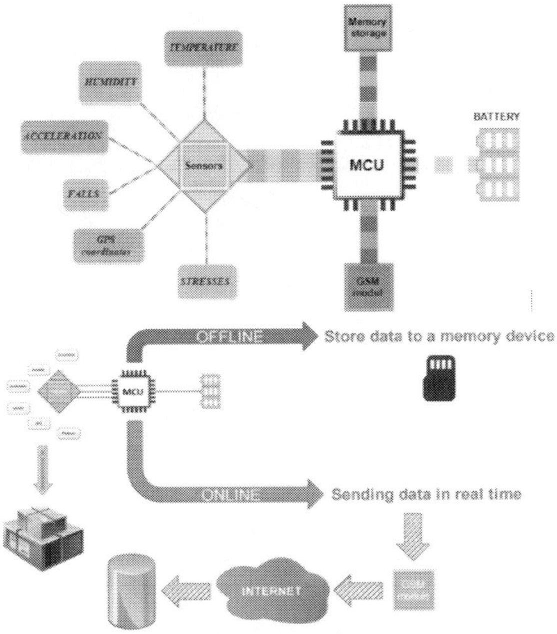

Figure 1. Concept of Smart agent.

Figure 1 represents two proposals for a smart agent. The difference is access to recorded information. The online version of the smart agent is accessing data in real time. The off-line version of the smart agent has access to the data after completion of the transport process.

IV. MEASUREMENT METODOLOGY

The main impetus for the implementation of smart tools agent was needed to identify the factors that may affect the postal parcel dispatch time after transport. After the implementation of a smart agent and related laboratory performance tests, realistic tests were performed. Our measurements were carried out at an unnamed postal operator. For the purposes of this article, we will refer to it as a general postal operator.

Now, we proceed to the preparation process and implementation of measurement. As already mentioned, the subject of our measurement was to capture the negative influences that can affect the content of postal parcels. We chose a trio of sensors. For this measurement, we activated the following sensors:

- Temperature (° C - Celsius),
- Humidity (% RH - Relative Humidity),
- Accelerometer and gyroscope ($m.s^{-2}$).

Through these sensors, we were able to determine the degree of humidity, temperature, acceleration in each vectors direction of postal parcel and of course location of the package through the gyroscope. Beside general acceleration, we also considered acceleration toward Earth´s surface. All these data were recorded on a storage medium (external memory) connected to the smart agent. Other data that were used for efficient analysis data were obtained from the postal operator. We used information on the arrival and departure times of the postal rate for loading and unloading, and of course, the approximate time of manual and mechanized handling parcels. Basic statistical methods [13] were used for processing and analysis of these values.

A. The principle of treatment of postal parcels

Phase 1. Within first phase, we obtained the pre-sorted parcels coming from processing node. In next step, the parcels were sorted at central processing center. Consequently, these consignments were transported at the appropriate time to a central processing center, where the scope of the processing node belongs. **Phase 2.** Here, the shipments are automatically processed and routed through sorting lines (see Figure 2). According to the site directed (resp. Sites) shipments, either transferred to other central processing centers (see Figure 2) or subsequently through non-mechanized (pedestrian) or mechanized centers delivered to the addressee (see the **Phase 3** Figure 2). The same procedure is repeated in other central processing centers.

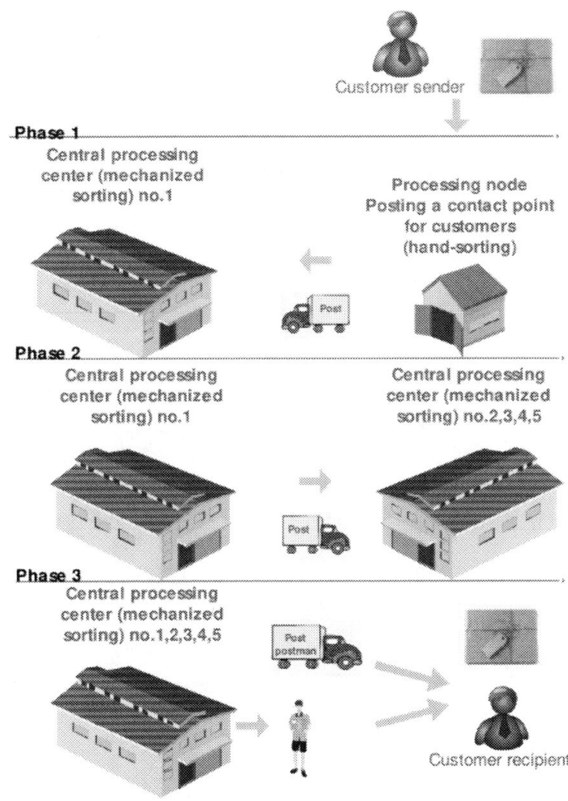

Figure 2. Principle of treatment of postal parcels.

B. Preparation of measurement

For our testing, we used standard cardboard packaging sizes 350x250x120mm. The weight of this packaging was 184 g. Our smart agent weighted 258 grams including batteries. Together, the smart agent with the envelope and the inner lining weighted 556 grams.

V. MEASUREMENT

In our measurements, we tested the consignment coming from the postal transportation network of postal operator. In our measurements we used just part of postal transport network described in Figure 2. This particular consignment is characterized in the context of Figure 2, the first phase. So, we filed a smart agent in the aforementioned packaging to transport node. From there, the shipment was transported to a central processing center and went through the whole process of sort order. Based on the agreement with the workers of sorting facility, the package was removed with a smart agent at the end of the sorting process and the following day handed over to our team. The entire schedule is more evident in Figure 3.

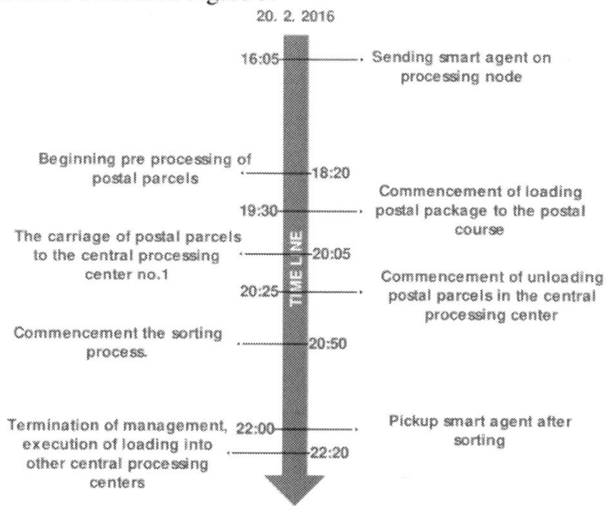

Figure 3. Time line of measurement.

The entire schedule is more evident in Figure 3. There was only one group of data which had a higher value. And this value is 7.345 ms2 and the directional vector 'Z' at position 1, see in Figure 4.

VI. MEASUREMENT RESULT

Through this measurement, we were able to obtain 339,303 groups of values. Each group contained five values. Now, we can move on to concrete results.

A. Position of the postal parcel

The whole measurement took less than six hours. During this period the consignment of several position changes. From the data analysis it is quite difficult to ascertain the exact number of these changes, because in many cases postal parcel remained on one edge. If we exclude these values, the number of position changes would equal 14th. The following Table 1 and Figure 4 represent the time duration in the different positions within the measurement.

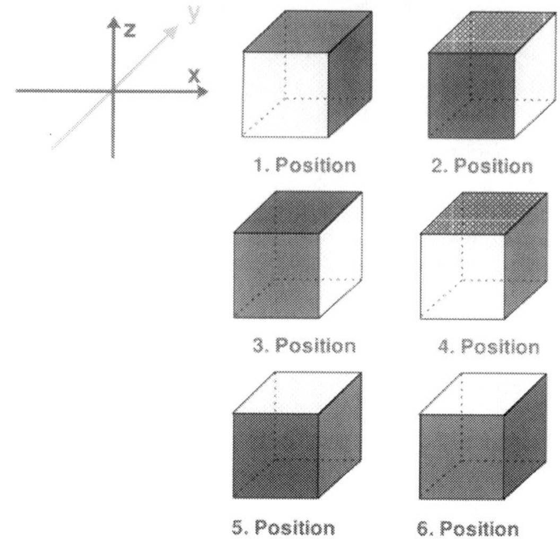

Figure 4. Position of postal parcel.

TABLE I. %TIME SPENT IN EACH POSITION

Position 1	Position 2	Position 3
71,12%	*0,62%*	*3,62%*
Position 4	**Position 5**	**Position 6**
12,24%	*3,67%*	*8,74%*

We find it very difficult to establish clear position of mailings. The reason for this is again the case that a considerable number of values are already on the edge; see Table I that represent % time which smart agent spent in each position. As expected, the largest shipment time was spent in position 1. The reason is simple, because at this postal operator, there is a regulation that says that all the postal parcel must be addressed side up. This regulation is intended to eliminate the time required for changing the position of postal parcel before entering the sorting device. This fact is important for the correct load the address side of the postal parcel by barcode reader on the sorting line. In general, this regulation sets specific parameters for postal parcels. In this regulation postal parcel need to be set with the address side facing up.

As we can see in Table I, over 28% of time spent by the smart agent was in other position at the transport process. In the largest extent, this consignment was incorrectly positioned on processing node.

B. Acceleration of postal parcel

In the laboratory testing we received information from smart agent based on acceleration. We used the same smart agent parcel for real and also laboratory conditions. From the large amounts of data, it was found that most of the data acceleration ranges from range from (0,22; 5,936) $m.s^{-2}$ in all three directional vectors.

There was only one group of data which had a higher value. And this value is 7.345 $m.s^{-2}$ and the directional vector 'Z' at position 1; see Figure 4. In terms of time data provided to us by postal operator, it could be just about downhill shipments sorting line. In the phase postal parcels moved from sorting line to belt conveyor and fell down through the slip. This value corresponds to the base data during laboratory testing. This value corresponds to a fall from a height to 80 cm, which can be described as acceptable value. That postal operator gives one specific information regarding the nature of the postal parcel and said, "Cover postal parcel must be modified so that the content of postal parcels withstands a fall from a height of 120 cm".

C. Temperature and humidity

The sudden change in temperature or excessive humidity can to some extent negatively affect the contents of the consignment. It was the reason why we used these two sensors (temperature and accelerometer sensor). On the temperature, we were interested primarily in a sudden change in temperature. We have assumed a large change in temperature between output and input into organizational units of transport. Unfortunately, this effect appeared. There were several reasons. The first of them was the precision packing of our postal parcel and the other too little variance in temperature. Summary of temperatures is given in Table II.

TABLE II. SUMMARY OF TEMPERATURE

Temp-min	Temp-max	Temp-avg
6,50	*11,00*	*8,37*

TABLE III. SUMMARY OF HUMIDITY

HR-min	HR-max	HR-avg
48%	*74%*	*66%*

Unfortunately, the same problem also affected moisture data. Each measurement depends on the forecast condition. Summary of humidity is given in Table III.

VII. CONCLUSION AND FUTURE WORK

The current results of the smart agent are foundations for its own improvement. Through this measurement, we gained a large amount of data; but, without precise identification of the specific area where data originated. In the results, we relied on data obtained from the postal operator, which ultimately appeared to be too inaccurate. Therefore, we want to equip our smart agent with additional sensors that will help us to eliminate the negative aspects of data processing. One of them is the GPS module and the second is an electronic compass. We currently have in development an on-line version of the smart agent, i.e., a version that will allow batch sending this data via services of mobile networks.

Despite all the difficulties, we believe that the concept of smart agent represents a further step not only to eliminate bottlenecks shipping process but also to connect IoT with reality.

ACKNOWLEDGMENT

This article was created to support project named as:
IV -Institutional research - 9/KS/2016 - Intelligent package as a tool for research on physical influences on parcels at selected postal operators.
E!7592 AUTOEPCIS - RFID Technology in Logistic Networks of Automotive Industry

EUREKA

Centre of Excellence for Systems and Services of Intelligent Transport II ITMS 26220120050 supported by the Research & Development Operational Programme funded by the ERDF

REFERENCES

[1] F. Beneš, L. Kubáč, P. Staša, and V. Kebo, "RFID and Augmented Reality," proceedings of the 14th International Carpathian Control Conference (ICCC): Rytro, Hotel Perła Południa, Poland, 2013, pp. 186-191.

[2] V. Hunt, A. Puglia, and M. Puglia, "RFID: A Guide to Radio Frequency Identification." New Jersey (USA), John Wiley & Sons, 2007, pp. 28-176.

[3] M. Kendra, J. Lalinská, and J. Čamaj, "Optimalization of transport and logistics processes by simulation," in ISTEC; Proceedings of the 3rd International Science, Technology and Engineering Conference, Dubai, United Arab Emirates (UAE), Dec. 2010, pp. 886-892.

[4] V. Klapita and J. Mašek, "Processes solution in the warehouse by the queuing theory application," in Horizons of Railway Transport: scientific papers, vol. 3, no. 1, 2010, pp. 64-66.

[5] P. Kolář, "Container shipping market dimensions and customer orientation in the Czech Republic," Central European Business Review, 2013, pp. 115-127.

[6] P. Kolář and J. P. Rodrigue, "Improving the Bottlenecks: The Czech Republic as a Central European Intermodal Transport and Logistics Platform," in IAME Conference 2014. Norfolk: Maritime Institute, Old Dominion University,

[7] R. Madleňák, L. Madleňáková, and J. Štefunko, "The variant approach to the optimization of the postal transportation network in the conditions of the Slovak Republic," in: Transport and Telecommunication, Vol. 16 (3), 2015, pp. 237-245.

[8] M. Maslarić, A. Groznik, and N. Brnjac, "Distribution Channel Reengineering: A Case Study." PrometTraffic&Transportation, 2012, pp. 35-43.

[9] F. Thornton and Ch. Lanthem, "RFID Security. Rockland (MA, USA),: Syngres Publishing," 2006, pp. 229.

[10] J. Vaculík and J. Tengler, "Potential of new technologies in logistics services," in CLC 2012 - Carpathian logistics congress: Jesenik, Czech Republic, 2012.

[11] J. Tengler and Z. Kolarovská, "The sensor logistics," in Company diagnostics, controlling and logistics 2016, Zuberec, University of Žilina, Slovak republic, 2016, pp. 300-305.

[12] L. Vojtěch and M. Neruda, "Application of Shielding Textiles for Increasing Safety Airborne Systems - Limitation of GSM Interference," in The Ninth International Conference on Networks (ICN 2010). Los Alamitos: IEEE Computer Society, 2010, pp. 157-161.

[13] H. Bakytová, M. Urgot, O. Konštelová, "Základy štatistiky." Bratislava (Slovak republic), publishing: Alfa, 1975, pp. 92-111.

Intelligent Shopping Trolley (IST) System by WSN to Support Hypermarket IoT Service

You-Chiun Wang and Chang-Chen Yang
Department of Computer Science and Engineering
National Sun Yat-sen University
Kaohsiung, Taiwan, R.O.C.
Email: ycwang@cse.nsysu.edu.tw; m003040070@student.nsysu.edu.tw

Abstract—**The Internet of Things (IoT) technology allows physical objects integrated with sensors to monitor and communicate with the outside world. The paper develops an Intelligent Shopping Trolley (IST) system to provide IoT service in a hypermarket. Each trolley is equipped with sensing modules to cooperatively monitor its customer's behavior. The sensing data is sent to a server through the ZigBee network to analyze the customer's preference. Then, the retailer can notify the customer of sales information about interesting products in real time. Also, a customer can query the trolley for product data such as where it is. Then, the system schedules an obstacle-free shortest path to guide that customer. The paper reports both system design and implementation experience. A prototype is also deployed in a real-life hypermarket to verify the feasibility of IST system.**

Keywords–customer behavior; indoor navigation; Internet of Things (IoT); shopping trolley; ZigBee.

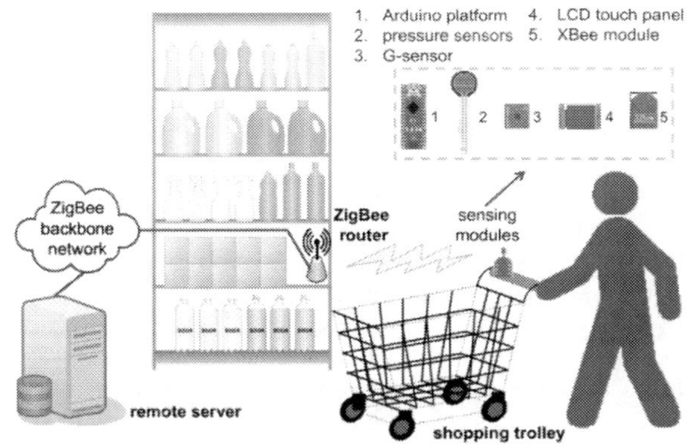

Figure 1. The architecture of our IST system.

I. INTRODUCTION

Today, Internet of Things (IoT) has attracted considerable attention from academic, industrial, and commercial communities. It is a burgeoning technology to let devices and physical objects connect with each other by their sensing, communicating, and processing capabilities. Wireless Sensor Network (WSN) is a critical technique of IoT [1], which uses many sensor nodes to jointly monitor the environment. WSN has various applications such as animal tracking, oceanic exploration, traffic control, and urban monitoring [2]. The great progress of WSN, together with other techniques like big data, social network, and cloud computing, promote the development of IoT [3].

This paper introduces IoT to hypermarkets by exploiting WSN's sensing ability, as shopping plays an important role in our economic activity. Many retailers use member cards to record the products sold to customers, and analyze their preference accordingly. However, this method is *offline*, in the sense that the retailer has no idea what products the customers may have interest (but did not buy) when they were shopping in the hypermarket. Some systems such as video surveillance could monitor a customer's activity [4]. However, it requires huge computation to conduct analysis [5]. Besides, such systems cannot provide real-time interaction with customers. Therefore, our goal is to develop an online, interactive system to detect the preference of customers and feed them back in real time, so as to assist customers when they are shopping.

Figure 1 gives the architecture of our Intelligent Shopping Trolley (IST) system by WSN to provide hypermarket IoT service. We equip a trolley with multiple sensing modules to monitor the behavior of its customer. Each product shelf is also placed with wireless routers. These routers, together with trolleys, connect with each other via the ZigBee protocol, and organize a *hybrid WSN* [6] in the hypermarket for communication and detection purposes. Specifically, when a customer is using the trolley, its sensing modules can monitor the customer's activities (e.g., is the customer walking or stopping?). The sensing data is sent to the remote server via a ZigBee router placed on the product shelf that the customer visits. Thus, the retailer can analyze the consumer's behavior and provide feedback to him/her about sales information. For example, when the trolley detects that its customer is stopping by some product shelf for a while, the server can quickly notify the customer of the promotion or discount for the products on that shelf. It can be realized by showing information on the trolley's Liquid Crystal Display (LCD) touch panel. In this way, the retailer could increase the opportunity that a customer is willing to buy the product, since the information of sales promotion is sent to the customer at the right time.

Moreover, the IST system also helps a customer find the desired product and guide him/her to the product's location. Specifically, conventional hypermarkets are operated by self-service. Customers search for the products on their own, place them in trolleys, and proceed to the checkout counters. However, without any assistance, finding the products may be time-consuming [7]. Although Global Positioning System (GPS) is a mature technology to guide people, it is hard to use GPS in a hypermarket due to satellite signal loss. Thus, we develop a lightweight guiding scheme modified from the popular A* algorithm [8]. Our scheme models the hypermarket by grids and computes the shortest path to help a customer detour obstacles and crowds, so that he/she can easily get the desired product. Consequently, we could improve the shopping experience of that customer.

Our contribution is to introduce WSN's sensing capability to common shopping trolleys, and apply IoT to the daily shopping in hypermarkets. The retailer can use our IST system to analyze customers' behavior in real time, and send various information like sales promotion, catalogue, or advertisement to customers to increase potential sales. Besides, IST can suggest the shortest, obstacle/crowd-free path for a customer to get the interesting product in an easy way. Both system design and implementation detail are presented in this paper. We will also develop a prototype and deploy it in the Carrefour hypermarket to demonstrate the proposed idea.

The rest of this paper is organized as follows. The related work is given in Section II. Section III proposes our IST system. Section IV details the hardware implementation. Our prototyping experience is described in Section V. Finally, Section VI concludes this paper and gives some future work.

II. RELATED WORK

Several studies use image or signal processing to facilitate shopping. Tomizawa et al. [9] develop a shopping robot to purchase things for the people who cannot go by themselves to the hypermarket. A user can select the desired product and ask the robot to pick up that product for checkout. To do so, the robot recognizes the target object by a laser range finder and a camera, and uses its hand to grab the recognized object. In [10], volunteers wear electroencephalogram (EEG) caps and eye-tracking systems to do shopping. EEG helps neurologists to observe the brain activity, while the eye-tracking system allows them to see the volunteer's field of view. The data is used to measure the effect of marketing campaigns. Obviously, these studies have different goals with our work.

In [7], store items are tagged with Radio Frequency IDentification (RFID) to identify their positions. This data is registered to an information retrieval system. Then, customers can query the system to search and locate their desired items. Kitazawa et al. [11] design an agent-based in-store simulator to model the shopping behavior of customers. They equip market trolleys and shopping places with RFID tags. Then, purchased items are collected with the point of sales information gathered at the cash desk. The shopping paths and purchase data can be fed as parameters of the simulator to improve its performance. However, [7] and [11] aim at back-end management (i.e., item administration or simulation), rather than front-end management to monitor the behavior of customers.

Some work uses RFID to guide shoppers. In [12], customers carry public cards for identification and mobile phones for navigation. As products are tagged with RFID, each customer can query the product data (e.g., name, manufacturer, and price) via the phone. The system also guides a customer to get the interesting product by sending a route to the phone. Then, the customer can use the card to do checkout. The work of [13] aims at assisting visually impaired people in shopping. To do so, RFID is used to identify products, and people are navigated by audio instructions to obtain products. Besides, an autonomous billing system is built by using ZigBee to send the information. However, neither [12] nor [13] consider analyzing customers' preference and proving them feedback.

Using sensors to enhance shopping trolleys is also discussed. In [14], trolleys are equipped with sensors to record their moving distances and orientations, so as to track customers. Besides, when detecting obstacles, the trolley's velocity can be slowed down for safety. Rupanagudi et al. [15] attach a camera on each trolley to guide a customer based on the shopping list. To simplify image processing, the hypermarket is mapped with only three colors (i.e., blue, light orange, and dark orange). Then, each trolley identifies the color read from its camera to estimate the position. However, these studies do not use trolleys to analyze customers' preference on products.

On the contrary, our work discusses how to apply IoT to hypermarkets through WSN-based trolleys. By detecting the activity of a customer related to the trolley, we can analyze the preference of that customer. Moreover, an efficient guiding scheme is developed to help customers detour obstacles and beat the crowds, so as to improve their shopping experience. These features distinguish our work from others.

III. IST SYSTEM DESIGN

This section presents the IST system for hypermarket IoT service. We first give the whole picture of our system. Then, we discuss how to analyze customers' behavior via shopping trolleys, and guide them in the hypermarket.

A. System Architecture

Figure 1 presents the IST architecture with three components: *shopping trolleys*, *ZigBee routers*, and a *remote server*. Through ZigBee communication, they form a hybrid WSN in the hypermarket. Specifically, each trolley is a *mobile sensor* that moves in the WSN and produces sensing data, while ZigBee routers act as *static sensors* to provide connectivity and relay messages [16]. Then, the server is a *sink node* to gather data from trolleys and send commands to the network. Below, we detail the function of each component.

1) Shopping Trolley: A trolley plays the role of *user interface* for each customer. It detects the customer's movement and checks if he/she is griping the trolley's handle. Such data is sent to the remote server to analyze the preference of that customer. Based on the analysis result, the server sends relevant information (e.g., sales promotion or activities) to the customer. Moreover, the customer can query the location of desired product via the trolley, and our system then schedules a walking path to help the customer detour obstacles and crowds.

To do so, each trolley has five sensing modules shown in Figure 1. First, the *Arduino platform* works like a motherboard to connect all modules. Specifically, both pressure sensors and G-sensor periodically send their sensing values to Arduino. It also establishes full-duplex links with the LCD touch panel and XBee module to interact with the customer and connect with ZigBee routers, respectively. Besides, Arduino processes input and sensing data, deals with the server's commands, and sends its computation results to other modules for action. Thus, Arduino is also viewed as the main controller of a trolley.

Second, two *pressure sensors* are installed on the trolley's handle to detect whether the customer is using the trolley. Such a sensor can dynamically change its electric resistance based on the pressure exerted on it. When the customer is griping the handle, he/she is exerting a large amount of pressure to the sensor, which results in resistance decrease and voltage increase. Thus, by detecting the voltage change, the trolley can determine whether the customer is griping (and using) it.

Third, the *G-sensor* detects the acceleration G_X, G_Y, and G_Z on the X, Y, and Z axes, respectively. When the trolley stops, its G-sensor reports that $G_X = 0$, $G_Y = 0$, and $G_Z < 0$ (i.e., the acceleration direction on the Z axis is toward earth). When the trolley is moving, we have $G_X \neq 0$ or $G_Y \neq 0$, depending on the direction. With this property, the G-sensor can determine the status of a trolley (i.e., moving or stopping), and also estimate its moving direction.

Fourth, the *LCD touch panel* is an I/O device for a customer to interact with the trolley. The customer can use LCD to search for desired products. In addition, when the server replies the sales promotion or suggested path to the trolley, this information will be shown on LCD.

Finally, the *XBee module* provides communication for a trolley. It follows the IEEE 802.15.4 standard [17] to support low-power transmission ($<$2mW), and adjusts transmission power to provide different range (40$\sim$120m). The trolley uses its XBee to join the hypermarket WSN and exchange messages with a nearby ZigBee router.

2) ZigBee Routers: We place each product shelf with ZigBee routers to provide full coverage [18] of the hypermarket. A router is given one unique ID (e.g., MAC address) for identification. Once a router finds that a trolley is stopping at its shelf, it can notify the server that the customer may have interest in some products. Besides, all routers organize themselves into WSN backbone for communication. A trolley can report its sensing data to the server via the visiting router. The server also uses the backbone to send commands to an individual trolley, or broadcast information to the WSN. We use the Ad-hoc On-demand Distance Vector (AODV) protocol [19] to route packets in the network. Moreover, the routers help estimate the positions of trolleys. So, our system can track every trolley in the hypermarket.

3) Remote Server: The server is the decision center of our system. It connects to the retailer's database to access product information (e.g., prices, discounts, and activities). The server has four missions. First, it checks the health of all components. When there is something wrong with a component, the server notifies an employee to examine that component. To do so, the server records for each component the most recent message sent from it. If a component did not send any message for a threshold time (e.g., 1 hour), the server sends a Hello message to that component and checks if any response is returned. After several failed tries (e.g., 3 times), the server marks that component as broken, and sends a notification to employees. The duration of two successive Hello messages can be set to, for example, 1 minute.

Second, when a trolley transmits its sensing data to the server, the server will analyze the customer's behavior accordingly. The analysis is conducted based on the combination of two actions: 1) the customer is griping the trolley's handle and 2) the trolley is moving. Such analysis result can be recorded in the retailer's database. For example, the retailer can count the number of times that each kind of products have ever been reviewed by customers. Then, the retailer can gather statistics for the reference to adjust its marketing strategy. The analysis is online, which means that the retailer can observe the preference of customers when they are shopping in the hypermarket. Then, the retailer can find out potentially popular products. Moreover, since each trolley reports only its status and there is no linkage between the customer's personal data and that trolley, we can protect the privacy of customers.

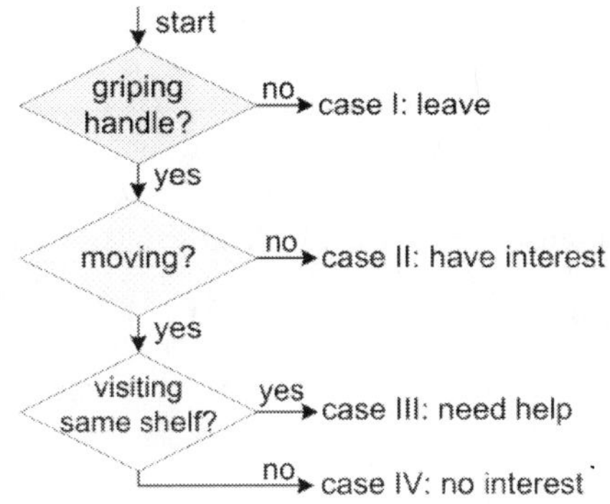

Figure 2. The flowchart to determine the behavior of a customer.

Third, if the server finds that a customer has interest in some product (e.g., he/she stops by a product shelf for a while), it can refer to the database to see if there is sales promotion for the product. If so, the server can unicast such information to the trolley via AODV. Moreover, the server can announce messages to a subset of nodes in WSN. In this case, the server can construct a multicast tree [20] to send its data more efficiently.

Finally, as ZigBee routers will estimate the position of each trolley, it allows the server to keep track of the distribution of trolleys in the hypermarket. Then, once a customer queries a walking path to get the desired product, the server can take such distribution as reference to find a shortest path to detour obstacles and beat the crowds. In Section III-C, we will discuss how to efficiently find such a path.

B. Determining Behavior of Customers

Without using cameras to monitor the behavior of customers, which may involve in complex image processing, we adopt both pressure sensors and G-sensor equipped on each trolley to conduct the monitoring job.

Figure 2 gives the flowchart to determine the behavior of a customer by the trolley. In each case, the remote server can feed back some information to the customer, which is shown on the trolley's LCD panel. Below, we list the four cases:

I. The customer may leave to do something (e.g., looking for products). In this case, the relationship between customer and trolley is temporarily broken. When the customer returns, the trolley can show the advertisement of nearby products to draw his/her attention. However, if the trolley's handle is not gripped for a long time (e.g., $\geq$ 30 minutes), we treat the trolley as unused, so the server will notify an employee to retrieve that trolley.

II. There is a high possibility that the customer is checking some product, which means that he/she may have interest in that product. Thus, the server can send the customer sales promotion or special activity (according to the retailer's database), so as to increase the purchase intention.

III. The customer has visited the same product shelves multiple times. It means that the customer is searching for some products and may require help. So, the server can ask nearby employees to assist that customer.

IV. The customer may be walking aimlessly and have no interest in nearby products. Therefore, we can show the product catalogue for his/her reference.

When the trolley detects that the customer has interest in certain products, the server can also record the statistics for these products in the database. It helps the retailer to adjust sales policy or product arrangement in the future.

C. Navigating Customers in the Hypermarket

There are *fixed* and *movable* obstacles in a hypermarket. Fixed obstacles include walls and product shelves, while movable obstacles are crowds (i.e., other trolleys). A customer cannot cross fixed obstacles, but he/she may pass through a region with only one or two trolleys. To help a customer detour obstacles and fast get the desired product, we model the hypermarket into grids, where the grid length allows two trolleys to pass through. Since each trolley periodically reports its position to the server, the server can keep track of the number of trolleys in each grid. Then, we define a *crowded grid* to be a grid with more than two trolleys. It is difficult for the customer to move the trolley through such grids.

Given the customer's location (denoted by grid g_s) and the destination (denoted by grid g_e), we modify the A* algorithm to find an obstacle-free shortest path. Specifically, we compute the cost to reach each grid g_k by:

$$\hat{C}(k) = \hat{A}(k) + \hat{M}(k), \tag{1}$$

where $\hat{A}(k)$ is the accumulative cost from g_s to g_k, and $\hat{M}(k)$ is the minimum cost from g_k to g_e. We define the cost of a crowded grid and a grid with fixed obstacle to ∞. Thus, the walking path will not contain such grids, and the customer can detour obstacles and crowds. Then, we conduct the following steps to find the shortest path:

1. Let sets L_C and L_S contain candidate and selected grids, respectively. Initially, $L_C = \{g_s\}$ and $L_S = \emptyset$.
2. Select the grid g_k from L_C that has the minimum cost $\hat{C}(k)$. However, if no grid can be found, there is no path between g_s and g_e. So, the scheme terminates.
3. We calculate the cost of each adjacent grid by (1). If the grid with a finite cost is not included in L_S, we add it to L_C. Then, we view g_k as the starting grid, remove it from L_C, and add it to L_S.
4. Steps 2 and 3 are repeated until we select g_e from L_C. Then, we add g_e to L_S.
5. The walking path is included in L_S. However, it may contain some redundant grids. Therefore, we traverse all grids in L_S to obtain the final (shortest) path.

Notice that trolleys will dynamically move in the hypermarket. When a customer is walking along the suggested path but some grids on the residual path become crowded, we can adaptively compute a new path by the above scheme for the customer.

IV. Hardware Implementation

In this section, we discuss the hardware implementation of IST. Figure 3 shows the sensing modules installed on a shopping trolley. We use Arduino Mega2560 [21] to coordinate all modules, which has a 16MHz ATmega2560 microcontroller, 8KB Static Random Access Memory (SRAM),

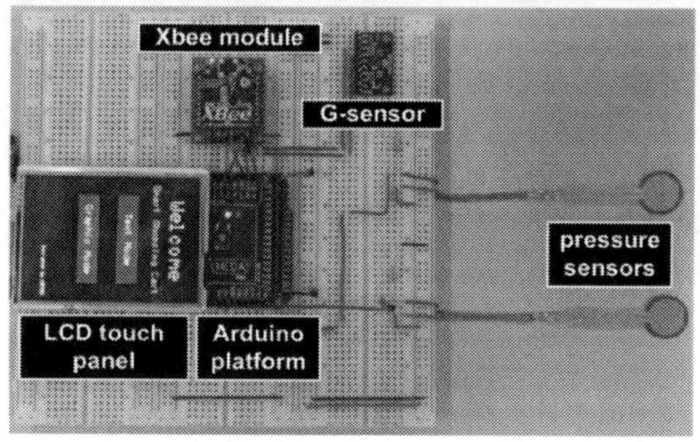

Figure 3. The sensing modules installed on a shopping trolley.

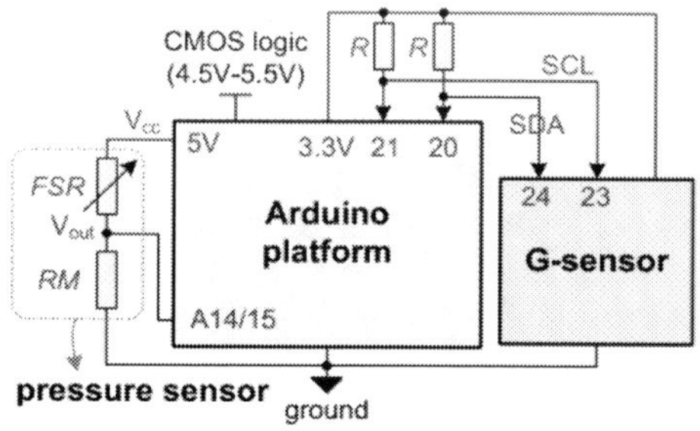

(a) pressure sensor and G-sensor

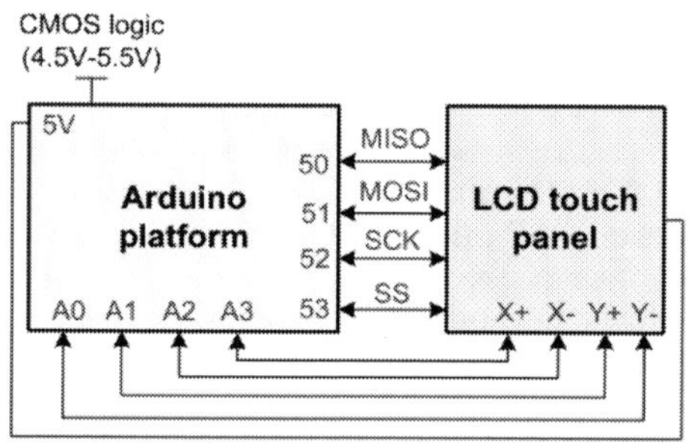

(b) LCD touch panel

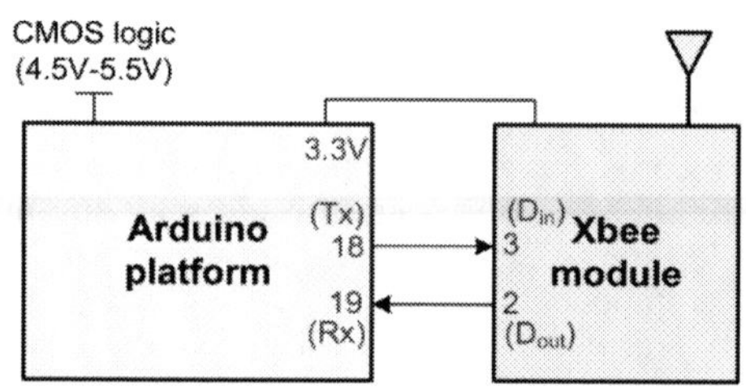

(c) XBee module

Figure 4. The circuit connections between the Arduino platform and other modules, where 'CMOS logic' denotes the external circuit.

4KB Electrically Erasable Programmable Read Only Memory (EEPROM), and 256KB flash memory. Its operating voltage is 5V, and the input voltage is 7∼12V. Arduino also supports multiple protocols for IC communication, such as Inter Integrated Circuit (I^2C) and Serial Peripheral Interface (SPI).

Arduino uses 54 digital I/O pins and 16 analog pins for communication, where the direct current for an I/O pin and a 3.3V pin is 40 and 50mA, respectively. Figure 4 shows the circuit connections between Arduino and other modules.

Specifically, Arduino supports a *reference voltage* V_{cc} to the two pressure sensors, and uses A14 and A15 analog pins to get the *output voltage* V_{out} from them, as shown in Figure 4(a). The operating principle of a pressure sensor is the *voltage divider rule* [22]:

$$V_{out} = \frac{RM}{FSR + RM} \times V_{cc}, \quad (2)$$

where FSR and RM are changeable and fixed resistances, respectively. When a customer gives a force to the pressure sensor, FSR will decrease. Based on (2), it results in the increase of V_{out}. Then, by reading V_{out} from A14 and A15 pins, Arduino can detect whether the customer is holding the trolley. In the implementation, we use Sparkfun FSR402 force-sensitive resistor [23] to be the pressure sensor, where $FSR = 1\text{M}\Omega$ (initially) and $RM = 10\text{K}\Omega$ ($\pm 0.25\%$).

Figure 4(a) also shows how to connect Arduino with a G-sensor, where 'R' denotes a resistance. G-sensor is used to detect the trolley's movement by estimating the acceleration along three axes. To obtain the estimation, Arduino uses its 20th and 21st pins to read the data from both Serial Data Line (SDA) and Serial Clock Line (SCL) of the G-sensor, respectively. The communication between Arduino and G-sensor follows the I^2C protocol. Besides, Arduino supports 3.3V operating voltage to trigger the G-sensor. In our implementation, we adopt InvenSense MPU9250 accelerometer [24] as G-sensor.

Each trolley has an LCD touch panel to interact with its customer. Here, we use Thin Film Transistor (TFT) touch shield [25]. It has a 2.8-inch display with 240×320 resolution and 18bit colors. The display is a 4-wire resistive touch screen, and has a visual angle of $60° \sim 120°$. The shield has an ILI9341 controller with built-in RAM buffer, and 8bit digital interface plus 4 control lines. Arduino uses the SPI protocol to communicate with LCD, where Arduino serves as the master while LCD acts as the slave. To instruct LCD, Arduino uses its 50th, 51st, 52nd, and 53rd pins to respectively connect LCD's controlling pins: Master Input Slave Output (MISO), Master Output Slave Input (MOSI), Serial ClocK (SCK), and Slave Select (SS). LCD uses four data pins, X+, X−, Y+, and Y−, to report the position where the customer touches the screen. Thus, Arduino connects these pins via its A0, A1, A2, and A3 analog pins to get the data, as shown in Figure 4(b).

Through the XBee module, Arduino can communicate with a nearby router. We use XBee Series2 [26] in our implementation. It provides a transmission distance of 40m and 120m indoors and outdoors, respectively. The supply voltage is $2.1 \sim 3.6$V, and the transmission power is 2mW. XBee operates on the 2.4GHz band, and supports point-to-point, star, and mesh topologies. The receiver sensitivity is -96dBm and the data rate is 250Kbps. We use two XBee pins for communication: *data out* (D_{out}, the 2nd pin) and *data in* (D_{in}, the 3rd pin). Thus, Arduino uses the 18th and 19th pins to connect with XBee, as shown in Figure 4(c).

V. PROTOTYPING EXPERIENCE

We demonstrate our IST system in Carrefour, as shown in Figure 5. All sensing modules are encapsulated in a control box for easy deployment, and we entwine pressure sensors on the trolley's handle to detect the usage by a customer, as illustrated in Figure 5(a). A customer can push the trolley to do shopping

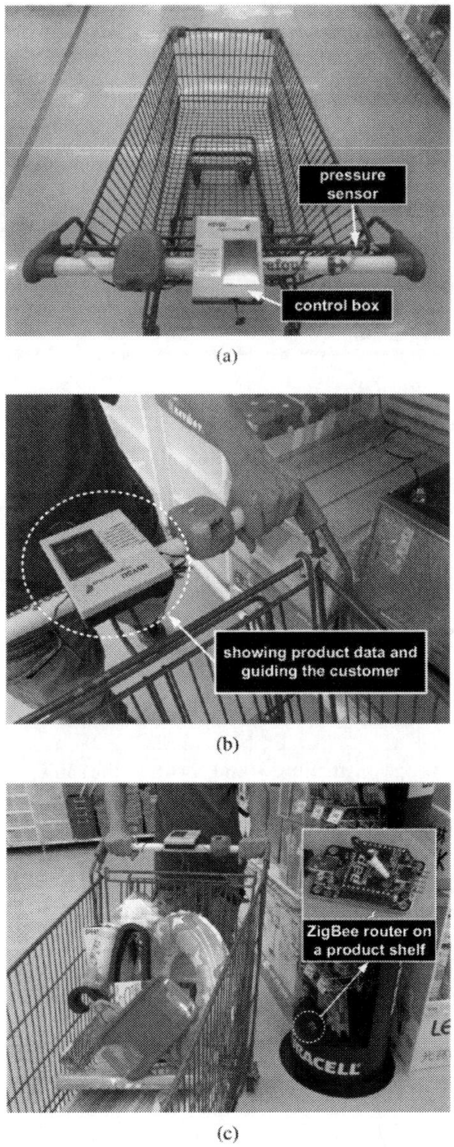

Figure 5. IST system deployment in Carrefour: (a) encapsulate all components into a control box, (b) the LCD touch panel shows the product data and guide the customer (by the moving direction), and (c) the shopping trolley communicates with the ZigBee router placed in a product shelf.

in the hypermarket. Then, the trolley will not only show the product-discount information when the customer stops to check products, but also navigate the customer via an arrow sign, as presented in Figure 5(b). Besides, when the customer moves close to a product shelf, the trolley can exchange the data with a ZigBee router, as shown in Figure 5(c). Therefore, the server can obtain the up-to-date position of that trolley. Through this way, we can apply the IoT technology to our daily shopping in hypermarkets.

Moreover, we develop a Java-based interface at the server to calculate the walking path for each customer, as Figure 6 shows. The layout of product shelves refers to Carrefour and we divide the hypermarket into 22×15 grids. A customer can select two non-obstacle grids to be g_s and g_e, which are

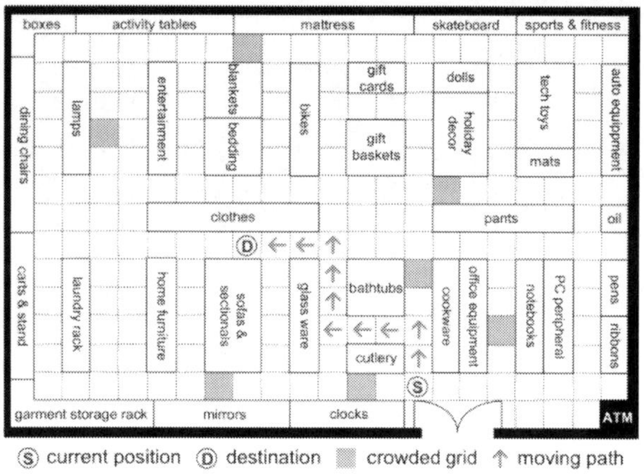

Figure 6. An interface (at the server) to show the walking path for a customer.

respectively denoted by 'S' and 'D'. Crowded grids (i.e., ≥ 3 trolleys) are marked by gray, and our scheme will then prevent the customer from passing through these grids. Finally, the walking path is shown on the interface by arrows.

VI. Conclusion and Future Work

Many retailers use member cards to record the preference of customers, but the method is offline and non-interactive. Therefore, this paper embeds WSN's sensing ability in common shopping trolleys, and brings the IoT technology to our daily shopping. Our sensor-based trolley can monitor the behavior of each customer when he/she is shopping in a hypermarket. The retailer can thus quickly provide necessary information to the customers who have interest in some products. Besides, we also develop a navigation scheme from A* to help customers easily get their desired products. Both the designing architecture and implementation detail of our IST system are reported. Furthermore, we also test a prototype in Carrefour to demonstrate its practicability.

For the future direction, we will integrate IST with some existing systems such as visual surveillance or RFID to improve the accuracy of monitoring customers' behavior and preference. In addition, we can apply the energy harvesting technique to extend the system lifetime. One possibility is to obtain energy from the trolley wheel's movement.

Acknowledgements

You-Chiun Wang's research is co-sponsored by the Ministry of Science and Technology under Grant No. MOST 104-2221-E-110-036-MY2 and MOST 104-2628-E-110-001-MY2, Taiwan.

References

[1] A. Al-Fuqaha, M. Guizani, M. Mohammadi, M. Aledhari, and M. Ayyash, "Internet of Things: a survey on enabling technologies, protocols, and applications," IEEE Communications Surveys & Tutorials, vol. 17, no. 4, 2015, pp. 2347–2376.

[2] Y. C. Wang, "Mobile sensor networks: system hardware and dispatch software," ACM Computing Surveys, vol. 47, no. 1, 2014, pp. 12:1–12:36.

[3] F. daCosta, Rethinking the Internet of Things: A Scalable Approach to Connecting Everything. New York: Apress, 2013.

[4] W. Lao, J. Han, and P. H. N. de With, "Automatic video-based human motion analyzer for consumer surveillance system," IEEE Transactions on Consumer Electronics, vol. 55, no. 2, 2009, pp. 591–598.

[5] Y. C. Tseng, Y. C. Wang, K. Y. Cheng, and Y. Y. Hsieh, "iMouse: an integrated mobile surveillance and wireless sensor system," IEEE Computer, vol. 40, no. 6, 2007, pp. 60–66.

[6] Y. C. Wang, "A two-phase dispatch heuristic to schedule the movement of multi-attribute mobile sensors in a hybrid wireless sensor network," IEEE Transactions on Mobile Computing, vol. 13, no. 4, 2014, pp. 709–722.

[7] D. Hicks, K. Mannix, H. M. Bowles, and B. J. Gao, "SmartMart: IoT-based in-store mapping for mobile devices," in International Conference on Collaborative Computing: Networking, Applications and Worksharing, 2013, pp. 616–621.

[8] H. Wang, J. Zhou, G. Zheng, and Y. Liang, "HAS: hierarchical A-star algorithm for big map navigation in special areas," in International Conference on Digital Home, 2014, pp. 222–225.

[9] T. Tomizawa, K. Ohba, A. Ohya, and S. Yuta, "Remote food shopping robot system in a supermarket–realization of the shopping task from remote places," in IEEE International Conference on Mechatronics and Automation, 2007, pp. 1771–1776.

[10] S. F. Sands and J. A. Sands, "Recording brain waves at the supermarket: what can we learn from a shopper's brain?" IEEE Pulse, vol. 3, no. 3, 2012, pp. 34–37.

[11] M. Kitazawa, M. Takahashi, T. Yamada, and T. Terano, "Analyzing supermarket shopping paths from indirect observation and simulation study," in IEEE International Conference on Signal-Image Technology & Internet-Based Systems, 2013, pp. 939–943.

[12] R. Chen, L. Peng, and Y. Qin, "Supermarket shopping guide system based on Internet of things," in International Conference on Wireless Sensor Network, 2010, pp. 17–20.

[13] M. Mathankumar and N. Sugandhi, "A low cost smart shopping facilitator for visually impaired," in International Conference on Advances in Computing, Communications and Informatics, 2013, pp. 1088–1092.

[14] S. Gai, E. J. Jung, and B. J. Yi, "Localization algorithm based on Zigbee wireless sensor network with application to an active shopping cart," in IEEE International Conference on Intelligent Robots and Systems, 2014, pp. 4571–4576.

[15] S. R. Rupanagudi et al., "A novel video processing based cost effective smart trolley system for supermarkets using FPGA," in International Conference on Communication, Information & Computing Technology, 2015, pp. 1–6.

[16] Y. C. Wang, F. J. Wu, and Y. C. Tseng, "Mobility management algorithms and applications for mobile sensor networks," Wireless Communications and Mobile Computing, vol. 12, no. 1, 2012, pp. 7–21.

[17] IEEE Std 802.15.4-2011, "IEEE standard for local and metropolitan area networks–part 15.4: low-rate wireless personal area networks (LR-WPANs)," 2011.

[18] Y. C. Wang, C. C. Hu, and Y. C. Tseng, "Efficient deployment algorithms for ensuring coverage and connectivity of wireless sensor networks," in IEEE Wireless Internet Conference, 2005, pp. 114–121.

[19] C. E. Perkins and E. M. Royer, "Ad-hoc on-demand distance vector routing," in IEEE Workshop on Mobile Computing Systems and Applications, 1999, pp. 90–100.

[20] X. Xiang, X. Wang, and Y. Yang, "Supporting efficient and scalable multicasting over mobile ad hoc networks," IEEE Transactions on Mobile Computing, vol. 10, no. 4, 2011, pp. 544–559.

[21] Arduino, http://www.arduino.cc/, retrieved: June 2016.

[22] C. K. Alexander and M. N. O. Sadiku, Fundamentals of Electric Circuits. New York: McGraw-Hill Education, 2012.

[23] Sparkfun, https://www.sparkfun.com/, retrieved: June 2016.

[24] InvenSense, http://store.invensense.com/, retrieved: June 2016.

[25] Adafruit, http://www.adafruit.com/, retrieved: June 2016.

[26] Digi International, http://www.digi.com/, retrieved: June 2016.

Time Synchronization on Android Devices for Mobile Construction Assessment

Maik Benndorf and Thomas Haenselmann
University Of Applied Sciences Mittweida
Faculty of Applied Computer Sciences & Biosciences
Germany, Mittweida 09648
Email: {benndorf,thomas.haenselmann}@hs-mittweida.de

Abstract—**Within this work we aim to assess the structural integrity of buildings in the case of catastrophic events using several off-the shelf smart phones featuring vibration sensors. In order to compare the vibration samples obtained from different devices, precisely synchronized clocks are needed. In this article, we suggest how to align clocks based on sound beacons to mutually take clock drift and skew into account, in a precision which can be expected from traditional synchronization approaches like Network Time Protocol (NTP).**

Keywords–sensor networks; time synchronization; clock skew; clock drift

I. Introduction

In cases of natural disasters like flooding, timely access to information about transport infrastructure is crucial for the first-aider. In particular, bridges could be fit for traffic, partially usable or be completely destroyed. During this research project we scrutinize, whether destruction influences the resonance frequency of a bridge. For that reason, we applied vibrometers of the type "Beitzer System 9000" [1].

Figure 1. This figure shows the bridge for our tests.

However, in many cases such a device is not available in a timely manner in the areas struck by a disaster. Nonetheless, information about the state of transport routes is crucial for affected people as well as for aid organizations [2]. Hence, we scrutinized how the experiment mentioned above can be conducted with the help of acceleration sensors in mobile phones. During our experiments, the sensors were positioned at different points on the surface and the beams of the bridge. In order to compare vibrations of the devices every vibrometer is at least equipped with two mobile phones. Figure 1 shows the bridge of our tests. The bridge has a length of 30 meters, a width of 4 meters and weighs about 75 tons.

Figure 2 shows the recorded vibrations caused by a walking pedestrian. A large difference between both systems is the sample rate. While vibrometers measure with approximately 2,500 Hz, the sensors of mobile phones only

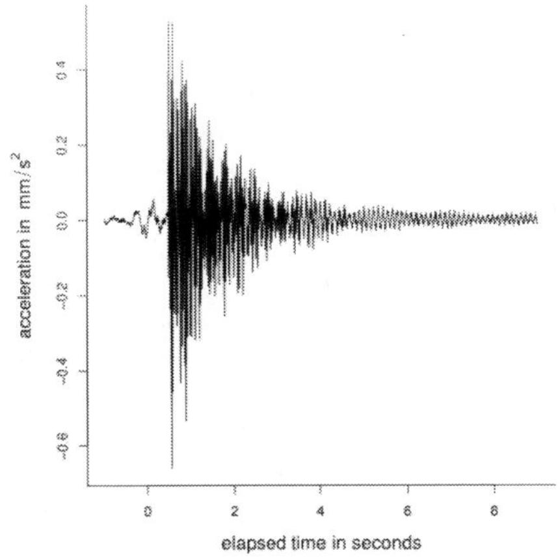

Figure 2. Vibrations of the bridge recorded by the vibrometer and triggered by a walking pedestrian.

measure with 100 Hz. In order to sample with a much higher virtual frequency, many mobile phones should be connected with each other. The start of measurements from different devices are naturally shifted against one another. In an ideal case, this leads to a higher sampling rate. For that purpose, the offset between these devices needs to be exactly determined, which requires all of them to agree on a common time base. Therefore, the time source should be the hardware clock. The literature follows different approaches to synchronize those devices. Most of these methods have limitations, e.g., a network connection for a NTP-based synchronization. In this article, we introduce an approach making use of the microphone of a mobile phone in order to synchronize the time and align the vibrations of different devices.

This paper is organized as follows: Section II is devoted to explain the related work in the field of synchronizing methods. Section III explains in detail our approach. Section IV shows how the clock-skew influences synchronization methods. A summary and an outlook for further research are shown in Section V.

II. Related Work

The problem is related to the time synchronization in sensor networks. A lot of research has been done in this area. There are several methods for synchronizing physical clocks. These methods can be classified as "internal" and "external" synchronization. For an internal clock synchronization, all nodes accept the time of a reference node in a network [3].

In external clock synchronization, the value is taken from an external clock source, such as a common time service (e.g., NTP) or the Global Positioning System (GPS) [4].

A. Synchronization by NTP

NTP is a protocol for synchronizing computer clocks using a set of distributed servers around the world. This protocol is also known as Simple network time protocol. It is built on top of the User Datagram Protocol (UDP) [5]. The protocol was announced with a precision in the range of nanoseconds [6] [7].This protocol has been utilized in numerous clients for several years. Juda Levine [8] reports in 2011 about 5×10^9 requests per day. The accuracy of the Protocol and the related assets have been studied in numerous works [9]–[11]. The network latency has a major impact on the accuracy. Zhao et al. [10] evaluated the accuracy with less then 10 ms under Local Area Network (LAN) condition and less then 100 ms under Internet conditions. As a reference for their evaluations they used the time of the GPS.

B. Synchronization by GPS

The Global Positioning system was designed and is still under the control of the United States Department of Defense. Nevertheless, it is also freely accessible by anyone. The system consists currently of 32 operating satellites that are orbiting the earth at an altitude of approximately 20,000 km. Every satellite contains multiple atomic clocks that support very precise timing data [12]. For determining the position, the receiver needs signals from at least three of these satellites. The position of the receiver can be calculated by the difference between signal sent and received by the receiver. With this ability to receive very accurate data from multiple sources an accurate time can be obtained. In 2015 Mazur et al. [12] designates the accuracy of such time synchronizations within up to billionth of a second. This system is available anywhere in the world and has a very high accuracy. But it requires a direct line of sight to the satellite and an initial connection takes a long time in some cases.

C. Clock-Skew and Drift

Most computing devices are equipped with a hardware oscillator assisted computer clock. The frequency of the hardware oscillator determines the rate at which the clock runs [13]. This clock becomes inaccurate because the frequency varies. Figure 3 shows the difference between the clock drift - in this case the clock is below or ahead by a fix offset, the clock skew - here the offset is growing during the time, and the jittering - in this case the device clock is affected by internal (e.g., processor utilization) or external (e.g., temperature, humidity [14]) fluctuations. To keep these clocks in time, Zhenjiang Li et al. [15] uses the flickering lights of fluorescent lights.

D. Time Synchronization on Mobile Devices

One recent work in this area is provided by Lazik et al. [17]. They used ultrasonic beacons to synchronize the time on mobile devices. Therefore, they built up a network with one network master. The master is connected to a GPS receiver and transmits ultrasonic chirps in a frequency that is outside of the human hearing but still detectable by the microphone of smartphones. They reported that the devices could be synchronized with an average accuracy of 720 μs. At the beginning of their experiments they investigated devices with Android and iOS. They reported a high level jitter on the Android device (in the order of milliseconds and higher) and chose the iOS devices for the rest of their experiments. The high jittering is justified by Android's task scheduler. Within this work they also benchmarked the NTP timing performance (on iOS). They ran their experiments with three different communication channels, Long Term Evolution Technologie (LTE), Wireless Local Area Network (WLAN) and one idle WLAN router that is directly connected to a Stratum 1 NTP server fed by a dedicated GPS clock. Using LTE they measured an average jitter of 47 ms, the average WLAN jitter is measured with 30ms and finally the average jitter in the ideal case with the WLAN router connected to NTP Server is measured with 19.3 ms.

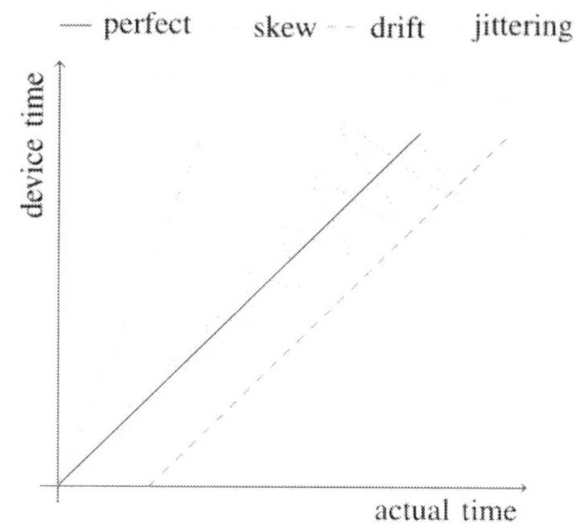

Figure 3. This figure shows the difference between a perfect clock, one with drift, one with a skew and one, as it is likely to occur in real [16].

III. SYNCHRONIZATION

In the previous section, we explained some synchronizing methods. Synchronization with a common time service will not be considered at the moment. This is because we can not make any assumptions about the availability, connection and bandwidth. A prerequisite of a synchronization among different devices is that they share the same network. In order to make the use case as simple as possible, it is not planned to create a network between those devices. A quite simple example for synchronization comes from sports. With a 100 m sprint, eight athletes stand in starting blocks. The race starts with an external signal which is same for each athlete.

This idea will be applied here. First, a sender and a receiver needs to be chosen. The sensors of modern mobile phone are suitable as receivers. A mobile phone is equipped with numerous sensors, e.g., accelerometer, gyroscope, microphone, etc. For synchronizing the time, a sensor with the highest possible sampling rate is required. The sample rate of the accelerometer is nearly 100 Hz. The gyroscope samples at a frequency up to 200 Hz. For these sensors, there is no advantage to the outlined problem. In contrast, the microphone samples up to 44,100 Hz. Therefore, we chose the microphone as receiver.

The sender (sound source) in our experiments is a choke used in athletic sports. This sound creates a distinctive peak (up to 93 dB) in the amplitude. It has almost no reverberation. Hence the time can be determined exactly. During our test the distance between sender and receiver was up to one meter almost the same for all devices. So the velocity of sound did not influence the result. The recorded peak and the corresponding timestamp can be used to determine an exact timestamp for the start. So, the data of different devices can easily be aligned.

A. Devices used

During the experiments, we used three smart phones with android operating system (Table I).

TABLE I. DEVICES USED

Manufacturer	Model	OS Version	Microphones
Motorola	MotoG (2nd Edition)	5.1.1	2
Sony	Xperia M2	5.1.1	1
Samsung	Galaxy A3	5.0.1	2

These devices are equipped with up to three MEMS-Microphones (micro-electro-mechanical-systems).

B. Specifics

Due to the operating system, there are some specifics that need to be mentioned.

- The sound is encoded by 16 bit. So values in the range from -32,768 to 32,767 with a maximum signal to noise ratio of 96.33 dB can be achieved.
- The audio samples are provided by the operating system as chunks. So only the time when a package is received can be measured. The time for the samples is calculated from the sample rate by interpolation. The size of the chunks depends on the buffersize that is proposed by android (for the three devices with 3,584 samples per chunk the same).
- There are many discussions about the usage of the function *System.nanoTime* [18]–[20]. So we choose the function *System.currentTimeMillis*. This function returns the elapsed time in milliseconds since midnight, January 1, 1970 (UTC).

To reduce external influences, we disable most of the applications on the device. In addition, the recorded data during the process is only held in memory and written after completion. While using this synchronization method, other mechanisms resulting in a synchronization, e.g., synchronization by local time with NTP Server, need to be switched off.

C. Experiments

We conducted about thirty experiments in six days. Within each experiment we created several peaks at distances between 5 seconds up to 1 minute. So we can compare the results from 5 seconds up to 24 hours. Figure 4 shows one raw experiment within four peaks at 0 s, 10 s, 30 s and 60 s. The data in this figure is aligned by the time on device. Please note that, there is an initial offset for each clock in the beginning. To align these samples by the amplitude, we first calculated their absolute values.

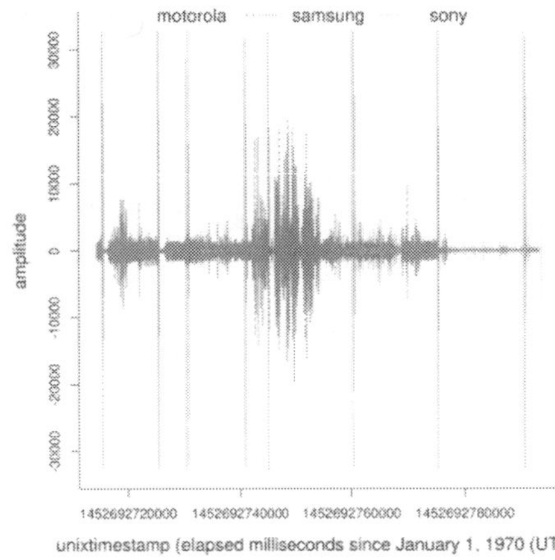

Figure 4. In this figure, the peaks are aligned by the unixtimestamp. Please note the offset between the devices, especially, the samsung is 20 seconds ahead of the other devices.

In this example, the first peak is used to align the samples of different devices. The alignment result for these three devices can be seen in Figure 5a. In Figure 5b, the data is reduced to an absolute amplitude above 32,000. In this perspective, all the data is aligned. By zooming in at 60 seconds (Figure 5c) an offset between these devices can be seen. It can be noticed that the offset between the devices becomes significantly larger during the time. This fact leads us to look deeper into the clock skew of the devices.

IV. Clock Skew

Since the figures show an obvious offset after only 60 seconds, we scrutinize the skew of the clocks further.

TABLE II. THE DISTANCES BETWEEN THE DEVICES CALCULATED BY THE PEAKS IN MILLISECONDS.

time	Motorola - Samsung	Motorola - Sony	Samsung - Sony
10 s	-1	5	6
20 s	-8	-26	-18
30 s	-9	-21	-12
50 s	-13	-10	3
60 s	-15	-6	9

Table II depicts the offset of the clocks from the above illustrated Figure (5c).

TABLE III. THIS TABLE SHOWS THE MEAN DISTANCES BETWEEN THE DEVICES AND THEIR STANDARD DEVIATION AFTER ELAPSED TIME IN MILLISECONDS.

	Motorola - Samsung		Motorola - Sony		Samsung - Sony		
time	mean	std	mean	std	mean	std	values
5 s	-0.57	3.45	0.14	7.10	0.71	4.38	7
10 s	-0.31	4.39	-0.22	4.63	0.0	4.42	105
20 s	0.56	5.16	0.36	5.13	-0.2	4.091	80
30 s	0.42	6.71	0.19	5.94	-0.22	3.91	127
60 s	-0.09	6.32	-0.12	5.46	-0.02	4.88	72
90 s	-0.16	5.08	-0.81	4.19	-0.65	4.68	49
2 m	-0.30	4.52	-1.27	5.25	-0.96	5.12	33
1 h	-8.71	4.68	-19.09	4.32	-10.38	4.28	21
6 h	-54.44	8.53	-99.22	7.32	-44.77	3.34	9
12 h	-158.33	4.22	-424.67	2.16	-266.34	4.92	6
24 h	-212.33	3.21	-531	6.55	-318.67	4.16	3

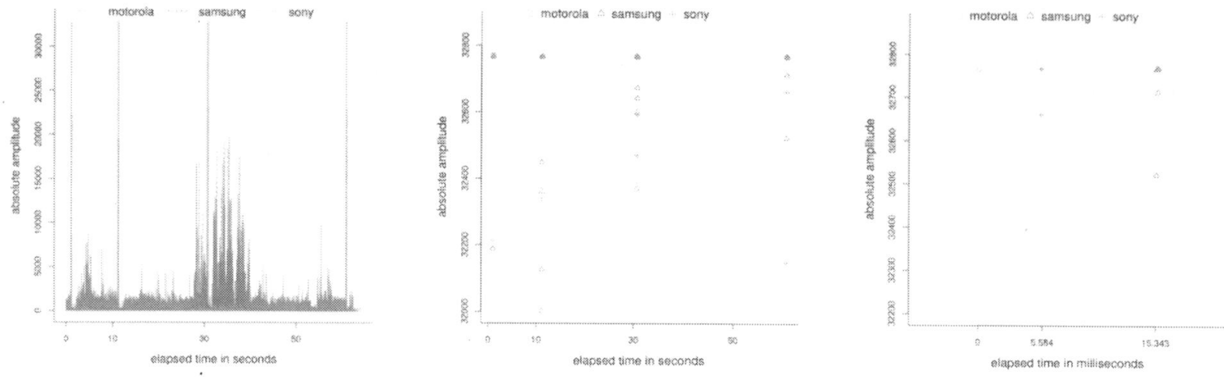

(a) aligned data (b) aligned data filtered by maximum amplitude (c) offset after 60 seconds

Figure 5. Figure shows an aligned Result (a) full plotted, (b) reduced to the peaks and (c) the offset in this experiment after 60 seconds.

While the distance between Motorola and Samsung is growing, the other distances are jittering. Over all the measurements, there is an error between these devices. Table III provides an overview of the distances between the devices. For this purpose, the mean value and their standard deviation is given. The results in this table vary very strongly and become stable only over longer periods of time when the standard deviation can be neglected. To reduce the errors, these experiments must be repeated for synchronization of the devices. One reason for this may be the jittering, that is also mentioned by Lazik et al. [17]. In order to evaluate the skew of the devices, we also set up a GPS timing within our experiments. The Figure 6 shows the time on device compared to the GPS time.

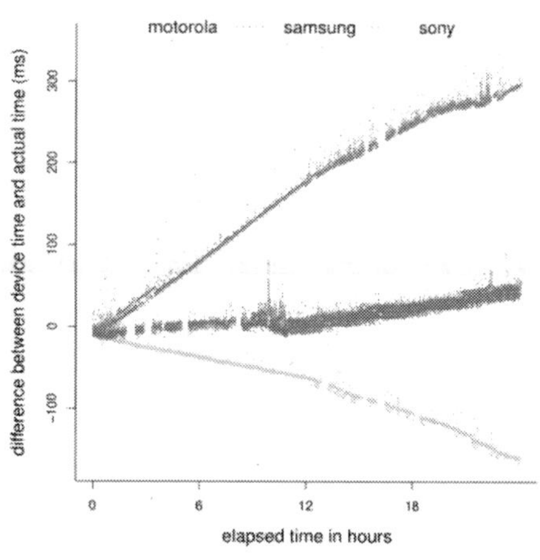

Figure 6. The clocks skew of the devices within 24 hours compared to the timestamp given by GPS.

So we can confirm the above measured distances between these three devices. Furthermore, we can calculate an average offset for this (Table IV). This offset can be used to interpolate / extrapolate the time on device. Thus, the data of the synchronized devices can be aligned. One example of such an alignment can be seen in Figure 7, where the data of two

TABLE IV. THE AVERAGE OFFSET PER SECOND ON DEVICE IN NANOSECONDS.

Motorola		Samsung		Sony	
mean	std	mean	std	mean	std
23.59	366.33	0.73	7.35	15.79	356.34

different devices (positioned at 1/6 of length and 1/2 of width of the above mentioned bridge) is aligned by the synchronized time.

V. CONCLUSION

In this article, we introduced an approach that synchronizes the time between mobile phones. Therefore, the microphone sensors were utilized. The devices were synchronized by an external sound event. This event can be recognized by observing the amplitude of the built in microphones and the corresponding timestamp. Besides the synchronization of time, the individual clock skew and drift can be derived. So we can achieve an accuracy of up to 5 ms. One reason for this value is the strong jittering on these devices. Theoretically, the achievable resolution is up to the order of microseconds, since the microphones work with a sample rate of 44,100 Hz. Thus, this approach would provide a more accurate result than the synchronization via NTP but would still be behind than the synchronization using GPS. Therefore, further investigations of the jittering is necessary, which will follow.

One advantage of this approach is that network, data or GPS connections are not necessary. The only limitation is the distance between the sound source and the devices. This means that this approach is highly suitable for areas where the above mentioned services are not available.

REFERENCES

[1] M. Messtechnik., "Frequenzanalyse durch fft," 2009, (retrieved: 31-May-2016). [Online]. Available: http://www.beitzer.de/products/FFT.html

[2] L. Özdamar, E. Ekinci, and B. Küçükyazici, "Emergency logistics planning in natural disasters," Annals of operations research, vol. 129, no. 1-4, 2004, pp. 217–245.

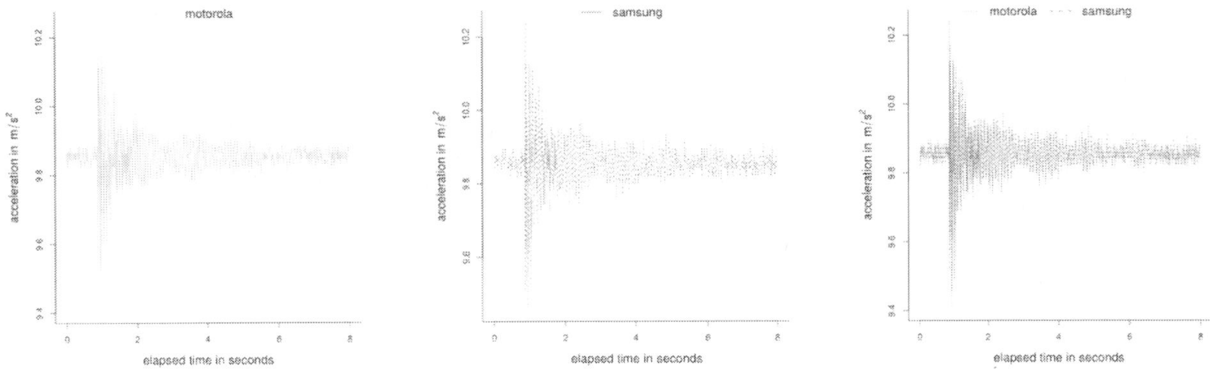

(a) vibrations of motorola (b) vibrations of samsung (c) vibrations of both devices combined

Figure 7. This figure shows same vibrations as Figure 2, recorded by the smartphones. Figures (a) shows the vibrations recorded by motorola, (b) recorded by samsung and (c) the data of both devices aligned after time synchronization.

[3] K. Sun, P. Ning, and C. Wang, "Tinysersync: secure and resilient time synchronization in wireless sensor networks," in Proceedings of the 13th ACM conference on Computer and communications security. ACM, 2006, pp. 264–277.

[4] B. Kusy et al., "Elapsed time on arrival: a simple and versatile primitive for canonical time synchronisation services," International Journal of Ad Hoc and Ubiquitous Computing, vol. 1, no. 4, 2006, pp. 239–251.

[5] J. Postel, "Rfc 768 - user datagram protocol," Isi, 1980.

[6] D. L. Mills, "Network time protocol (ntp)," Network, 1985.

[7] ——, "Internet time synchronization: the network time protocol," Communications, IEEE Transactions on, vol. 39, no. 10, 1991, pp. 1482–1493.

[8] J. Levine, "Timing in telecommunications networks," Metrologia, vol. 48, no. 4, 2011, p. S203.

[9] A. N. Novick and M. A. Lombardi, "Practical limitations of ntp time transfer," in Frequency Control Symposium & the European Frequency and Time Forum (FCS), 2015 Joint Conference of the IEEE International. IEEE, 2015, pp. 570–574.

[10] K. Zhao, A. Zhang, and K. Liang, "Research on the uncertainty evaluation of network time service system," in European Frequency and Time Forum (EFTF), 2012. IEEE, 2012, pp. 122–125.

[11] S. Ping, "Delay measurement time synchronization for wireless sensor networks," Intel Research Berkeley Lab, 2003.

[12] D. C. Mazur, R. A. Entzminger, J. A. Kay, and P. A. Morell, "Time synchronization mechanisms for the industrial marketplace," in Industrial & Commercial Power Systems Technical Conference (I&CPS), 2015 IEEE/IAS 51st. IEEE, 2015, pp. 1–7.

[13] F. Sivrikaya and B. Yener, "Time synchronization in sensor networks: a survey," Network, IEEE, vol. 18, no. 4, 2004, pp. 45–50.

[14] J. Aron, "Flickering lights could help smartphones keep time," New Scientist, vol. 215, no. 2874, 2012, p. 22.

[15] Z. Li et al., "Flight: Clock calibration using fluorescent lighting," in Proceedings of the 18th annual international conference on Mobile computing and networking. ACM, 2012, pp. 329–340.

[16] T. Haenselmann, Wireless Sensor Networks: Design Principles for Scattered Systems. Oldenbourg Verlag, 2011.

[17] P. Lazik, N. Rajagopal, B. Sinopoli, and A. Rowe, "Ultrasonic time synchronization and ranging on smartphones," in Real-Time and Embedded Technology and Applications Symposium (RTAS), 2015 IEEE. IEEE, 2015, pp. 108–118.

[18] A. Shipilv, "Nanotrusting the nanotime," 2014, [retrieved: 2016-05-16]. [Online]. Available: http://shipilev.net/blog/2014/nanotrusting-nanotime/

[19] S. Kobylansky, "What is behind system.nanotime()?" 2012, (retrieved: 16-May-2016). [Online]. Available: http://stas-blogspot.blogspot.de/2012/02/what-is-behind-systemnanotime.html

[20] M. Kuperberg, M. Krogmann, and R. Reussner, "Timermeter: Quantifying properties of software timers for system analysis," in Quantitative Evaluation of Systems, 2009. QEST'09. Sixth International Conference on the. IEEE, 2009, pp. 85–94.

International Academy, Research,
and Industry Association (IARIA)
412 Derby Way
Wilmington, DE 19810

ISBN 978-1-5108-2691-5

CURRAN ASSOCIATES INC.
proceedings.com